Sex Media

Sex Media

Feona Attwood

polity

First published in 2018 by Polity Press

Polity Press
65 Bridge Street
Cambridge CB2 1UR, UK

Polity Press
101 Station Landing, Suite 300
Medford, MA 02155, USA

ISBN-13: 978-1-5095-1687-2
ISBN-13: 978-1-5095-1688-9(pb)

A catalogue record for this book is available from the British Library.

Library of Congress Cataloging-in-Publication Data
Names: Attwood, Feona, author.
Title: Sex media / Feona Attwood.
Description: Malden, MA : Polity Press, [2017] | Includes bibliographical references and index.
Identifiers: LCCN 2017013930 (print) | LCCN 2017029093 (ebook) | ISBN 9781509516902 (Mobi) | ISBN 9781509516919 (Epub) | ISBN 9781509516872 (hardback) | ISBN 9781509516889 (paperback)
Subjects: LCSH: Pornography--Social aspects. | Pornography in popular culture.
Classification: LCC HQ471 (ebook) | LCC HQ471 .A88 2017 (print) | DDC 306.77--dc23
LC record available at https://lccn.loc.gov/2017013930

Typeset in 11 on 13 pt Adobe Sabon by
Servis Filmsetting Ltd, Stockport, Cheshire
Printed and bound in Great Britain by Clays Ltd, St Ives PLC

For further information on Polity, visit our website: politybooks.com

Contents

Acknowledgements

Thanks to all at Polity for making the process of completing this book so pleasant and straightforward – Elen Griffiths, Ellen MacDonald-Kramer and Mary Savigar – and to Tim Clark for copy-editing.

I would not have been able to write the book at all without the many inspiring scholars working in gender and sexuality and media and cultural studies – especially Kath Albury, Martin Barker, Meg John Barker, R. Danielle Egan, Alan McKee, John Mercer, Susanna Paasonen, Julian Petley and Clarissa Smith – whose work I repeatedly return to.

Big thanks to Julian, Meg John, Danielle and Clarissa who read individual chapters early on in the process and helped me to work out whether I was on the right track. Thanks to the Wellcome Trust for funding a small project on sexualization and public engagement and to all the academics who contributed to *The Sexualization Report* (Attwood et al., 2013) and other experiments in making academic work more accessible. For inspiration in this area, thanks in particular to Meg John Barker, Justin Hancock, Petra Boynton and Clare Harris.

Introduction

Sex sells. Our world has been pornified. Culture is sexualized and it's making our children grow up too quickly. Porn is everywhere. Porn changes your brain. There is an epidemic of porn addiction. Porn is a public health crisis. Sexting is a growing problem. Raunch culture is damaging girls. Virtual reality is the future of porn. The future of sex is with robots.

These kinds of sensationalist claims are made repeatedly in the public discussion of sex media.[1] While sex media are part of many people's lives, they are increasingly used as a focus for discussing a range of other questions – what access we should have to the internet, what it means to be sexually healthy, how men and women differ in their relation to erotic and intimate life, what the relations between media, fantasy and sexual practice are.

This book is about sex media – those media forms in which sex is the primary focus of representation. As studies of pornography and other sexually explicit media have shown, sex media are diverse, interesting in and of themselves, and worthy of study.[2] They are also a good starting point for thinking about sexuality and gender, the body, fantasy and representation. They provide interesting ways into considering how policy and regulation work, how norms, customs and values develop and the ideas they depend on.[3] They allow us to consider how media are increasingly part of public and private life; part of people's practices and their sex lives. They can help us to think about the changing place and significance of sex in contemporary society.

1

My argument in this book is that we need better and more critical frameworks and approaches for understanding sex media. While being 'critical' is often associated with being condemnatory or 'pessimistic' about something, critical thinking does its best to avoid a binary approach which sets up a 'debate' in terms of whether we should be pessimistic or optimistic about it, or which asks us to decide definitively whether something is 'good' or 'bad', healthy or unhealthy, progressive or oppressive.

A critical approach to sex media questions assumptions about the way things are or appear to be, draws on insights from disciplines that acknowledge the complexity of culture, and takes into account the shifts and continuities in the ways that sex and media are constructed historically. It understands that research is framed by asking particular kinds of questions, and recognizes that both advantages and problems arise from doing things in particular kinds of ways. It considers the contexts of sex media – their relation to other media genres, forms and aesthetics and to the broader social and cultural frameworks of regulation, work, leisure, intimacy, health and education.[4]

I have not been able to cover everything that I would have liked to in this book. The book is also focused primarily on examples, histories and debates from English-speaking countries, and the arguments I make about these do not necessarily apply to other countries. For example, while I have spent quite a bit of time talking about the ways in which pornography has been an important issue for feminists, this has played out in quite different ways in different countries.

The book begins with an overview of what is meant by sex, gender and sexuality, moves on to questions of regulation and the issue of sexualization, and then considers a range of sex media and their relation to labour, leisure, education and health.

Chapter 1 introduces the terms sex, sexuality and gender, and shows how definitions and representations of these often depend on a hierarchy that marks out 'good' and 'bad' and presents sexuality and gender as binary – where there are only two ways of being: heterosexual or homosexual, male or female, masculine or feminine.

While definitions and representations can work to restrict and police the way sex and gender are understood, they can also be used to challenge norms and create new types of experience, community and ways of thinking. I describe how sexual politics that attempt this have developed since the 1960s, and how countercultures and political activists have worked to shape these politics. I also show how critical approaches – in lesbian and gay studies, queer theory, sexuality and gender studies – have provided frameworks for understanding sex and sexuality.

The chapter ends with a look at how some contemporary forms of sex advice often privilege certain kinds of practices and identities, while others suggest a move towards different ways of thinking about sex. This is happening in a context where both sex and the media are increasingly central to our culture and a range of technologies play an increasingly important role in our experiences and understandings of sex.

Chapter 2 considers the regulation of sex and sex media, showing how concerns about sex have come to focus particularly heavily on media. It shows how regulation often takes the form of categorizing and labelling texts, for example in the kinds of classification used by the British Board of Film Classification or the use of terms such as pornography and obscenity in law.

The regulation of sex and sex media tends to focus on what is considered excessive, extreme, playing with power or pushing the body to its limits – as in the kind of pornography created by the American producers, Larry Flynt and Extreme Associates. It also often focuses on young people, as in the recent attempts to police 'sexting'. This kind of regulation may be presented and intended as a protective measure, but it also often operates according to a sexual double standard and works to restrict and shame young people – especially young women and girls.

The chapter ends by considering some contemporary trends in the regulation of sex media. While it is often argued that sex and sex media are now less heavily regulated than in the past, there is nevertheless evidence of a process of juridification – an expansion and intensification of regulation as part of a broader move towards the surveillance of communication. This increasingly involves an interest in regulating people's creative and fantasy worlds.

Chapter 3 examines the claim that contemporary mainstream media and culture have become 'sexualized'. It considers the development of a 'sexualization debate' that has become the most public and visible way in which sex and media are discussed and a means of expressing concerns about children, young people and women. The chapter looks at the approaches and evidence used in policy reports on sexualization and how these relate to other sorts of evidence about gender and sexual equalities, young people and sex, relationships, crime, education and well-being. These reports do little to shed light on the conditions experienced by women and girls around the world, or on the experiences of young people. They do not explain the advances in the situation of some groups, for example in terms of access to education, or the continuing inequalities that others face in terms of health and well-being, or vulnerability to poverty and violence.

The chapter shows that while the sexualization debate tends to focus on an abstract figure of the child, research with actual young people reveals complex and varied relationships with media and suggests that these can be resources and spaces for talking and learning about sexuality, relationships and pleasure.

The chapter ends by concluding that while it is true that sex has become particularly visible – or 'onscene' – in Western cultures, various forms of sexism and double standards around sexual behaviour persist, and these are far from new. Yet, if culture is now sexualized, this is marked not only by sexism but by a diverse range of sexual communities, representations and ideas about sex.

Chapter 4 looks at a broad range of sex media and the similarities and differences between them. It begins by examining ideas about aesthetics, cultural capital and value and the place of sex media in relation to these. Sex media tend to be placed low down in a cultural hierarchy which is suspicious of media forms that invite the viewer's involvement.

Although forms of sex media are often depicted as lacking in variety, they include a wide range of conventions and characteristics. Broad categories mark out hardcore from softcore, and art from porn and erotica, but these frequently overlap and there are further distinctions within these categories too. For example, there

4

are a wide range of pornographies – in this chapter I look at drawn pornography, gonzo porn and amateur porn – and many more divisions within each type. There are also other genres that have a distinctive set of conventions for representing sex; for example, the various types of sexploitation movie, sex comedy and erotic thriller.

As well as tracing the variety of sex media, the chapter considers how they are related to mainstream culture and to entertainment. It ends by looking at the various ways media have come to provide new spaces for sexual interaction in cybersex, online sex games and virtual worlds. It considers the development of interactive and immersive sex media and the overlapping of media, space, representation and communication in the development of apps and networks for dating and hooking up. As with other aspects of life, sex is increasingly intertwined with media.

Chapter 5 puts sex media into a broader social context. It shows how sex can be seen as a form of intimate labour, both in terms of paid sex work and of 'sex as work' performed on the self and within relationships. Sex is also increasingly related to leisure, with particular types of sex seen as recreational and a developing range of sex leisure products. The chapter considers how the ways in which we experience and understand sex are linked to changing intimacies, relationship structures and sexual cultures. They also depend on the use of media and other technologies that are becoming steadily more important in the way we live, and that make possible new forms of public and private life. As these technologies become involved in the fashioning of our bodies and selves, they complicate our ideas about what is natural and authentic about human life and sexuality.

I end the book by discussing developing ideas about sex media in relation to healthy sexual development, sexual ethics, sex and sexuality education, and sexual citizenship. The book is designed to provide an accessible introduction to the area of sex media. I hope it will be useful for people at advanced school level who want to read more widely, and for undergraduates – and indeed anyone else – who wants a broad and critical introduction to the topic.

1

Sex, Gender and Sexuality

This chapter covers:

• Changes and continuities in the way sex, gender and sexuality have been understood in Western cultures.

• How definitions and cultural representations depict 'good' and 'bad' sex and how norms of gender and sexuality are produced in definitions and representations.

• The development of sexual politics since the 1960s, the 'sexual revolution' and the role of countercultures and political activists.

• The development of traditions for studying sex and gender and the importance of critical sexuality and gender studies.

• The growing role of media and a range of technologies in our experiences and understandings of sex and the increasing centrality of both sex and media in culture.

What is Sex?

Sexuality refers to 'all erotically significant aspects of social life and social being – desires, practices, relationships and identities' as well as sexual 'interests, acts, expressions, and/ or experiences'.

What is sex? The term is used in a range of different ways and has a wide set of associations. It is used to refer to men and women and the way they are classified as male or female on the basis of their chromosomes, hormones, genitalia and reproductive organs. Here, sex has 'the meaning of . . . biological differentiations'.[1] Sex also refers to particular *acts* – summed up in the idea that we can 'have sex'. A broader range of things are seen as 'sexy': a particular quality or look, 'the ability to excite desire and stimulate attraction'.[2]

Sexuality is a related word used for categories such as heterosexual and homosexual, bisexual, asexual and so on. It may refer to *orientation* or *preference* (the way someone experiences attraction and desire[3]), or to *identity* (how they define themselves sexually). Sexuality is also used more broadly for 'all erotically significant aspects of social life and social being – desires, practices, relationships and identities'[4] as well as sexual 'interests, acts, expressions, and/or experiences'.[5] It is 'a drive, an impulse or form of propulsion', 'a series of practices and behaviors involving bodies, organs, and pleasures', a matter of identities and 'a set of orientations, positions, and desires, which implies that there are particular ways in which the desires, differences, and bodies of subjects can seek their pleasure'.[6] Sexual identity has often been seen as related to gender – most commonly in the idea that sexuality depends on the gender of the person you are attracted to. But gender may not be a factor in the way a person experiences their sexual desire or identity at all; this may depend instead on how a person has sex or the kinds of sexual practices they are attracted to, along with a range of other things.[7]

Gender refers to the 'social production and reproduction of male and female identities and behaviors'.[8] It can be understood in terms of 'gender identity' (the gender a person identifies with), 'lived sex' (a person's experiences of being of a particular sex/ gender), and 'gender expression' (a person's presentation of appearance, interests and mannerisms that are usually considered to be feminine or masculine).[9]

Although masculinity and femininity are often presented as though they are related to biology, they actually describe practices

7

and characteristics that can belong to both men and women, regardless of their biological sex.[10] 'Female masculinity' includes identities such as 'tomboy', 'butch' and 'drag king'. 'Butch' (masculine) and 'femme' (feminine) are terms usually associated with lesbians.[11] 'Effeminate' is a term used to describe feminine men, along with other labels like 'sissy' or 'queen'. As sexism and effeminophobia – a means of pressurizing boys and men not to act in feminine ways[12] – show, femininity has a lower status in society than masculinity.

As we can see, 'sex', 'sexuality' and 'gender' can be confusing terms because they refer to such a wide range of things: acts and practices; categories of person; identities; orientations and preferences; urges and instincts; feelings and desires; appeal, appearance and the power to attract; ways of engaging with and relating to others; communities and cultures.

All of these aspects have varied across time and place and they are often the subject of debate and disagreement. They are also used in different contexts: sometimes as part of an *essentialist* argument to suggest that sex, gender and sexuality are 'essences' determined by biology; as *identity labels* to explain to others how a person believes they 'fit ... into the world';[13] or as *umbrella terms* to draw various groups of people together. All of our terms, new and old – 'lesbian', 'trans', 'heterosexual', and so on – 'are imperfect, historical, arbitrary, and temporary',[14] and new terms are emerging all the time as part of the way that people think about and live gendered and sexual lives.[15] Boxes 1.1 and 1.2 list some of the recent terms used to describe sexual and gender orientations and identities.

Attempts to capture this kind of variety are also becoming more mainstream. In 2014 Facebook made it possible to customize the gender options on people's profiles (see Figure 1.1).[16] Some of these terms are used as umbrella terms to describe groups and to 'form alliances between disparate people who share some obstacle or form of discrimination in common'.[17] These include 'trans', used 'to describe all people who defy straight mainstream notions regarding gender'; 'queer' to describe LGBTQQIA+ (lesbian, gay, bisexual, trans, queer, questioning, intersex, asexual) people,

Box 1.1: Sexual orientations and identities

Asexual describes people who may not experience sexual attraction or arousal, or people who experience these things without feeling the need to act them out sexually or with a partner.

Bisexual describes people who may be attracted to more than one gender, or for whom gender isn't a factor in who they are attracted to.

BDSM or kink refers to people who engage in sexual practices that emphasize exchanges of power, restriction of movement, or intense sensations.

Homosexual refers to people who are attracted to people of the same gender.

Heterosexual refers to people who are attracted to people who they understand to be of the 'opposite' gender (men to women and women to men).

Monosexual refers to people who are attracted to people of only one gender.

Metrosexual describes someone whose sexual identity depends on media, consumerism and the development of lifestyle, rather than particular sex acts or sexual orientation.

people of non-binary genders, and people whose identities challenge binary ideas about gender and sexuality; and 'GSD' to include all forms of gender and sexual diversity.[18]

What is 'Normal' Sex?

'Normal' is often code for what someone thinks are 'natural', 'good' and 'healthy' kinds of sexuality and gender, and it is frequently found in conservative, conventional and moral views of sex and sexuality.

Box 1.2: Gender orientations and identities

Trans refers to those who move away from the gender they were assigned at birth.

Cisgender refers to people who are not trans and who remain in the gender they were assigned at birth.

Non-binary gender terms include:

Androgynous people whose identities incorporate aspects of gender associated with men and women.

Agender people whose identities are not based on gender.

Gender fluid people who move between genders.

Pangender people who move between multiple genders.

Third gender people who consider themselves to be of an additional gender.

Representations of sex and gender – in literature, art and media and in educational works like dictionaries and advice books – play an important role in circulating and challenging ideas about what sex is or should be.

Gender is very often presented in terms of a *hierarchy*, with some genders ranked as more important and 'better' than others. The same applies to sexuality, with heterosexuality and monogamy usually represented as the 'best' kind of sexuality. This is generally also linked to the idea that gender and sexuality are binary – where there are only two ways of being (heterosexual or homosexual, male or female, masculine or feminine). But the variety of ways in which people identify in terms of gender and sexuality demonstrate that this is not the case. Identities, appearances and forms of expression vary extremely widely, and bodies are also diverse when it comes to chromosomes, hormones, genitals and brain structures.[19] A significant number of people are born intersex – with a physiology that 'does not fall neatly into the categories of male or female'.[20]

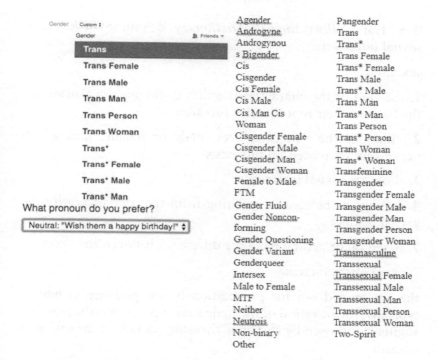

Figure 1.1   Gender options on Facebook.

Others identify as bisexual, trans, queer, asexual, androgynous or kinky.

In the dictionary definition in Box 1.3 we can see that sex is being related to reproduction and to the idea that male and female are 'opposite' sexes.[21] Sex and gender are presented as binary, taking two distinct forms: male and female. The definition also presents sex as a particular type of physical activity: penis-in-vagina sex. It links 'instinct', feelings, behaviour and appeal, as if all these things fit together in an orderly way. And it presents all of this as though sex is simply natural and biological. It is clear that the kind of sexual interest and activity being referred to is heterosexual.

It is not unusual to find biological sex, gender identification and sexual desires and practices linked together like this. The

Box 1.3: *Collins English Dictionary* definition of sex and sexual intercourse

sex *n.*

1. the sum of the characteristics that distinguish organisms on the basis of their reproductive function

2. either of the two categories, male or female, into which organisms are placed on this basis

3. short for **sexual intercourse***

4. feelings or behaviour resulting from the urge to gratify the sexual instinct . . .

7. based on or arising from the difference between the sexes

*** sexual intercourse** *n.*

the act carried out for procreation or for pleasure in which, typically, the insertion of the male's erect penis into the female's vagina is followed by rhythmic thrusting usually culminating in orgasm

bestselling self-help book *Mars and Venus in the Bedroom* suggests that heterosexual-monogamous-couple sex 'completes the person'.[22] 'Male' and 'female' sexuality are presented as very different things, with men 'needing' sex in the form of penetration and orgasm and women's desire 'triggered through love and romance' and focused on 'foreplay' – this term implying practices that happen before ('real') sex. While sex is presented as something that is very 'natural', it is quite clearly also a matter of culture – something we need advice about and help with.[23]

One of the most well-known advice books, *The Joy of Sex*, claims that what is 'normal' is what 'both' parties enjoy, though the repeated references to 'both' of you, and the illustrations of a man and woman alone together, make it clear what the limits of 'normal' are here. But ideas about sex are not static. When the book was updated in 2008 new topics such as internet pornog-

Figure 1.2   The bestselling sex-advice book, *The Joy of Sex: A Gourmet Guide to Lovemaking* (1972).

raphy, AIDS and Viagra were introduced, while the clitoris, which was mentioned only in passing in the earlier version, received much more attention.[24]

Sexuality, Gender and Normativity

The overwhelming focus on heterosexuality in Western cultures might lead us to assume that this form of sexuality is very old and well-established. In fact the idea of sexuality as an identity (being 'heterosexual' or 'homosexual'), as an essence which fixes and defines who we are,[25] is very recent indeed. Use of the word 'sexuality' to refer to a type of person[26] first appeared in the Oxford dictionary in 1800;[27] 'sexual passion' was used from 1821 and 'sexual instinct' from 1861. Using 'sex' to refer to particular acts became common in the 1920s, along with 'sexy' and 'sex appeal'.[28] The term 'heterosexual' was not in common use until the twentieth century and initially referred to an 'abnormal or perverted appetite toward the opposite sex' – abnormal because it did not focus on reproduction, the 'proper' sphere for sexuality. Only later was it used to mean 'sexual passion for one of the opposite sex; normal sexuality'.[29] The idea of the male homosexual emerged a little later, and that of the female homosexual later still.

The term 'normal' is sometimes applied to sexuality and gender as if it refers simply to the most common or typical forms, although many sexual identities, practices and fantasies that have been classed at 'not normal' are in fact very common. 'Normal' is often code for what someone thinks are 'natural', 'good' and 'healthy' kinds of sexuality and gender,[30] and it is frequently found in conservative, conventional and moral views of sex and sexuality. *Heteronormativity* is the term used to describe the way in which heterosexuality is almost always presented as the 'most normal' kind of sexuality, so natural that it is almost invisible.[31] It presents sex as a private matter, and associates community with 'intimacy, coupling, and kinship,[32] with family, reproduction, generations and the future. It makes other kinds of intimacy and other forms of sexual expression appear as 'pathological, deviant, invisible, unintelligible'.[33]

Heteronormativity and *cisnormativity* mean that heterosexuality and cisgender are associated with legal recognition and social privilege.[34] In contrast, being outside the 'norm' of sexuality or gender means that a person may be categorized as sick.[35]

Norms may be enforced through medical diagnosis. For example, the *Diagnostic and Statistical Manual of Mental Disorders* (DSM), published by the American Psychiatric Association, listed homosexuality as a category of disorder until 1973. Terms such as 'disorders of sex development' (DSD) have been used for intersex people[36] and 'gender identity disorder' for trans people,[37] giving the impression that these groups are suffering from some kind of physical or mental problem.

New Norms?

In Western cultures discourses of sex were once dominated by religious thinking and the institutions of the Church. Sex was associated with sin, and a Puritan view of sexuality that became steadily more influential also saw sex and sensual pleasures as undermining the family and devotion to work.[38] These associations are still important for some people today, but the invention of 'sex as we know it'[39] is more often framed as something we make sense of through law and science. The growth of *sexology* – a 'science of sex'[40] – in the late nineteenth century placed great importance on people's 'confession of the scientific truths of sex'[41] in order to define categories of individuals according to their sexual desires or practices, to diagnose sexual disorders and problems, or to discover new sites of sexual pleasure in the body.

Sexual acts and identities took on different meanings as part of this development. For example, autosexual practices such as masturbation and same-sex practices between men were once seen as sins but later became reclassified as illnesses, mental disorders or crimes, as forms of 'self-pollution' that could lead to disease and death.[42]

At any given time there are always 'major areas of contest'[43] where there are strongly opposing views about what sexual practices and identities mean, what their importance is, and what counts as good and acceptable. And, although we are used to thinking that we live in sexually 'liberated' times, sex is still often considered to be a dangerous or destructive force, needing to be 'redeemed' in a long-term coupled marriage, for reproduction or love ('sex negativity'). Good sex continues to be associated with respectability, legality, social and physical mobility, institutional support and material benefits ('the hierarchical valuation of sex acts'), and there is still often a refusal to recognize difference in sexual practices ('lack of a concept of benign sexual variation').[44] Here it is not so much sex 'itself', but particular kinds or contexts of sex that are seen as immoral, deviant, sick or dirty.

These ways of thinking are also often accompanied by ideas

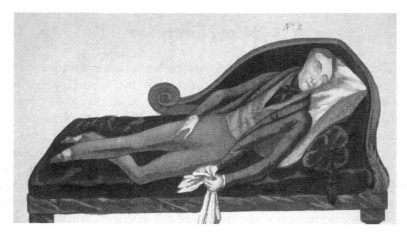

Figure 1.3 Masturbation was represented as causing disease and death in some medical works of the nineteenth century. 'Representing the last stage of mental & bodily exhaustion from self-pollution.' *The Secret Companion* (1845) by R.J. Brodie (Wellcome Trust).

about 'good' and 'normal' sexual practices and their 'opposites' – 'bad' and 'abnormal' sex. 'Good' sex is part of a 'charmed circle' of privilege, associated with heterosexuality and monogamy. It includes sexual encounters that take place within the same generation, involve couples, and are carried out in private. 'Bad' sex, at the 'outer limits' of acceptability, is associated with stigma and shame and includes encounters that are cross-generational, casual or sadomasochistic, those that involve solo or group sex, and those that are carried out in public.[45] The involvement of media, technology and commerce are also often seen as markers of 'bad sex', and pornography, sex work and the use of manufactured objects are associated with sex at the outer limits.

Politics

Debates about sexuality have also been shaped by secular philosophies such as liberalism and humanism. Unlike religious discourse, which focuses on sanctity and sin, these philosophies have usually

16

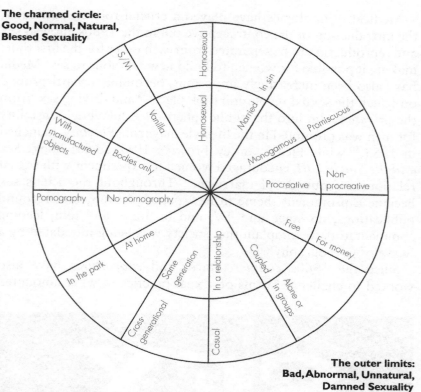

The charmed circle:
Good, Normal, Natural,
Blessed Sexuality

The outer limits:
Bad, Abnormal, Unnatural,
Damned Sexuality

Figure 1.4   The 'charmed circle' and 'outer limits' of sex (Gayle Rubin, 1984).

been more concerned with ideas about well-being, living a good life, the freedom of the individual and equality. They have taken shape within movements concerned with sexual politics,[46] but not always in the same way. For example, critiques of women as sexual 'objects' and commodities and an understanding of women as workers with rights are drawn on in different ways when people discuss sex work.

Developing approaches to research on sexual behaviour have also helped to shape debates about sex; for example, studies that received widespread publicity in the late 1940s and early 1950s suggested there was less difference between men and women sexually and that sexual orientation was less fixed and rigid than had been assumed.[47]

17

Medical technologies have played a crucial role; in particular, the introduction of the contraceptive pill in the 1960s allowed sex and reproduction to be separated from each other for the first time, making it possible for women to build new relations to sex. Media have also been increasingly important, becoming a 'battleground on which the sexual revolution took place'[48] and driving sex 'from the private realm into the public sphere'.[49] A 'playboy' sensibility for men was promoted in the lifestyle magazine *Playboy*, launched in 1953,[50] while Helen Gurley Brown's 1962 advice book, *Sex and the Single Girl*, encouraged women to experiment with sexual relationships outside of marriage.[51] Throughout the 1960s sex became a prominent theme in newspapers, novels, underground publications, on stage and TV, and in music and film, leading commentators to complain that society was being inundated by a 'wave of pornography'.[52]

Since the 1960s *countercultures* and *subcultures* have also worked to challenge norms of sexual practice in what amounted

Figure 1.5 Sex became a prominent theme in media in the 1960s. *Sex and the Single Girl* was a 1964 American comedy film, featuring a character based on Helen Gurley Brown, author of the bestselling book of the same title.

18

to a sexual revolution. The hippie movement promoted 'free love' while gay cultures grew to become more visible, with their own urban spaces, dress codes, media and places to meet for sex. Political movements such as feminism, gay liberation, sexual liberation and sex-worker movements, and forms of queer, trans and bi activism, have all played an important part in the way that sex is understood as part of public life.[53] The gay liberation movement challenged discrimination against gay people and pride marches have made gay culture more visible in city spaces. Sex-worker activism fought for work in the sex industry to be recognized as labour and for an end to the criminalization and stigmatization of sex workers.[54] The women's liberation movement focused on a range of issues such as equal pay, education and job opportunities, reproductive rights and access to childcare, violence against women, as well as sex and sexuality. Queer, trans and bi activism have worked to highlight the particular forms of discrimination experienced by people who identify as queer, trans and bi and to widen understanding of sexual and gender identity.

The Sex Wars

Feminists have taken a wide range of approaches to issues of sex and sexuality, with strong divisions and disagreements between different forms of feminism. Some feminist positions have emphasized the importance of women's sexual satisfaction, desire and pleasure, while others have focused on sexual dangers such as violence and harassment. Sexuality became a particular focus of debate in the 1970s, partly because many women felt that the sexual revolution had introduced new pressures on them to be sexually available while failing to challenge the sexual double standard.[55] Feminists called for women's right to a sexuality that was not linked to reproduction and motherhood, and drew attention to men's violence towards women and to the long history of patriarchal relations in which men assumed dominance over women.[56]

One area of conflict among feminists concerned sexual practices and identities that played with roles, power or performance, for example women practising BDSM or using sex toys, and lesbians adopting butch or femme roles.[57] For some feminists this reinforced the oppressive practices of patriarchal heterosexuality[58] and they argued that women should embrace a form of 'feminist sex' that was 'antiphallic, antirole-playing, and fundamentally egalitarian'.[59] Others argued that these practices were potentially challenging to existing ideas about 'normal' sex and opposed a feminist 'sexual correctness' that was oppressive of sexual minorities.[60]

The uncovering of the extent of violence – rape, harassment and abuse – suffered by women and children during this period became a major focus of feminist debate and activism, along with the role that media and culture might play in this.[61] A variety of groups engaged in political activism around the media; some focused on media sexism, some on sexual violence in media, others on violent pornography, and others still on all forms of pornography.

Of all the issues discussed by feminists during this period, it was pornography that became the most high profile and the most divisive.[62] Increasingly feminists clashed with each other over the issue, with some groups making it the focus of their politics, and anti-censorship feminists opposing them. Increasingly too, there were overlaps between the activism of anti-porn feminists and moral and religious groups who 'opposed abortion, homosexuality, child care, sex education, sexual freedom' and promoted 'a return to traditional religious and moral values, and a recommitment to the supremacy of the heterosexual, patriarchal, family'.[63]

A feminist conference, 'Towards a Politics of Sexuality', held in New York in 1982, marked a turning point in these debates, not only because it adopted a more critical and wide-ranging approach to sexual norms, values and politics, but also because it made the relations between sex, media and commerce more visible as the subject of academic and political debate.[64] With a focus on *pleasure* and *danger*, the conference tried to stimulate discussion on a number of controversial issues, but it became the focus of controversy itself when anti-porn feminists accused the conference organizers of promoting sadomasochistic sex and pornography.

The politics and the study of sex, sexuality and media have continued to be controversial, but from these starting points – and later in lesbian and gay studies and queer theory – a body of knowledge dedicated to investigating how sex, its norms, its representation and its regulation are socially and politically constructed and contested has developed.

Sex Critical, Sex Radical, Sex Positive

Instead of being positive or negative about sex we should subject all 'forms of sexuality and all sexual representations . . . to critical thinking' and be 'sex critical'.

Debates about sex and sexuality continue to take place around pro/positive and anti/negative views. These sometimes view sex as essentially good or bad; as liberating and empowering or as dangerous and oppressive. The term *sex critical* has been used as part of an argument that it does not make sense to be either wholly positive or wholly negative about sex – instead we should subject all 'forms of sexuality and all sexual representations . . . to critical thinking', and question how the idea of 'sexuality' impacts on the way we experience ourselves and others.[65] Yet there have always been shades of difference within the 'negative' and 'positive' positions. While some anti-sex or sex-negative positions have seen sex as inherently 'problematic, disruptive, dangerous',[66] others have focused on drawing attention to the problems associated with sexuality, particularly for women: rape, violence and harassment and 'oppressive mandates and requirements'.[67]

The terms pro-sex and sex-positive have most often been used to represent the view that sex is 'a potentially positive force', or to mark the celebration of 'sexual diversity, differing desires and relationships structures, and individual choices based on consent'.[68] A related term – *sex-radical* – has been used to describe 'those seeking and advocating more egalitarian, experimental and challenging forms of sex'.[69] The term sex-radical feminist has also been used to describe an approach to sexuality which is different both

Figure 1.6   Slutwalk Toronto, 2011. The slutwalks, held around the world to protest against rape and slut-shaming, continue a long tradition of activism around sex and gender. They began in 2011, after a policeman in Toronto, Canada, said that women should 'avoid dressing like sluts' to avoid sexual assault (Wikimedia Commons).

from libertarian 'positive' and radical feminist 'negative' views of sex because it critiques inequality without moralizing.[70]

Being sex-positive or sex-radical is often also associated with opposition to the regulation of sexual practices, the censorship of sexual representations, and restrictions on sex education. In a similar way, while disputes about pornography continue to be described in terms of anti-porn and pro-porn, it would be more accurate to say that many groups and individuals who have been labelled as pro-porn are actually anti-anti-porn; that is, critical of attempts to censor sexual representations.

Critical Sexuality and Gender Studies

The academic study of gender and sexuality has developed alongside these political debates, including a broad range of critical sexuality studies.[71] These are based in a variety of disciplines – history, literature, sociology, cultural studies and so on – but all take as their starting point the idea that 'human sexualities emerge through complex symbolic systems in specific social worlds (or cultures), grounded in material, biographical and bodily lives and embedded in wider historical structures', and the recognition that 'human sexualities are multiple, varied and contradictory'.[72]

A similar set of developments have taken place in the study of gender. A move towards *intersectional* feminist approaches has made it possible to think about the differences in women's experiences and priorities around the world, and to consider the ways that gender intersects with sexuality, race, ethnicity and other aspects of identity.[73] While earlier forms of gender studies focused mainly on women, and sexuality studies on gay men, developments in both have opened up debates about sex, sexuality and gender.[74]

Trans and queer thinkers and activists have challenged older ways of thinking about gender and sexuality and their significance for different communities and individuals. There have been calls for gender and sexual politics that take into account 'new forms of family, intimacy, and belonging'[75] and changes in 'the meaning of sexual contact',[76] that welcome diversity,[77] and that are committed to fighting the 'countless different sexist double standards'.[78] These kinds of approaches consider not only 'women's rights, issues, and liberation' but 'all forms of sexism', including those that oppress sexual and gender minorities.[79]

Sexism refers to all 'double standards based upon a person's sex, gender, and/or sexuality'; traditional sexism is 'the assumption that femaleness and femininity are inferior to, or less legitimate than, maleness and masculinity'.[80] *Heterosexism* is 'the institutionalized belief that heterosexual attraction and relationships are considered valid and natural, whereas same-sex attraction and relationships are not'. *Cissexism* is where trans 'gender identities, expressions, and sex embodiments are typically viewed as being less valid and natural'.[81]

These are forms of *oppositional sexism,* in which 'certain attributes are viewed as natural, legitimate, and taken for granted in one sex, and unnatural, illegitimate, and questionable when expressed in the other'. Sexism presents femininity, same-sex desire and gender diversity as 'inferior copies' of masculinity, heterosexuality and cisgender.[82]

These attempts to control and categorize suggest a strong belief that sex, sexuality and gender are, or should be, binary and dichotomous, that people should be male or female, masculine or feminine, gay or straight – that these are 'opposites' and are all that it is possible to be. They also suggest that sex, gender and sexuality should be linked to each other in a uniform way. Clearly this isn't the case, given the variety of practices and identities that people take up and the wide range of connections that they make between their bodies, identities, desires and practices.[83]

Sex and Media Studies

Today, sex 'assumes many forms' and 'is bound up with more things' than in the past, joining together bodies, technologies and media in new ways. The relations between sexual practices, media, identities and communities have become increasingly complex.

The study of sex and media has also developed dramatically over the same period. In the 1970s and 1980s, debates about sex and media focused on *objectification*, and anti-porn feminists saw pornography as 'propaganda that incites violence against . . . women and children'.[84] The growth in media and cultural studies since then has shown that we cannot simply divide representations of gender into positive and negative images or assume we know what effects media have in the world. Views that assume 'a simple link between words/images and behaviour'[85] have been challenged by a variety of new approaches and by studies of media genres, producers, audiences and institutions.[86]

The study of the representation of sexual groups, especially of gay men and lesbians, has also emerged,[87] and the relations between media and culture, gender and sexuality have become the focus of new interest. Today in Western societies, sex has become much

24

Figure 1.7 New norms? The charmed circle and outer limits of sex (Monique Mulholland, 2011).

more visible, particularly in the media.[88] It 'assumes many forms' and 'is bound up with more things' than in the past,[89] joining together bodies, technologies and media in new ways. The relations between sexual practices, media, identities and communities have become increasingly complex. Because sex has become easier to separate from reproduction and love, it has become possible to see it as *plastic*,[90] something we can rethink and change.

There are major areas of contest – aspects of sexual practice which people disagree on, while some forms of sex remain at the outer limits. However, some forms that were previously frowned upon are much more acceptable to many people today. Heterosexuality remains at the centre of the charmed circle, but may include frequent 'fun' sex and forms of 'raunch culture'.[91] In line with the neoliberal politics of Western societies, where the emphasis is on individual 'choice' and self-regulation,[92] there is some acceptance of sexual and gender politics so long as these are moderate and mainstream, not challenging to the status quo.

In this context a kind of homonormativity emerged – a politics that 'does not contest heteronormative assumptions and institutions' and promotes 'a privatized, depoliticized gay culture anchored in domesticity and consumption'.[93] Forms of sexuality which fit with heteronormativity – for example gay couples focused on monogamy and marriage, and other sexual identities that conform to conventional ideas about gender expression – have become more acceptable.[94]

These new norms of sex and their alternatives can be seen in the range of ways that contemporary sex-advice books speak to their readers. Some focus on *relationships*; *Hot Sex: How to Do It*, for example, is described as 'perfect bedtime reading for two' and aimed at 'Everyday Couples' who want 'Exceptional Sex'.[95] Some are aimed at developing slow intimate sex – *Slow Sex: The Art and Craft of the Female Orgasm* focuses on developing a 'deeper spiritual and physical connection'[96] – while *Just F*ck Me! What Women Want Men to Know About Taking Control in the Bedroom* prioritizes speed and spontaneity.[97] Some books are aimed at teens (*Sex: A Book for Teens. An Uncensored Guide to Your Body, Sex and Safety*[98]) and others at older people (*He Never Saw Me Naked. Sex After 60: Enjoying Sex After Turning 60*[99]). Some are aimed at men (*The Thinking Man's Guide to Pleasuring a Woman: 6 Powerful Keys to Unlocking the Elusive Female Orgasm*[100]), while many, such as *Naughty Girl: A Sex Guide to What Men Want, Sex Tips for Straight Women from a Gay Man*[101] and *The Good Girl's Guide to Great Sex*,[102] are aimed at women.[103]

Others are concerned with health. In *The Great Sex Guide* some kinds of sex are described as being forms of 'preventative health measure'[104] and part of a 'therapeutic' culture. Some books concentrate on the sacred meanings of sex, as in *Urban Tantra:*

Sacred Sex for the Twenty-First Century.[105] Another type of book focuses on sex as recreation; *RecSex*, for instance, provides a guide to hook-up sex.[106] A focus on sex as play is evident in a number of publications: *The Ultimate Guide to Strap-On Sex*[107] says that 'sex is one area of life in which two trusting adults can truly relax, let their guard down, and throw themselves into the sensuality and eroticism of play . . . Your goals are to explore, experiment, and – above all – to have fun.'[108] Many books show how sex has become 'a statement of lifestyle and fashion', involving dressing up, body adornment, playing games, role play, using toys and props, stripping, making porn, or throwing a sex party.[109]

Sometimes sexual expertise, skill and performance is emphasized: *How to Do Everything*[110] is 'a sex book for people who like having sex, who want to have more, and want to know how to do everything better', while *The Sex Instruction Manual* offers 'Techniques for Optimum Performance'.[111] Some books, such as *The Seductive Art of Japanese Bondage*, focus on particular types of sexual practice.[112] *Fetish Sex* shows readers how to 'enjoy sexual fetishes as a healthy sex toy just like any other, no matter how ordinary or unusual'.[113]

What these guides suggest is that it is not so obvious what 'sex' is today. It may be promoted as a way of caring for the self and developing 'a sexual lifestyle';[114] or presented as 'a source of happiness, a form of relaxation, a site of pleasure . . . a means of achieving spiritual wholeness';[115] or it may be a way of connecting with the body and developing or maintaining a *sense of self*.

Although they offer a set of norms about what sex should be, to some extent these guides also reflect the fact that people's sex lives are very diverse. Sex may take place between lovers, friends or strangers – up close or at a distance in chatrooms, by text, phone, or through sharing images. It might but needn't be focused on genitals and it might but needn't lead to orgasm. People may be more interested in feet and earlobes, toys and outfits, or writing and drawing than they are in genitals.[116]

Sex may vary in character – be rough, gentle, tender, athletic, experimental or routine. And people have sex for many reasons: for pleasure, out of duty, to connect with others, to earn money,

With thanks to Kirstin Rohwer.

Figure 1.8 Make Your Own Relationship User Guide. Some contemporary sex and relationships advice is less prescriptive, more inclusive and reflective of diversity. (By permission of Meg John Barker and Justin Hancock.)

for excitement, to relax, to be playful, to experiment, to escape boredom or to let off steam. Sex may be experienced in a variety of ways: as uplifting, funny, embarrassing, hurtful, as 'a tiresome chore, a painful imposition, or simply tedious', and, perhaps more commonly than is ever represented, as 'an everyday activity, not particularly important to the individual' or 'a functional way of keeping oneself healthy and in touch with a partner'.[117] It seems that 'the lines we draw between sex and other activities such as play, leisure, spirituality, art, and relaxation'[118] may not be as clear as many people like to think.[119]

There are similarly blurred lines between sex and work, or intimacy and commerce. While these are often presented as mutually exclusive, sex involves commercial transactions of all kinds wherever it takes place, and people often 'mingle economic activity with intimacy'.[120] People may marry for money or stay together because they cannot afford to separate. Marriage comes with costs as well as tax incentives. Sex work and unpaid sex both involve 'emotional labour', and some sex work may involve care and affection while some unpaid sex may not.[121] And of course, sex is now intimately linked to media, technologies and a range of commercial products which may involve purchases, subscriptions and fees. The question of what sex is – which in some ways seems to be so straightforward – becomes much harder to answer once we start to think about these factors.

Sex, Media and Technology

There is 'a long-standing and well-recognized link between sex and technology throughout history and through many different cultures'.[122] Technologies often make it possible to change the way things are done, and specific types of technology can become part of the way we live out our sexualities.[123] For example, drugs can be used to enhance sexual performance,[124] while surgery can alter the appearance of genitals. Media and communication technologies have become especially important for how we learn to become more sexually skilled or attractive, as well as

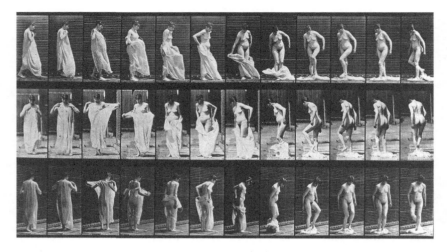

Figure 1.9 A Woman Undressing, 1887. Technologies such as photography are not only for recording, but a site for producing visual pleasure and knowledge about bodies and sex. Edward Muybridge's nineteenth-century studies of human motion mark an important moment in this process (Wellcome Trust).

providing sexual entertainment and ways of interacting sexually with others.

Technologies also alter what and how we can see. Microscopes and telescopes literally changed our view of the world, allowing us to see closer and further than had been possible before. They may become extensions of our bodies – for example the invention of photography made cameras an extension of the eye, as well as appearing to offer a way of preserving 'the trace of a once-present person or object' and the possibility of a 'relation to the real' through media.[125]

In Western cultures, the development of a science of sex[126] has focused on what can be known intellectually about sex, rather than on sexual pleasures and skills. This has been closely linked to the idea that scrutinizing the body can reveal the 'truth' of sex. Early pornography appeared to capture the evidence of sexual pleasure through maximum visibility, documenting sex through what has been called a 'frenzy of the visible',[127] played out through highly lit close-ups of body parts, moving through 'thousands of scenarios, angles, positions, and partners'.[128]

Over time technological processes have continued to provide 'the most vivid possible equivalent of sensory stimuli'.[129] Video made it possible to watch pornography in private, and the development of mobile and social media have continued to afford new ways of dividing the sexually public from the sexually private.[130] The internet made it possible to integrate porn more easily into our interactions with other people,[131] in line with the search for 'community, interactivity and personalization' in much new media use.[132]

In addition, new forms of sexual performance, game play and communication have become possible, allowing for a 'fusion of image and act'.[133] Sexual representations and practices are no longer so distinct from one another. People connect across real and virtual environments and there are 'diminishing boundaries between online porn and real life sexuality'.[134] Sex is part of the development of the internet[135] and it has been claimed that it actually drives technological innovation.[136] For example, demand for pornography has hastened the development of servers, e-commerce systems, DVD, mobile phones and broadband.[137] It has worked to accelerate the 'diffusion of new products and services', and to push the legal and social boundaries that have constrained porn production in the past.[138]

Yet the tendency to conceptualize sex in terms of 'good' and 'bad' persists. For example, while many advice books now include a wider range of practices than they did in the past, these are often presented as extras to the 'main event' of penis-in-vagina sex. Most are aimed at heterosexual couples and very few are addressed directly to men. Most assume that sexuality and gender are binary and that sex takes place in monogamous relationships, which the books aim to spice up by introducing new skills, techniques and pleasures. However the responsibility for managing all of this is assumed to be something that women will take on. There is still often a 'hierarchical valuation of sex acts' and the lack of a concept of 'benign sexual variation'.[139]

These and other kinds of representations work to regulate the ways in which we talk and think about sex. In the next chapter I examine the regulation of sex media in more detail, and the way

31

that concerns about sex have come to focus particularly heavily on media.

Summary

- Cultural representations often embody norms, presenting sex and gender as part of a hierarchy and as binary.

- Definitions and representations may work to police the way sex and gender is understood but they can also be used to challenge norms and create new identities, communities and ways of thinking.

- Sex often tends to be discussed in terms of either pleasure or danger, but critical approaches acknowledge that it is much more complex than this.

- Technologies and media are increasingly important to the way we experience and understand sex.

2

Regulating Sex Media

This chapter covers:

- The regulation of representations of sex in literature, art and film.

- The importance of cultural figures and media texts in regulation.

- The development of particular spaces, terminology and forms of classification for regulating sex media.

- The regulation of sexual representations and practices which are presented as 'extreme' and 'perverse'.

- The regulation of 'sexting' focused on young people, particularly girls.

- Contemporary trends in the regulation of sex media.

What is Regulation?

Regulation is not simply repressive – preventing something from happening, as we often think – but productive: contributing to the way sexual issues are represented, imagined and understood.

Regulation takes many different forms. Explicit forms of regulation include laws, rules and policies, whereas implicit forms include customs and practices, norms about what is acceptable, appropriate or polite behaviour, and common-sense views that make it difficult to express different ways of thinking. Regulation can work to support media freedom, for example by preventing monopolies, but it often closes down that freedom through forms of regulation such as censorship. Bans and blacklists can prevent and control the material being produced.[1] Licensing controls who can produce material or what its content should be, for example through the classification of films.[2]

Some forms of regulation are violent, such as the murder and intimidation of journalists or the destruction of works of art and literature.[3] There are also types of market censorship, for example when media owners have too much power, when relationships between governments and media corporations are too close, or when entertainment is prized over information, meaning that some types of content do not appear in the media at all.[4] Finally, there is the self-censorship involved when producers tone down their own products or publishers refuse to print controversial material for fear of reprisals.[5]

In Western societies ideas taken from science and the law have become important means by which people monitor their sexual behaviour. While religion continues to be an important justification for regulation, science and the law identify acceptable forms of sex, defining those that are legal or healthy and those that are illegal and unhealthy. These definitions encourage us to display the 'correct' kinds of sexual behaviour and desire, and to suppress or conceal those that are forbidden or frowned upon.[6] They also shape ideas about what 'sex' is. For example, in the UK until 1885 the law had forbidden non-reproductive sexual acts as immoral, whoever practised them, but when the Criminal Law Amendment Act of that year outlawed acts of 'gross indecency' between men it helped to create a category of a particular type of homosexual *person* whose activities should be regulated within law.

Around the same time, the scientific study of sex – sexology – was becoming a new and important area of expertise about sex. Sexologists were the forerunner of today's sexperts, counsellors and therapists. Towards the end of the nineteenth century, doctors and psychiatrists became especially concerned with categorizing sexual 'abnormalities', often presented as perversions and as congenital – inherited – conditions. New terms such as 'intermediate sex'[7] and 'invert' were used to describe people whose gender expression did not match their biological sex – 'manly' women and 'womanly' men – or people who were attracted to the same sex. For example, *Sexual Inversion*, published in 1897, argued that a female conventionally masculine 'congenital invert' would typically be attracted to a more conventionally feminine 'pseudo invert'.[8] Many modern assumptions about sexuality were established through this kind of writing, including the ideas that same-sex attraction might be a 'phase', that gay men are 'effeminate', or that lesbian couples are always made up of 'butch' and 'femme' partners.

Until this time there were no public figures associated with gay men and lesbians, but two trials – involving the writer Oscar Wilde in 1895 and Radclyffe Hall's novel *The Well of Loneliness* in 1928 – helped to change this. The trial of Oscar Wilde made public his relationships with male prostitutes and he was prosecuted for 'gross indecency'. Wilde pleaded not guilty, arguing that he was being attacked for 'the love that dare not speak its name', but he was convicted and sentenced to two years' hard labour, dying shortly after his release from prison.[9]

The main character in *The Well of Loneliness*, Stephen Gordon, is described as a 'narrow-hipped and wide shouldered' woman whose rejection of feminine things is 'queer', 'horrid', 'all wrong' and 'unnatural'.[10] Stephen falls in love with Mary, a more conventionally feminine character; giving her up to a man at the end of the novel, Stephen makes a plea that despite being 'flawed in the making' inverts should be tolerated by society and by God. Havelock Ellis, the author of *Sexual Inversion*, wrote the preface to *The Well of Loneliness*, describing it as the first English novel to present the 'poignant situations' of inverts in a hostile society.[11] The book was prosecuted and found obscene because it might 'encourage or legitimate lesbianism'.[12]

As the examples of Oscar Wilde and *The Well of Loneliness* show, cultural texts and 'figures' have become steadily more important in public debates about sex and sexuality, alongside

Figure 2.1 A photograph from the collection of the sexologist Richard von Krafft-Ebing. Krafft-Ebing's book *Psychopathia Sexualis* (1886) was part of the sexological interest in sexual 'perversions' (Wellcome Trust).

the law and science. Wilde's public presentation was as a flamboyant and 'effeminate' dandy, with long hair by the standards of the time, and 'aesthetic' dress which included velvet jackets and knee-length breeches. At the time this appearance was associated with being artistic[13] rather than with sexuality, but it was to become 'important in creating a public image of and for the homosexual; as decadent, artistic, white, upper class'.[14] Similarly, while Radclyffe Hall would not necessarily have been seen as such in the 1920s, her style came to represent a mannish and bohemian lesbian 'type', with her 'short hair, bow tie, chappish clothes, hand in pocket, lighted cigarette'.[15]

The trial of *The Well of Loneliness*, as in the case of Wilde, gave the depiction of homosexuality much wider publicity than it would otherwise have had. The trials show how regulation is not simply repressive – preventing something from happening, as we often think – but productive: contributing to the way sexual issues are represented, imagined and understood.

Regulation may shut down ways of talking and thinking about a topic, but it also contributes to ideas about the ways in which individuals and communities with particular sexual identities act and speak. This is important for groups who need a common language of expression in order to be visible to each other. It has been argued that, as a result of the development of sexology and new figures of sexuality, 'homosexuality began to speak in its own behalf', 'often in the same vocabulary' and using the language of science and law.[16] It became possible to create a shared identity and community for women who felt as Hall's characters did or men who shared Wilde's desires.[17]

Pornography and the Secret Museum

Of course, the main focus for the regulation of sexual representations has, over time, come to be pornography. Between 1500 and 1800 writings and images that would now be called pornographic were used by free-thinkers and libertines to test the limits of expression and challenge political authority and social and cultural norms.[18] When the development of printing and later photography made writing and pictures more accessible as part of a 'larger decentralizing trend in communications'[19] and a 'democratization of culture'[20] pornography was increasingly seen as in need of control.

The label 'pornography' is newer than we might think; dictionaries didn't include the word before the nineteenth century. It is

Figure 2.2 The trial of the writer Oscar Wilde in 1895 helped to create the public image of a flamboyant homosexual man (Wikimedia Commons).

also more closely connected to the broader categories of art and literature than we might expect. One dictionary definition from 1864 described pornography as 'licentious painting employed to decorate the walls of rooms sacred to bacchanalian orgies, examples of which exist in Pompeii'.[21]

The reference to Pompeii is to the sexually explicit statues, amulets and frescoes excavated there throughout the eighteenth and nineteenth centuries and removed to 'Secret Museums'. These were collections housed in museums such as the Borbonico Museum in Naples and the British Museum in London. The Secret Museum in London – originally called the 'Cabinet of Obscene Objects' – became an official collection in 1865, containing 'engravings of Roman bronzes and pottery lamps . . . eighteenth-century sketches of copulating couples, nineteenth-century Japanese colour porn cards, a Victorian reproduction of a medieval chastity-belt, early photographs of nudes in classical poses'.[22]

The discoveries at Pompeii and Herculaneum suggested that earlier societies may not have thought it important to hide away images of sex and fertility; many of the artefacts had been placed in public spaces – a statue of the god Pan having sex with a goat had been on display in the garden of a villa.[23] The setting up of Secret Museums to house these objects showed how different the Western view of sexual representation had become. It made literal the idea that access to sexual objects and images should be controlled and kept 'secret'.

Obscenity: Literature, Film and Art

The term 'obscenity' is used to indicate a representation that is 'indecent and vulgar, dirty and lewd, gross and vile and thus morally corrupting and potentially illicit'. It is linked to the Greek phrase 'ob skene' or 'off stage', suggesting that such representations are, or should be, kept out of sight.

In 1909 'pornography' appeared in the Oxford English Dictionary as a term to describe 'the expression or suggestion of obscene or unchaste subjects in literature or art'.[24] Categorizing something as 'obscene' has been one of the key ways of regulating media dealing with sexual subjects. Generally speaking, the term is used to suggest that an object or image is both sexual and offensive, though what counts as obscene varies across different times and

Figure 2.3 A statue of the god Pan and a goat found in the garden of a villa near Herculaneum and dating from the first century BC (Wikimedia Commons).

places. The term 'obscenity' is used to indicate a representation that is 'indecent and vulgar, dirty and lewd, gross and vile and thus morally corrupting and potentially illicit'.[25] It is linked to the Greek phrase '*ob skene*' or 'off stage', suggesting that such representations are, or should be, kept out of sight.[26]

In the UK a series of Obscene Publications Acts[27] have been used to regulate what can and cannot be represented within the law. The test of obscenity is whether a jury thinks that an image or text would be 'likely to deprave and corrupt' a viewer or reader who comes into contact with it.[28] In the US the test has been whether 'the average person, applying contemporary community standards', feels that sexual conduct is depicted in a 'patently offensive way' and whether it 'lacks serious literary, artistic, political, or scientific value'.[29] A similar defence 'in the interests of science, literature, art or learning, or of other objects of general concern' was added to the UK Act in 1959.[30] In the trial of *The Well of Loneliness* it had been argued that the novel's 'cleverness' made it more dangerous,[31] but in later trials the question of *value* became an important defence for writers.

D. H. Lawrence's novel *Lady Chatterley's Lover* is a good example of this. It was written in the UK in the 1920s but not published there till 1960 because of its depictions of sex between Lady Chatterley and her gamekeeper and because it used words like 'cunt' and 'fuck'. The publisher, Penguin, was taken to court, where, echoing earlier views of pornography as something particularly dangerous for 'vulnerable' groups, the prosecutor asked the jury, 'would you approve of your young sons, young daughters . . . reading this book . . . Is it a book you would wish your wife or servants to read?'[32] Thirty-five witnesses, including well-known authors such as Rebecca West, spoke in the novel's defence and Penguin was found not guilty of obscenity. A year later, the novel had sold two million copies, outselling the Bible. The trial had made the novel more visible and successful than it would have otherwise been.[33]

In the US, Allen Ginsberg's poem 'Howl', published in 1956, resulted in his publisher being charged with circulating obscene literature, but when literary experts defended the poem, the judge ruled that it was not obscene. In the UK guilty verdicts on the books *Last Exit to Brooklyn* and *Inside Linda Lovelace* were also overturned on appeal in 1966 and 1976.

Prosecutions for obscenity have continued to focus on literature and visual art, but as new kinds of media have emerged, rules aimed at regulating these have followed too. In the early twentieth century the British Board of Film Classification listed forty-three types of content that should be subject to censorship.[34] Many of these focused on sex (Box 2.1).

The US Motion Picture Production Code of 1930 placed restrictions on representations of adultery, scenes of passion, seduction or rape, perversion, sex between white and black people, the exposure of children's sex organs, nudity, undressing, and locations such as bedrooms.[35] It decreed that 'No picture shall be produced that will lower the moral standards of those who see it.' This was thought to be particularly important in the case of film due to its

Figure 2.4 *Lady Chatterley's Lover* was written in the UK in the 1920s but not published there until 1960 because of its depictions of sex (Wikimedia Commons).

Box 2.1: The British Board of Film Classification listed forty-three types of content that should not be shown, including many focusing on sex:

Vulgar accessories in the staging

Unnecessary exhibition of under-clothing

Nude figures

Offensive vulgarity, and impropriety in conduct and dress

Indecorous dancing

Excessively passionate love scenes

Bathing scenes passing the limits of propriety

Subjects dealing with White Slave traffic

Subjects dealing with premeditated seduction of girls

'First Night' scenes

Scenes suggestive of immorality

Indelicate sexual situations

Situations accentuating delicate marital relations

Men and women in bed together

Illicit relationships

Prostitution and procuration

Incidents suggestive of incestuous relations

Confinements

Scenes laid in disorderly houses

ability to reach 'every class of society' and because of its 'vivid' form of presentation.[36]

Art has also continued to be the target of accusations of obscenity. In 1989, the photographer Robert Mapplethorpe became the subject of controversy in the US when his exhibition, 'The Perfect Moment', was scheduled to open at the Corcoran Gallery of Art in Washington, D.C. The exhibition had been partially funded by a government grant and featured Mapplethorpe's X Portfolio – thirteen photographs showing gay sadomasochistic practices – and his Z Portfolio of black male nudes.[37] Senator Jesse Helms singled out as obscene images such as 'Mark Stevens', which showed a man in leather chaps with his penis exposed; 'Man in Polyester Suit', which showed the torso of a man with his penis exposed; 'Rosie', a partially naked girl; and 'Jesse McBride', which showed a naked boy. He argued that Mapplethorpe should not be allowed to show his work in the US. Under pressure, the gallery cancelled the exhibition, but artists then retaliated by projecting some of Mapplethorpe's photographs onto the Corcoran's facade. Demand to see the images increased dramatically thanks to the controversy, and the exhibition continued elsewhere.[38]

As this example shows, banning something may only end up focusing more attention on the offending item – a tendency demonstrated over and over again when the press reports on, and reproduces, images that it is arguing should not be visible, and when the law attempts to banish something from public view by making it the centre of attention.[39] This process has been called *on/scenity*, the 'gesture by which a culture brings onto the public scene the very organs, acts, bodies and pleasures' that were previously 'ob–off–scene, that is . . . needing to be kept out of view'.[40]

Labelling 'Pornography'

It has been argued that the failure to come up with a workable definition of pornography, over 150 years after the term began to appear in dictionaries, and its use for labelling such a wide range of different things – including Pompeiian frescoes, 'great chunks of

Shakespeare' and a variety of contemporary media texts[41] – should make us question the idea that there are things that are pornographic in nature.[42]

Although 'pornography' appears simply to describe particular kinds of content, it is part of a process of grouping things together in order to regulate them – a category used by relatively powerful groups such as middle-class white men 'on behalf of' more powerless groups such as women, children, the vulnerable and the working classes,[43] who, it is argued, need to be protected. This process of categorization often has very little to do with the characteristics of the texts themselves and more to do with ideas about standards, freedoms, rights and privacy, or about an object's imagined ability to 'deprave and corrupt' or to evoke feelings such as disgust. Similarly, while some kinds of subject matter might be understood as 'obviously' obscene – bodily functions, sex, violence and death – it is the idea that some texts are able to produce certain responses 'in ways . . . held to warrant repulsion'[44] that is more central to the notion of obscenity.

The label 'pornography' is also often used more generally today as a figure of speech to 'express many kinds of intense revulsion'.[45] News media often use the term 'porn' as a metaphor[46] for weakness or self-indulgence, to suggest a loss of contact with the world or other people, to imply the wasting of time, a lack of critical judgement, or paying too much attention to feelings, sensations and bodies that are felt to be intense and excessive.

Over time, pornography has become the key focus for testing ideas about what is obscene. Unlike art and literature, it is usually assumed to have no value, and when people argue in its defence it is more likely to be in terms of free speech and the right to sexual expression and representation.

Porn Producers and 'Extreme' Porn

The label 'extreme', like those of 'porn' and 'obscenity', becomes a way of establishing – and regulating – which kinds of representations are acceptable and which are not.

45

Box 2.2: Examples of the way the label 'porn' is used in British newspapers (Barker, 2012):

Nature porn: landscape porn, tree porn, gardening porn, horticultural porn

Food porn: gastro porn, potato porn, charcuterie porn

Property porn: real estate porn, homes porn, DIY porn

Techno-porn: car porn, bike porn, cathode porn, medical porn, brain porn

Emotional porn: grief porn, poverty porn, anger porn, death porn, misery porn

Status porn: servant porn, posh porn, aristo porn, fogey porn, political porn, anarcho porn

One area of pornographic regulation has focused on professional producers who are seen as 'libertarian' figures[47] concerned with individual sexual freedom and depicted as powerful men locked in battle with society. Hugh Hefner, the founder of the Playboy empire in the 1950s, is most closely associated with the promotion of sexual hedonism and a lifestyle which celebrates youth, pleasure and consumption[48] and resists the domestication of men into the roles of husband and breadwinner.[49]

In the late 1990s the kind of softcore imagery associated with *Playboy* magazine became fashionable again,[50] and Playboy became more visible as a brand through the use of its logo on clothing, jewellery and accessories. Despite this, Hefner has continued to be a focus for opposition to pornography, in campaigns such as the 'Eff Off Heff' protest in 2011 against the reopening of a Playboy club in the UK. The *Playboy* magazine itself, however, is increasingly seen as offering an outdated and mild form of pornography, a 'retro brand of "gentleman's porn"'.[51] The remark that contemporary pornography 'is not your father's *Playboy*',[52] widely repeated in the media, is used to suggest that there is a real difference between past and present pornographies, with increasingly cruel 'body-punishing' images becoming widely available.[53]

The *Hustler* porn empire, created by Larry Flynt, can be seen as the predecessor of much of the hardcore pornography that currently attracts this kind of criticism. Flynt became well known throughout the 1970s for transgressing 'in the most profoundly offensive way possible, each and every deeply held social taboo, norm, and propriety he could identify',[54] and was duly subject to 'an astonishing array of obscenity, libel, and criminal charges'.[55] *Hustler* adopted a graphic style in its magazine, not only in its representations of sex, but in its images of 'hugely fat women, hermaphrodites, amputees' and its 'explicit photo spreads of the consequences of venereal disease, graphic war carnage, and other in-your-face pictorials'.[56]

Graphic style and content emphasizing different kinds of excess are found throughout many kinds of hardcore porn. For example, men and women may be represented as absolute opposites, so that heterosexual sex 'becomes a near impossible play of colossal penises and the tiniest of vaginas'. Similarly, 'intensities of arousal, desire and pleasure', 'stamina and gratification' may be presented in fantastic and hyperbolic ways,[57] while sexual activity may focus on 'mechanized cycles of penetration from one orifice to another'.[58] The Cambria List, attributed to the US lawyer Paul Cambria, lists content that porn producers should not include if they want to avoid prosecution (Box 2.3).

Forms of hardcore porn that employ graphic style or content, or that push at the boundaries of what is familiar and acceptable in other ways, became the focus of two high-profile prosecutions of porn producers in the US in the early 2000s. In 2003 the premises of Extreme Associates were raided by federal agents and five videos were seized.[59] These featured actresses dressed like young girls, scenes of women drinking vomit, saliva and other bodily fluids, and plots that focused on the beating, rape and murder of women. Rob Black and Lizzie Borden, the directors, were indicted by a jury for the production and distribution of obscene pornographic materials and in 2009 they were jailed for a year and a day.[60] In the same year, Max Hardcore was found guilty

Box 2.3: The Cambria List – porn content likely to result in prosecution:

No shots with appearance of pain or degradation

No facials (bodyshots are OK if shot is not nasty)

No bukkake

No spitting or saliva mouth to mouth

No food used as sex object

No peeing unless in a natural setting, e.g., field, roadside

No coffins

No blindfolds

No wax dripping

No two dicks in/near one mouth

No shot of stretching pussy

No fisting

No squirting

No bondage-type toys or gear unless very light

No girls sharing same dildo (in mouth or pussy)

Toys are OK if shot is not nasty

No hands from 2 different people fingering same girl

No male/male penetration

No transsexuals

No bi-sex

No degrading dialogue, e.g., 'Suck this cock, bitch' while slapping her face with a penis

No menstruation topics

No incest topics

No forced sex, rape themes, etc.

No black men–white women themes

of obscenity relating to five movies and jailed.[61] His films showed vomiting, choke-fucking, 'pissing into the gaping orifices of female performers' and close-up shots of their faces covered in urine, semen, saliva and smeared makeup.[62]

Rob Black appealed to figures in the pornography industries for support, arguing that he was simply extending the boundaries of porn representation as Larry Flynt had done before him. But the president of *Adult Video News* president described Extreme Associates' films as 'horrible, unwatchable, disgusting',[63] while Larry Flynt condemned the depiction of 'forced sex' in their work.[64]

The condemnation of 'extreme' images shows that the depiction of any relationship between sex and suffering, fear and harm is generally interpreted as wrong and disturbing, though it is not particularly uncommon elsewhere in film, especially in the horror genre.[65] The label 'extreme', like those of 'porn' and 'obscenity', becomes a way of establishing – and regulating – which kinds of representations are acceptable and which are not.[66] What its use reveals is an insistence that sex should always be associated with pleasure rather than suffering, harm, trauma or disgust.[67]

Regulation and 'Perverse' Sex

Consensual 'perverse' forms of sexual practice have also been the subject of regulation. In the UK in 1990 sixteen gay men received fines or prison sentences following an investigation, 'Operation Spanner', during which a video showing men engaging in SM activity was seized by the police. Despite appeals, the convictions were upheld by both the Court of Appeal, the UK Law Lords and the European Court of Human Rights. The decisions were based on a ruling that bodily harm related to sexual activities (measured in terms of pain and marks on the body) could only be lawful if it was 'transient' and 'trifling'.[68]

More recently in the UK, Section 63 of the Criminal Justice and Immigration Act (2008) has focused on what it calls 'extreme pornographic' material that 'appears to have been produced solely or principally for the purpose of sexual arousal'.[69] Material is seen as 'extreme pornography' if it is 'grossly offensive, disgusting or otherwise of an obscene character',[70] and is subject to prosecution if it represents in 'an explicit and realistic way' an activity that could threaten the person's life or be 'likely to result in serious injury to a person's anus, breasts or genitals'.[71] Possession of such material can result in being placed on the Sex Offender's Register and jail terms of up to three years.

One attempted prosecution (*R v Holland*) which was brought (and later dropped) under this Act in 2010 concerned the possession of what became known as the 'Spankwire' video, a short montage aimed at body modification enthusiasts that depicted scenes of genital modification, mainly focused on 'cutting, binding, squashing or inserting objects into the penis'.[72] The video had been in circulation since 2007 and at the time of the attempted prosecution had logged almost 2 million hits on spankwire.com alone.[73] The popularity of sharing audience reactions to the video on sites such as YouTube suggests that there are pleasures in being 'shocked', 'horrified' and 'disgusted' and in performing this for the camera and other audiences.

What these cases suggest is the tendency of regulators to focus on images and practices that appear risky, play with power, or push the body to its limits, whether in terms of the content of porn or the bodily and sexual practices of particular individuals, communities and consumers, even if they are consensual. Yet these characteristics are accepted and even taken for granted in the case of activities such as boxing, rugby, mountain climbing and cosmetic surgery, which are also potentially dangerous and may result in pain and injury.[74] Neither are all forms of sexual activity judged in the same way – penis-in-vagina sex is almost always presented as 'good' sex, even though it may result in a lack of pleasure, disease or unwanted pregnancy.[75] It is the right to take sexual pleasure from the consensual giving or receiving of pain, and the challenge to norms of sexual activity and its significance, that are restricted. In particular it is representations of BDSM, 'queer erotic expression',[76] and images that challenge ideas of appropriate behaviour for women that are most vulnerable to regulation. In the process, acts, bodies and communities that are not heteronormative – or which challenge norms of sex and gender in other ways – are either made invisible, or made visible only in order to punish and stigmatize them.[77]

Sexting: 'Self-Produced Pornography'

Alongside 'extreme' sex and sex media, young people's sexual practices have become a major focus for regulators and are often used to justify new forms of regulation because young people are seen as 'vulnerable', 'high risk' and 'at the mercy of an adult sexuality that is alien to them and may well be harmful to them'.[78] In particular, a view that the internet is 'full of pedophiles, child molesters and child rapists' has fuelled a series of 'technopanics' and other 'media panics' and led to continual demands for increased legislation – and often to actual changes in regulation.[79]

One of the most high-profile examples of this has taken place around 'sexting' – a term that has come to refer to the circulation of naked or semi-naked images by mobile phone. Although this is something that a variety of age groups engage in, public interest has focused almost entirely on young women and girls. Studies have revealed quite differing levels of sexting amongst young people – one study in the US in 2009 found that only 5 per cent of fourteen to seventeen year olds had sent images of themselves and 18 per cent had received them.[80] Another in 2010 suggested that 8 per cent of seventeen year olds had sent explicit images,[81] while a European project in the same year found that 12 per cent of eleven to sixteen year olds had seen or received online sexual messages.[82] However an Australian study in 2014 found that over 50 per cent of students had received a sexually explicit text message while 43 per cent had sent such a message. Forty-two per cent had received a sexually explicit image of someone else and 26 per cent had sent a sexually explicit image of themselves.[83]

While concern around sexting has drawn on fears about young people being at risk from adults, it has focused on young people's sexual behaviour with each other. Sexting has been described as a disturbing 'epidemic' resulting in 'tragic consequences'[84] such as emotional and psychological damage and even suicide.[85] Clearly some forms of sexting may be risky, harassing or exploitative, for example where young people are seeking to hook-up with adults, where images are shared without consent, or where circulating images is used as a way of attacking and shaming girls.[86] But it is much more common for sexting to be 'experimental', taking place as part of an existing relationship, or between two people where one is hoping to be in a relationship with the other.[87] It may also take place between friends, as a joke, during a moment of bonding, or be the digital equivalent of 'truth or dare' games. Images may be created for flirting, to 'show off' or to 'gross out' others.[88] The rise of interest in young people and sexting can be seen as part of a much wider concern with age, technology and sexual representation. In Australia the law forbids not only the depiction of people engaged in sexual activity if they are not adults, but also the portrayal of adults who look as though they are under eighteen and of adults who are portrayed as minors.[89] In the UK too, images are treated as an image of a child if they convey an impression that the person depicted is not an adult, even if 'some of the physical characteristics shown are not those of a child'.[90] In the US, at least twenty states had introduced sexting legislation by the end of 2009,[91] and sexting was being described as 'self-produced child pornography'.[92]

A particularly high-profile case took place in 2008 when a District Attorney in Pennsylvania threatened to bring child pornography charges against four girls aged thirteen who had sent pictures of themselves bare-breasted or wearing bras and bathing suits. The DA claimed that the images showed a 'prohibited sexual act' because the girls were posing provocatively. They were threatened with being charged and made to register as sex offenders unless they submitted to probation and agreed to complete an education programme. When three of the girls' families sought a restraining order against the DA,[93] this became the first case to challenge the prosecution of young people for sexting.[94] The court agreed with the families, finding that 'an individual District Attorney may not coerce parents into permitting him to impose on their children his ideas of morality and gender roles'.[95]

Sexting, Double Standards and Shaming

Several teenage suicides have attracted publicity because of their links to sexting. Jessica Logan was an eighteen-year-old girl from Ohio whose former boyfriend forwarded a nude picture of her to people at her school. Logan was harassed and bullied as a result and she killed herself in 2008.[96] In 2012 her parents settled a case in which they had accused the school of not protecting Jessica from sexual harassment. The case established that School Districts could be liable if they failed to protect students from sexual harassment at school, and the 'Jessica Logan Act', which requires schools to prohibit cyber-bullying, was passed in 2013.

Hope Witsell was a thirteen-year-old girl from Florida who sent a photograph of herself to a boy she liked. This was forwarded by another girl, eventually being circulated around Hope's school. As a result, the school suspended her. She was later pressured by several older boys into sending them a photo of her breasts. When this was discovered the school refused to let her run for a student advisor position and the bullying began again.[97] She committed suicide in 2009.

Amanda Todd was a fifteen-year-old girl from Vancouver. She was stalked and blackmailed by someone she met online who circulated a photograph she had shared with him to her friends and family. She was driven out of school and moved to a new area, but the stalker followed her and the image was circulated around her new school. In 2012, Amanda shared the

Figure 2.5 Amanda Todd was blackmailed, bullied and harassed over an image circulated without her consent.

story of her bullying on YouTube. A few weeks later, she killed herself.

These cases have been taken up to argue that sexting does indeed have tragic consequences. But it is clear from the evidence that the problems are caused not by the sending or receiving of images but by harassment and bullying, by the failure of adults and institutions to protect and support the young people involved, and by the blaming of the girls whose images are circulated by others without their consent.

Part of the problem here is the sexual double standard involved when girls are expected by boys to engage in 'sexy' self-display but then 'face legal repercussions, moral condemnation and "slut shaming" when they do so'.[98] Amanda Todd was blackmailed, while Jessica Logan was 'viciously bullied, sexually shamed, and socially isolated' and, like Hope Witsell, was 'inadequately defended, and even further shamed and punished by teachers, school administrators, and parents'.[99]

Public campaigns around sexting have continued to address

Megan's Story

▶ ▶| ◀) 1:00 / 1:52   CC ⚙ 🔊 ⊹

Figure 2.6   Megan's Story, a campaign against sexting in Australia, 2012. Many campaigns of this type focus on shaming girls.

young people both as victims and as perpetrators of crime, warning them about the dire consequences for their reputations and careers. Yet there is little evidence that young people are being refused employment or university places because of this kind of activity,[100] and while some images are distributed without the sender's consent, this does not happen in the majority of cases.[101] It has been argued that the 'sexting panic' acts to produce fear, shame and the *'fear of shame'*,[102] through warnings that are 'repeated over and again in media and pedagogical texts'.[103]

These responses to sexting reveal how older sexual double standards continue to cause problems for young people, especially girls, as well as the challenges that new technologies pose for the privacy of both young people and adults. They are also part of a wider set of 'debates about the right of the child to choose their sexual preferences, explore their sexuality and make decisions about their body'.[104] As mobile technologies and social networks come to be a bigger part of our lives, young people use them in ways that challenge what it means to be a child,[105] and 'new communication and information technologies create qualitatively new types of relationships that . . . require some legal rethinking of identity'.[106]

Juridification

Although there is a common perception that sexual representations have become less heavily regulated in the sexually 'open' societies of the West, many kinds of sexual regulation are actually increasing. The idea that 'things become only more liberal, that society moves in an ever upward arc towards greater social and personal freedom', may be mistaken;[107] instead we have 'witnessed a flurry of regulatory controls across the globe'.[108] There are certainly more *types* of regulation today, including crime control, criminalization, 'administrative control' which takes place through licensing and inspection,[109] and forms of technological control using filtering and content blocking.[110]

The term *juridification* has been used to describe 'an increase in law through its expansion (where more social relations become legally regulated), and densification (where legal regulations become more detailed').[111] It refers to the 'proliferation of . . . bureaucratic regulation in the everyday world' and 'an expansion of the responsibilities that burden citizens in a way that reinforces and even multiplies the regulatory impact'.[112] This is partly because regulation has to try to keep up with new technologies as they appear, and partly because it is less and less clear how to differentiate between publishing and broadcasting, which were previously quite distinct activities, and between these and the ways that we use new technologies to communicate with each other. As a result, more forms of representation have come under scrutiny, including drawn and computer-generated imagery and online chat.

New measures are continually introduced and legislation is often extended; for example, in the UK, legislation on sexual images of children[113] was extended in 1994 to include 'pseudo-photographs',[114] in 2008 to cover images derived from photographs or pseudo-photographs,[115] and in 2009 to cover all images, including drawings and computer-generated images.[116] Laws no longer cover only the taking, making and distributing[117] of indecent images but also the possession of them,[118] and the original focus on images of under sixteen year olds has been extended to include images of under eighteen year olds.[119]

This shift is also part of a trend towards the increased regulation of the *fantastic*, the *fictional* and the *imaginary*. There are precedents, of course, for regulating fictional material, as the prosecutions of novels such as *The Well of Loneliness* and *Lady Chatterley's Lover* show. Regulation has also sometimes focused on sexual fantasies. For example, the 1990 US prosecution of Daniel DePew was based on his entrapment by undercover police officers during which he swapped fantasies with them about making a child porn 'snuff' film. It has been described as 'a crime that never happened' because there was no crime, actual or intended, and because the officers had 'invited him there in the first place, and . . . spurred him on by sharing their own equally kinky fantasies'.[120] All the same DePew was sentenced to thirty-three years in prison.

The ways in which fiction is regulated have also been extended. Child pornography legislation has been repeatedly expanded in some countries to include images of 'fictional' or 'imaginary' children.[121] In the UK, legislation was extended in 2015 to cover images of staged or fantasy 'rape'.[122] These extensions mark a move from using laws to prosecute people for making images that are records of actual sexual abuse to regulating images which depict performances or fantasies.

The extension of regulation in these particular ways can also be seen as part of a broader move towards mass surveillance. The sense of being under surveillance has become a key means of control in contemporary Western societies, where CCTV cameras film inside buildings and outside in public spaces, and where purchases and communications are tracked and data is mined to profile people for market research or to assess financial or criminal risk.[123]

The huge scale of government spying on the phone calls, browsing histories and online posts of citizens and their access to communications made through Google, YouTube, Skype and Facebook has become increasingly clear since 2013.[124] New legislation has also been introduced to support this; in 2016 for example, the UK government introduced an Investigatory Powers Act legalizing 'the most extreme surveillance in the history of western democracy',[125] and a Digital Economy Bill significantly extended its powers to censor the representation of consensual sexual acts.[126]

A move towards regulation that focuses on the 'possession' rather than the production, distribution or consumption of sexually explicit materials is also part of an attempt to regulate those materials in a context where producers and consumers may be in different parts of the world and subject to different forms of legislation. Consequently the net of regulation is cast much wider than in the past, with increased scrutiny on individual media producers, performers and consumers.[127]

Repeated technopanics are often fuelled by media reports and add to the pressure for new legislation, often based on appeals to the need to protect young people. Such appeals often depend on the fear of a 'paedophile gaze', and on the idea that we should regulate any texts that we worry might incite desire in a paedophile. Some artists' images of children have been removed from exhibition because of claims that they might be experienced in this way,[128] and sexting has also been described as 'dangerous because of the audience that it might find',[129] despite the fact that even when sexted images are distributed without permission, they are very rarely uploaded to public websites where they might become part of a paedophile collection.[130]

In the case of the now-criminalized drawn and computer-generated material, many young people – including girls and young women – are making, sharing and consuming such material in animation, comics and gaming (ACG) fan communities.[131] Rather than protecting young people, regulation in these areas impacts directly on them,[132] as it does in cases where sexting is understood as 'self-produced pornography'. But what is also happening here is that what we know about the contexts in which particular texts are produced and consumed by actual people is being disregarded in favour of what some people fear about the imagined response of imagined people.

Regulation also makes particular groups hyper-visible; for example, actions taken against sexting nearly always focus on girls and young women, rather than boys and young men.[133] At the

Figure 2.7   Feminist porn producer Pandora Blake and obscenity lawyer Myles Jackman lead a protest against the UK's Digital Economy Bill in 2016 (Backlash).

same time, spaces for young people to communicate and create in ways that may allow them to develop an understanding of sex and sexuality are diminished.[134]

As the focus of sexual regulation shifts increasingly to culture, the division between regulating representation and regulating speech, thought, fantasy and daydreaming is disintegrating, with some claiming that 'we have entered the era of thought crime'.[135] Culture and, along with it, the inner worlds of individuals and communication between groups seem to be regarded as inherently dangerous. This view is seen most clearly in the claims that media has become 'pornified' and culture 'sexualized', which will be the focus of the next chapter.

Summary

- Concerns about sex have come to focus particularly heavily on media.

- Regulation produces ways of thinking, feeling and talking about sex and sexuality.

- The regulation of sex and sex media often works by presenting these as 'excessive', 'extreme' and 'perverse' and focuses in particular on representations and practices that are non-normative, play with power or push the body to its limits.

- The regulation of sex and sex media often focuses on 'protecting' young people, but it also often operates according to a sexual double standard and depends on restricting young people's rights.

- A process of juridification – an expansion and intensification of regulation – is part of a broader move towards the surveillance of people's communication which increasingly involves an interest in regulating their creative and fantasy worlds.

3

Sexualization

This chapter covers:

- The claim that contemporary mainstream media and culture has become 'sexualized', and the development of a 'sexualization debate'.

- The claim that sexualization is oppressive to children, young people and women.

- The kinds of approaches and evidence that are used in policy reports on sexualization, and how these relate to other kinds of evidence about gender and sexual equalities and about young people's well-being.

- Research that focuses on young people's relations to sex and media.

- The sexualization debate in relation to the new visibility of sex in Western cultures and to 'onscenity'.

What is Sexualization?

Concerns about sexualization are part of a bigger tendency for the public discussion of sex to focus on media.

What is sexualization? At the most basic level, to 'sexualize' simply means to make something sexual. The term has been used

61

to indicate how visible sex has become in contemporary culture, how preoccupied we are with sexual values and practices, how new forms of sexual experience have emerged, and how access to sexual representations has increased to the extent that culture itself is 'sexualized'.[1]

However, this is not how the term is generally used in policy reviews in the US, Australia and the UK,[2] in popular media and even in some academic writing, in news media and in popular books with titles such as *So Sexy So Soon: The New Sexualized Culture and What Parents Can Do to Protect Their Kids*[3] or *Prude: How the Sex-Obsessed Culture Damages Girls (and America Too!)*.[4] Here, 'sexualization' is used to indicate a worrying process that is affecting people, particularly young people and children, in new, dangerous and harmful ways. For example, the former UK Prime Minister David Cameron referred to sexualization as 'dumping a waste that is toxic on our children', warping their minds and bodies and taking away their innocence.[5]

It has been claimed that 'what children are learning today isn't normal or good for them' and that the sexualization of childhood is 'having a profoundly disturbing impact on children's understanding of gender, sexuality, and relationships'.[6] It has also been argued that sexualization is associated with poor mental health, 'acts of self-harm', depression and thoughts of suicide,[7] and that pornography – a key feature in the sexualization of culture – is responsible for 'one of the most depressed, anxious and lonely generations of young people ever to inhabit the earth',[8] leading those who use it to 'neglect their school work . . . become isolated from others, and often suffer depression'.[9]

Originally used in the 1970s to describe the 'acquisition of sexual skills, knowledge, and values' and the 'development of sexual attitudes',[10] the term 'sexualization' has come to be used as a way of expressing concern about children and young people, most often as part of a discussion about girls 'growing up too quickly'.

Some see sexualization as evidence of moral decline[11] and argue for a focus on restoring 'the notion of sexual innocence to

Figure 3.1 Sexualization has become the focus of many popular books.

girlhood'.[12] But sexualization has also been seen as part of a back-lash against feminism, a means of hijacking feminist politics by repackaging consumer culture and the pursuit of sexiness as a way to feel 'empowered'. As a result, women come to 'participate in their own sexual exploitation'.[13] This process has been described as a new 'technology of sexiness' that relies on representing women as 'knowing, active and desiring', but actually works as a form of 'self-policing', in which women become responsible for cultivating a 'sexy body'[14] and forms of 'sexpertise'. This technology of sexiness is part of a wider 'postfeminist sensibility' which *seems* to emphasize women's choice while actually encouraging them to engage in self-surveillance.[15]

These kinds of discussions have become very familiar in the early twenty-first century, but the definitions of sexualization that are often used in them turn out to tell us very little when examined closely. For example, in the UK Home Office report on sexualization in 2010 the term is used to describe 'a number of trends in the production and consumption of contemporary culture' where 'the use of sexual attributes' is 'a measure of a person's value and worth',[16] but is also used to refer to 'sexual objectification'[17] and 'gender stereotypical ideas and images'.[18] In the UK Bailey Review carried out two years later, sexualization is used to refer to four very different things – the visibility of sexual content in public, misogyny, children's sexuality and 'deviant' sexual behaviours and lifestyles.[19] It is not clear why these are being linked together in this way.

According to the widely quoted American Psychological Association Report:

> Sexualization occurs when 1. a person's value comes only from his or her sexual appeal or behavior, to the exclusion of other characteristics; 2. a person is held to a standard that equates physical attractiveness (narrowly defined) with being sexy; 3. a person is sexually objectified – that is, made into a thing for others' sexual use, rather than seen as a person with the capacity for independent action and decision making; 4. sexuality is inappropriately imposed upon a person.[20]

Points 3 and 4 seem to be referring to problems of sexual consent or abuse, but if so, why not use those terms? The issue of attractiveness in point 2 suggests a more longstanding and familiar set of concerns with beauty and body image rather than something specifically to do with sex. It's not clear why any of these points are being presented as though they are connected to 'sexualization', which the report presents as a new phenomenon.

Policy reports also mix together views that promote gender equality and sexual well-being with normative and moralistic views of sexuality and gender. For example, the idea of 'healthy sexuality' used in the APA report makes a whole range of sexual practices and relations such as polyamory, online sex and sex work invisible.[21] It also ignores boys, focusing its discussion of sexualization entirely on girls.

Gender-stereotyping in clothing, products and services for children are largely ignored in the Bailey Review, despite this being a clear focus of parents' concerns according to its own research.[22] Indeed the report cites claims that gender preferences are part of 'a normal, healthy development of gender identity'.[23] Its discussion of magazines focuses on 'sexually suggestive' content and 'deviant' practices rather than the representation of women;[24] a framing that suggests a strong 'family values' approach, rather than one concerned with gender and sexual equality.[25]

Sexualization and the Figure of 'the Child'

The 'child' is often used as a metaphor for larger social issues, a figure representing innocence that must be protected from new social and cultural developments, or a future that we must fight to defend.

Concerns about sexualization are part of a bigger tendency for the public discussion of sex to focus on *media*.[26] For example, there is much more interest in young people's use of technologies for sharing sexual images than there is on other aspects of their lives such as the way they develop sexual feelings and desires or what their views about sexual practices are. Concerns about sex are often expressed in relation to media and technology – the possibility of young people becoming addicted to online porn, paedophiles lurking on social networking sites, the circulation of child porn, 'extreme' images, sexting, and so on. A wide range of media texts have also come under scrutiny – especially pornography, but also music videos and magazines, toys, clothes and accessories, and leisure practices such as pole exercise and 'sexy' dancing.

The expression of these kinds of concern, however, is far from being a modern phenomenon. Although sexualization is often presented as 'unlike anything faced by children in the past',[27] most public discussions about childhood sexuality since the late eighteenth century have taken exactly this concerned form, fretting about the corruption of childhood innocence and the need to protect young people by regulating their access to sex and to media.[28] Throughout this period anxieties about media influence on children and young people have focused on popular songs, novels, Shakespeare's plays, comic books, popular music,

Figure 3.2   The SPARK Movement activist organization was set up in 2010 to promote girls' healthy sexuality, self-empowerment and well-being and re-launched in 2016. Most campaigns concerned with sexualization focus on girls and women.

television and video, in addition to the more recent focus on online and mobile media.[29]

The 'child' is often used in this way as a metaphor for larger social issues,[30] a figure representing innocence that must be protected from new social and cultural developments, or a future that we must fight to defend.[31] Debates about sexualization do this when they focus on an abstract and imagined[32] 'child' rather than on real children and young people with differences and diverse experiences.

In particular, it is the figure of the sexualized girl that has become a way of expressing concern about a wide range of social issues that are seen as threatening. For example, in one account, the story of 'Emma' is used to represent the problems of sexualization. Emma 'struggles over her popularity with the boys in her class', begins to throw up after eating, gets a contraceptive injection which gives her 'severe body rash and fatigue', is dumped by her boyfriend, 'puts on weight and feels distressed' and becomes 'exhausted all the time'. Emma's 'school results plummet', 'there are fights at home', she 'becomes pregnant', 'has an abortion', is 'violently ill', 'has trouble sleeping and spends hours crying in her room', takes antidepressants, 'becomes the butt of jokes and gossip', and 'responds with outbursts of temper alternating with feelings of loneliness and bottomless despair'. Emma 'sees her future as bleak, not worth living for . . . She thinks all of this must be her own fault and believes she is a total failure.'[33]

Sexualization and Policy

'Concern' about sexualization may simply reproduce the idea that girls are passive, media are inherently problematic and sex is dangerous, while doing nothing to challenge the real inequalities in the way that gender and sexuality are experienced.

Of course Emma is a fictional character, invented to represent girls in general. But even the more apparently factual accounts such as policy reports and some academic papers link together multiple problems in this way in narratives of risk, danger and a downward spiral of harm.[34]

In some accounts, 'child pornography; children being targeted by any form of marketing; young people becoming sexually active; sexual abuse of children; raunch culture; protecting children from any sexualised material in the media; and body image disorders' are presented as though they are all part of the same problem and connected to one another. Writers 'slip from one to the other as though any of them were saying the same thing, with any of them either being a cause or an effect'.[35] Rather than working to define and analyse sexualized culture as they claim to be doing, these accounts are more often simply 'a means of expressing dismay at many unconnected behaviours'.[36]

They also frequently draw on poor-quality or irrelevant information, muddling together academic studies with market research, 'common-sense' views, anecdotes, and claims made by campaigners which have not been verified, so it is hard to know how seriously to take them. Some of the most striking claims are made without proper evidence; for example, in the 2010 UK Home Office report

Box 3.1: The UK Home Office report on sexualization was published in 2010 and was widely criticized for its use of evidence:

'Sexualisation is tied to economic markets in the forms of beauty and sex industries, that both open and restrict the breadth and variety of identities and ambitions open to young women. A growing number of girls are setting their sights on careers that demand a "sexy" image. Surveys have found for instance that a high proportion of young women in the UK aspire to work as "glamour models" or lap-dancers.'

on sexualization, it is claimed that many girls now aspired to be glamour models and lap-dancers. This was widely repeated in the news, despite being based on a non-existent study.[37] Research that does not support the report's claims is simply left out of the discussion.[38] The statistics and surveys that *are* used are often not referenced. A great deal of relevant information – for example the evidence that men report feelings of body dissatisfaction as well as women – is ignored.[39]

Many of the studies used in these reports come from a media-effects tradition of research which has been widely criticized for its simplistic view of the role of media in people's lives and a tendency to present this solely in terms of what media 'do' to people that is 'harmful' and 'risky'.[40] Work by researchers who specialize in media and cultural analysis is often not included in the reports, nor is work that 'might have contributed young peoples' voices to the mix'.[41] Different types of studies are also bundled together even where they do not clearly relate to sex or sexualization.[42] For example, one study included in the APA report focused on the way girls' 'self-objectification' impacted on their performance while throwing a ball, and another on 'menstrual shame' and body discomfort. Many of the studies were carried out with adults rather than children or young people, and many of them come from before the period during which sexualization is thought to have accelerated. It is hard to see how these can tell us much about young people in contemporary societies where forms of media production and consumption have changed dramatically in the last ten years.

These kinds of reports also imply that sexualization is a major concern for all adults, and certainly all parents, though there has been little effort to gather adults' views on this. Where they have been collected, they are often ignored, but when adults are listened to they present more complex views than the sexualization debate suggests. For example, although parents are often said to be worried that their children are growing up too quickly, they may actually see them as pretty sophisticated in their use of media, but less grown up than previous generations when it comes to getting employment, taking responsibility and running households. They often believe that young people should have the right to make their own decisions and to express themselves, and while they may worry about their children's choices and tastes, they do not want them to be left out or bullied because they are too different from their friends. They tend not to see their *own* children as 'sexualized', or to think that images and products are *inherently* sexual. They are also often sceptical about whether legislation is the right way to address concerns about sexualization.[43]

In conclusion, the sexualization debate, as it tends to be presented, is often unproductive: 'a distracting and disorienting context in which to think about contemporary gender relations',[44] about sexuality, and about solutions to the problems and inequalities that young people face. 'Concern' about sexualization may simply reproduce the idea that girls are passive, media are inherently problematic and sex is dangerous, while doing nothing to challenge the real inequalities in the way that gender and sexuality are experienced.[45]

The dismay that these accounts express represents different things for different groups of people. For some, the figure of the sexualized girl is 'an emblem of the erosion of the patriarchal family', while for others, she is proof of the decline of feminism.[46] And although these are stories that appear to be propelled by concern, there is also often a strong sense that their authors see girls as out of control, as 'skanks' who are 'sexually precocious' or 'slutty'.[47] Such stories express hostility and distaste rather than empathy with young people and curiosity about what they do, think and feel.

Sex, Gender and Equality

It is clear that gender and sexual equalities are extremely uneven around the world. The rights of lesbian, gay, bisexual and transgender people vary dramatically. In a number of countries they may not have protection in the workplace or under the law, or be allowed to adopt children. They have the fewest rights in African and Asian countries, and in some countries they face imprisonment, violence, torture and execution.[48] Transgender and gender non-conforming people face high levels of harassment and discrimination and are much more likely to attempt suicide than the general population.[49] Suicide attempts are also high for LGB people, especially gay or bisexual men.[50] Many LGBTI people experience harassment, abuse, prejudice and stigmatization and suffer from poor health.[51] Of all sexual groups it is bisexual people who most frequently have mental health problems, including depression, anxiety and self-harming.[52] The debate about sexualization has little to tell us about this.

Women make up two-thirds of the world's adults who are illiterate.[53] Caring for family members and unpaid domestic work is still largely performed by women and, in less developed regions, also by young girls.[54] Women are rarely employed in jobs with status and power or in decision-making positions in government. A pay gap between men and women exists pretty well everywhere and women represent 70 per cent of the world's poor.[55] Yet there have been advances in the position of women and girls. Two-thirds of countries now have equal numbers of boys and girls in primary education, and in over one third girls outnumber boys in secondary education. More women than men now attend universities and in 2008 women represented more than 40 per cent of the labour force worldwide.[56]

Violence against women is also a global problem: 30 per cent of women worldwide have experienced intimate partner violence and over 7 per cent have experienced non-partner sexual violence. Violence against women is one of the least reported crimes – in a European survey only 13–14 per cent of women had reported their most serious incident of violence to the police.[57] Yet while violence

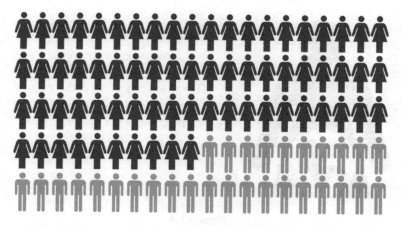

Figure 3.3 Women represent 70 per cent of the world's poor.

occurs around the world, it varies across countries, with the most affected regions being Africa and South-East Asia. It is associated particularly with beliefs in the patriarchal control of the family, sexual purity and male sexual entitlement, with weak legal sanctions for sexual violence, and with the unequal position of women relative to men.[58] The most serious inequalities affect girls and women much more severely in countries where sexualization has not been claimed to be taking place.[59]

Young People, Sex and Well-being

Although debates about sexualization are often presented as being concerned with the rights of women and girls, their claims do little to shed light on the conditions experienced by women and girls around the world. In the same way, they have little to tell us about the experiences of young people in developed countries and about how these relate to ethnicity, class and age.

Comparing claims about the negative impact of sexualization on 'cognitive functioning, physical and mental health, sexuality,

71

Teen pregnancy rates were the lowest in thirty years.

There was a decline in the rate of girls aged 15–17 who gave birth – from 39 per 1,000 in 1991 to 15 per 1,000 in 2011.

Figure 3.4

and attitudes and beliefs'[60] with other sorts of information about young people is a useful way of contextualizing debates about sexualization. For example, if we look at other measures of young people's sexual behaviour in the US at the time of the sexualization debate we can see that:

- girls reported waiting longer to have sex than in the past,[61] and relatively few young people had had oral sex,[62] vaginal sex[63] or anal sex.[64]
- the most common sexual practice for girls aged fourteen to fifteen was masturbation; fourteen to seventeen year olds were more likely than any other to have had safe sex when they had vaginal intercourse,[65] and condom use had increased.[66]
- teen pregnancy rates were the lowest in thirty years[67] and there was also a decline in the rate of adolescent girls who gave birth.[68]

More general measures of young people's well-being and achievement also contradict the picture of failing youth that is suggested in the sexualization debate. For example, in the US:

- substantiated cases of childhood sexual abuse had decreased,[69] as had sexual assault rates against young people.[70]

The number of young people aged 18–24 completing high school with a diploma had increased from 84% in 1980 to 91% in 2011.

The number of young people enrolling in college after high school had increased from 47% to 65% for males and from 52% to 72% for females.

Figure 3.5

- the rate of serious violent crime involving youth victims had decreased,[71] as had the rate of serious violent crime offending by young people.[72]
- the number of young people completing high school with a diploma had increased,[73] as had the number of young people enrolling in college after high school, and the increase was higher for females than for males.[74]
- the percentage of children with serious emotional or behavioural difficulties had remained the same,[75] while the percentage of young people who had had a major depressive episode during the past year had decreased slightly.[76]

Of course, statistics don't give a complete picture of a situation and numbers can increase or decrease for a variety of reasons. For example there may be differences in the way that information is collected and categorized over time. Reports of emotional difficulties and abuse may increase during periods when these become matters of news coverage because people feel more confident about reporting them. On the other hand, many people's experiences may not be reported at all.

However, these figures certainly don't fit with the stories of decline and tragedy that are told about young people in debates about sexualization, and they don't support the claim that young people's lives are becoming harder because of sexualization – instead they suggest that there has been widespread improvement in most indicators of children's well-being in the world's most advanced economies.[77] It's odd then, that there is such an overwhelmingly negative tone to the way that children and young people are discussed in sexualization debates.

At the same time, those debates fail to pick up the stark differences in the experiences of young people. For example, in the US:

- black, non-Hispanic youth were more likely than white, non-Hispanic youth and non-Hispanic youth of two or more races to be victims of a serious violent crime.[78]
- higher rates of maltreatment were reported for girls than boys;[79] younger children were more frequently victims of child maltreatment than older children, especially those under the age of one, and black, non-Hispanic children had the highest rates of maltreatment.[80]
- more males than females were reported by a parent to have serious emotional or behavioural difficulties,[81] but major depressive episodes among young people were more than twice as high among females as among males.[82]
- girls were more likely to report attempting suicide than boys but boys were much more likely than girls to die from suicide. Of the reported suicides in the ten to twenty-four age group, 19 per cent were females and 81 per cent were males.[83]

These figures suggest a much more complicated picture of young people's lives and well-being, with differences linked to gender, age and ethnic background.

So although debates about sexualization are often presented as being concerned with the rights of women and girls, their claims do little to shed light on the conditions experienced by women and girls around the world. In the same way, they have little to tell us about the experiences of young people in developed countries and about how these relate to ethnicity, class and age. They ignore what we know about the experiences of GSD people and about the varieties of sexism that many people face. They gloss over the way that heteronormative views of sexuality and gender frame the experiences of young people, and they often caricature girls as 'skanks' or helpless victims, and boys as predatory and cruel or 'addicted' to porn. Overwhelmingly, they focus on girls as a problem and on 'changing girls' attitudes and behaviors to solve the problem of sexualization'.[84]

Researching Sexualization

It is only by looking at the particular contexts in which people encounter representations of sex that we can begin to understand what their significance is.

Claims made in debates about sexualization don't fit convincingly with other evidence about young people's lives. They tend to draw on stories told elsewhere about sexualization as a dangerous or risky process and on the figures of the young person and child. They are often characterized by a strong lack of interest in young people's understandings of their own practices. For example, concerns about young people and 'sexting' have become a key feature of debates about sexualization, but this is not a term that young people themselves use.[85]

Between 2008 and 2013, one research team catalogued 400 news stories related to 'sexting', presenting it as a social problem and legal issue, but rarely talking to young people about the place and meaning of this practice in their lives.[86] Young people's 'experiences of doing, being and becoming sexual are often sensationalized, silenced, caricatured, pathologised and routinely undermined' in these debates.[87] But what does research which includes young people's voices tell us about the relation between young people, sex and media?

It is perhaps not surprising that when young people are invited to comment on sexualization as adults present it, they do just that, often beginning their discussions with researchers by reproducing a 'public account' of sex and media as risky and harmful, drawing on the figures of the young person and child. Usually these focus on the dangers for *other* – particularly younger – children.[88] But their accounts of their *own* experiences, feelings and practices are dramatically different. So, while debates about sexualization suggest that young people are presented with a barrage of media which encourages them to be sexy, young people themselves say that they encounter a diverse range of sexual material in mainstream media. They also say that media often contain very mixed messages about sex – it is presented as desirable *and* dangerous – and that finding out about sex is 'surrounded by shame, embarrassment and ambivalence'.[89]

Despite this, young people value media as a source of information about sex.[90] They often engage with media in ways that are varied, critical or resist 'obvious readings',[91] and they may be sceptical, moralistic or indifferent about the way sex is represented in media.[92] The meanings of sexual media and goods are also highly dependent on context.[93] For example, clothes that might appear sexy to one person are not seen in this way by another, and their sexiness might also depend on whether they are worn at school or for a party. Items like the Playboy bunny logo that have been described in popular and policy reports as clearly 'sexualizing' may be understood by young people as simply fashionable, as 'cute' and 'childish', or as representing innocence and sexiness at the same time.[94]

Young people also see media as providing languages to speak with and a 'place to speak from'.[95] For example, pre-teen girls use magazines as a source of knowledge about sex and a starting point for talking about sex with their friends.[96] These kinds of engagement provide them with 'adult-free and education-free zones' where they can 'collectively negotiate what is acceptable, desirable and what is "too much"'.[97] New media spaces such as online fan forums, blogs, tumblrs and vlogs have also become places where young people can engage in debate about issues of sex,[98] while practices such as sending messages about sex can work as sites for learning about sexuality.[99] A study in 2015 found that 30 to 50 per cent of thirteen to seventeen year olds in the US had used social media to flirt or interact with someone they were attracted to and that media and communication technologies were woven into their romantic lives.[100]

In sexualization debates the focus is often on the 'exposure' of young people to sexual media by accident, especially online, because of popups, poor search techniques or weak safety measures.[101] But it is mostly younger children who experience this, while older children also seek out sexual media. Levels of engagement with online pornography are lower than many people think[102] – a major European study found that 23 per cent 'had encountered sexual images, online or offline',[103] mainly older children. Relatively few reported being upset by sexual images that they saw online,[104] and the majority coped well and got over the experience quickly.[105] This suggests that 'social, policy and academic concerns regarding the impact of pornographic content on young people are seriously overstated'.[106]

Young people learn about sexuality from a range of sources, and they use media, and the internet in particular, to find out about the 'erotic',[107] relationships and pleasure.[108] They seek out sexual materials of various kinds out of curiosity, for sexual satisfaction, for entertainment, to relieve boredom, to be transgressive, or to develop their sexual knowledge, skills and capabilities.[109] Increasingly pornography is something that young people engage with and talk about in order to negotiate ideas about gender.[110] For some young people, pornography is not considered a source of information,[111] while for others it is a learning resource but also 'a means of bonding in friendship groups, sexual communities or intimate relationships', and 'a source of arousal, of laughter, of disgust'.[112]

Young people may engage with porn before they are in a sexual relationship, so that it becomes part of the way they reflect on whether they are ready for sex, what their tastes, orientations and preferences might be, and what they hope for and expect from sex and relationships. They may use it as a way of exploring and trying out sexual practices, fantasies and identities, and as a way of feeling, experiencing and attending to their bodies, of 'discovering potentialities and possibilities' as part of a process of 'becoming aware'.[113] Engaging with sexual material becomes part of the way young people work out their understanding of sex and sexuality.[114]

Onscenity

What then can we make of the claims that society is becoming more sexualized? Certainly sex has become particularly visible – 'onscene' – in Western culture,[115] both as a source of leisure, entertainment and self-discovery and as a site of fascination and concern; indeed, sexualization debates are part of this process itself. What is particularly distinctive about sex in our time is the way that media and communication technologies have become part of everyday life, making possible new kinds of sexual interaction. Glossy porn-chic representations are widely noted in mainstream culture,[116] alongside an expansion of the pornosphere, while pornography has also become easier to access, though it remains an 'outlaw' form. This peculiar and complex situation in which sex is simultaneously celebrated and feared, familiar and shocking, means that sex is 'onscene' in new ways.[117]

At the same time we can note a continued conservatism in many depictions of sex which rely on 'normative constructions of gender and sexuality' and on a view of sexual diversity as scandalous and deviant.[118] And it is still largely the bodies of women and girls that are used to express and embody sex, whether this is in terms of sexual display or sexual concern.

Yet a detailed consideration of sexual representations – even those that are considered the most 'mainstream' – reveals considerable complexity. For example, claims that the Miley Cyrus music video 'Wrecking Ball' simply 'depicts a woman exploring the iconography of porn'[119] miss its significance as part of music video culture in general, and its reference to specific videos like Sinead O'Connor's 'Nothing Compares 2 U', as well as its use of fashion and aesthetics which are not particularly recognizable as a form of 'pornostyle'.[120]

Claims that performers like Miley Cyrus are simply sexualized – or that we can categorize them clearly in relation to ideas about being 'sex positive' or 'sex negative' – miss the very real differences in style and approach across a range of music videos and performances. They also fail to capture the variety and change within the

Miley Cyrus - Wrecking Ball

▶ ▶| 🔊 0:48 / 3:41   HD 🔲 ⊹

Figure 3.6   Concerns about sexualization have focused on female performers and music videos, such as Miley Cyrus in Wrecking Ball, 2013.

self-representation of many such performers; for example, after 'Wrecking Ball' Cyrus quickly moved on to more androgynous and gender-fluid performances in support of her charity organization The Happy Hippie Foundation, which is concerned with homeless and LGBTQ youth, and described herself as pansexual.[121]

In addition we shouldn't assume that we know how young people will respond to sexual representations. In fact, some studies have suggested that, because of the way that 'sexualization' discourse links girls' sexuality 'to morality, appearance and age', they have to carefully monitor their relation to performers such as Miley Cyrus.[122] As this and other studies suggest, what young people say about sex and media often demonstrates the presence of a double standard around sexual behaviour which is far from new. There is pressure on girls to be sexy but not too sexy, to take responsibility in sexual encounters with boys, and to police their own behaviour and that of other girls.[123] Young women feel concerned about being labelled as 'slags', and wish they were more confident about their bodies and appearance.[124] Pre-tween girls worry about how to display 'appropriate sexuality' for their age group and struggle to find ways of balancing sexiness and respectability, for example by wearing leggings under short skirts and keeping 'showy' clothing for special occasions.[125] But women of all ages also come under intense scrutiny, and disapproval is as likely to focus on women covering up their bodies and not being sexy 'enough' as it is on women who dress in skimpy clothing and are 'too sexy'.[126]

At the same time there has been a real growth in the diversity of sexual communities and representations. Claims about sexualization often make this invisible, as well as ignoring the many ways in which people of all ages challenge sexist media representations. They fail to recognize that young people and women are not homogeneous groups, that the place of media in their lives depends on 'age, individual preferences, peer networks . . . familial relations, access to particular technologies and texts', and that people engage with media in a range of different ways.[127] It is only by looking at the particular contexts in which people encounter representations of sex that we can begin to understand what their significance is.

To understand the contemporary relations of gender, sexuality and media in a meaningful way we need to disentangle the questions we want to ask from the kinds of sweeping claims that have been made about the sexualization of culture. The terms we use need to have the power to explain how the things that we study 'operate in particular contexts'.[128] This means that we also need to pay more attention to the diversity of contemporary media[129] and the 'very real differences and contradictions within media content',[130] including not only more mainstream representations, but also those that are produced by independent and niche producers, communities and subcultures, amateurs and fans. We need a much better language for describing the different kinds of sexual media that circulate in our cultures. The next chapter discusses these in detail.

Summary

- The 'sexualization debate' is the most visible way in which sex and the media has been recently discussed in public and has become an established way of expressing concerns about children, young people and women.

- Many claims made in this debate focus on an abstract figure of the child, are selective in the way they use and interpret evidence, and are often underpinned by normative views of sex, media and young people.

- Research suggests a much more complicated picture of young people's lives and of their relationships with sex and media.

- Sexualization is better understood as describing the ways that sex has become particularly visible – onscene – in Western cultures, and the sexualization debate is part of this process itself.

4

Forms of Sex Media

This chapter covers:

- Ideas about aesthetics, cultural capital and value in relation to sex media.

- The terms that are used to mark the differences between sex media: hardcore/softcore, art/porn/erotica, and domesticated pornographies.

- A range of pornographies such as drawn pornography, gonzo porn and amateur porn.

- Genres that have a distinctive set of conventions for representing sex, 'porno-chic' in mainstream media, and the relation of pornography to other popular forms of entertainment.

- Media spaces for sexual interaction in cybersex, online sex games and virtual worlds.

- The development of interactive and immersive sex media and the increasing overlapping of media, space, representation and communication.

Categorizing Sex Media

How we categorize media texts depends on a number of sometimes contradictory and shifting factors. For example, pornography is often defined by its content (sex), its intention (to sexually arouse), or the way it transgresses respectable styles of representation (showing sex 'for its own sake, for the sheer hell of it').[1] For some people, porn is porn simply because it depicts a particular set of acts in the form of 'sexual numbers'[2] – standard scenarios featuring oral sex, anal sex and so on. For others it is primarily about intention (did the producer of the work intend it to be seen as pornographic?) or consumption (do audience members read or experience it as pornographic?).

Context – where a media text is placed, how it is framed, who is invited to look at it – is also important, and of course is always changing, which is why some images may be considered pornographic in one decade or century and not in another. Porn may be understood as whatever is contained in the 'pornosphere . . . the space in which explicit sexual discourse is circulated', including through 'the written word, as well as pictures, photography, moving images and sound'.[3]

The style of a text may also be seen as making something pornographic – and pornographic style is usually considered to be one that depicts bodies and sexual practices graphically, explicitly and perhaps crudely. Aesthetics or form refers to the formal qualities and stylistic conventions of a text and to the meanings and feelings that they evoke.

The study of aesthetics was once associated with the study of high culture – art, music and literature, with a strong focus on their worth and beauty. This relied on the idea that cultural and media texts were arranged in a hierarchy with high-culture forms such as opera and ballet prized over forms of low, mass or popular culture such as gangster films and romances, which were seen as offering 'satisfaction at the lowest level'.[4] Yet these categories change – both opera and Shakespeare's plays, for example, which are often seen today as a form of high culture, were forms of popular entertainment before the nineteenth century.[5]

Aesthetic hierarchies also have clear associations with class and gender; for example, opera is seen as 'better' than soap opera because of its association with upper-class audiences, while genres aimed at female audiences – the romance, chick-lit, boy-band

83

music – may be seen as trashy or lacking in value. Media enjoyed by mass rather than niche or specialized audiences may be seen as uninteresting and 'mainstream'.

Today a much greater variety of texts are valued and studied, including many popular works that were 'once dismissed as aesthetically unworthy'.[6] Yet the idea of a cultural hierarchy of texts, with some deemed to be better than others, remains. In particular, an aesthetic which is thought to encourage detachment and contemplation in the viewer is seen as more 'cultured' than one that invites participation and involvement.[7] Refinement, intellect and distance continue to be associated with high culture and art, while vulgarity, emotion and expressiveness are associated with popular and especially low culture and entertainment.[8]

The persistence of this kind of aesthetic hierarchy is especially obvious when it comes to images of sex and the body. The genre most closely associated with sex – pornography – has been described as being at the very bottom of the cultural hierarchy. Porn is seen as 'the lowest of the cultural low', beneath 'opera, serious theater, gallery art, the classics, the symphony, modernist literature . . . art-house and European films . . . public television, Andrew Lloyd-Webber . . . teen-pics, soap operas, theme parks, tabloid TV, the National Enquirer, Elvis paintings on velvet'.[9]

Pornography is one of the *body genres*: those 'that focus on particular kinds of body movement and body spectacle – musicals, horror films, low comedies, "weepies"'.[10] All of these genres have an effect that 'is registered in the spectator's body'; 's/he weeps, gets goose-bumps, rolls about laughing, comes'.[11] All are associated with low culture.[12] Genres which invite this kind of reaction often arouse concern because of the sensory responses of their audiences and because they suggest too much closeness between what is represented and their audiences, with no space for contemplation or reflection. Pornography, in particular, is seen by some as breaking down the 'limit between viewer and image', producing an 'instability of the distinction between subject and object of representation'.[13]

Pornography is often discussed in relation to the category of art, and the comparison can help us understand how similar content may be valued quite differently according to its style and context. For example, the female nude in fine art has often been seen as representing cleanliness and order, as 'a symbol of the pure, disinterested, functionless gaze'. Naked women in pornography have, in contrast, been associated with dirt and disorder and the stimulation of desire.[14] The pleasures of looking at the art nude are presented as those of 'contemplation, discrimination and transcendent value', while those associated with the porn performer are often seen in terms of 'motivation, promiscuity and commodification'.[15]

Yet both art and porn involve the production of commodities and there is no reason to suppose that the modes of looking and pleasures associated with them are those that are always experienced by viewers. Even if they were, it is not clear why one set of pleasures should be seen as obviously 'better' than the other. In fact, neither set of representations have any inherent meaning;

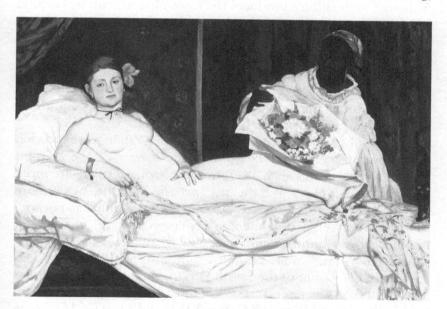

Figure 4.1 *Olympia*, by French artist Édouard Manet, drew on the tradition of the female nude, but depicted a contemporary prostitute rather than an idealized woman. The painting caused a scandal when it was exhibited in 1865 (Wikimedia Commons).

art and pornography depend on each other for their 'meaning, significance and status',[16] each being understood as what the other is not. Indeed, it is the process of distinguishing media texts from each other in this way that can be said to create the categories of what is 'beautiful and . . . ugly . . . distinguished and . . . vulgar'.

Cultural Capital and Value

Such distinctions between texts can also be used to distinguish ourselves from others; by showing our taste we say something about who we are: our lifestyle, social position, values and membership of particular groups. It is a way of marking ourselves out as tasteful, and of producing cultural capital[17] – a kind of wealth that can be converted into prestige, social standing and belonging. Although high culture produces the most obvious cultural capital within Western societies, it is also produced *within* cultures. For example, music subcultures produce cultural capital which affords status within the subculture. This capital can be *objectified*, for example in haircuts, dress codes, record collections; *embodied*, by being 'in the know' or performing particular dance styles; and *converted*, for example into occupations such as DJ, style journalist, record industry professional, club organizer.[18]

It is useful to consider how issues of *value* relate to sex media. While pornography may be seen as the lowest of the cultural low, other sex genres such as erotica and erotic thrillers are more highly valued, and sex as a theme in art and literature much more so. Content that is considered obscene when presented as pornography is also found in contemporary 'performance, film, video, photography, painting, sculpture, and writing', where it can be considered as art.[19] Some art-house films also feature explicit sex, such as *In the Realm of the Senses* (1976), *Romance* (1999), *Baise Moi* (2000), *Intimacy* (2001), *9 Songs* (2003), *Nymphomaniac* (2013), *Blue is the Warmest Color* (2013) and *Love* (2015). Some of these films have been described as 'part of a trend towards a "new extremism" in contemporary European filmmaking', with brutal images that 'appear designed deliberately to shock or provoke the spectator', using 'techniques that heighten the sensory and affective involvement of audiences'.[20] What this shows is that the differences between art and porn are not absolute and that the distinctions people make between them, as well as what is considered to be acceptable and unacceptable, depend on context and change over time and across place.

Sex and Art

If a text shows explicit sexual content and uses techniques to involve its audiences' senses, how do people decide whether it is pornographic or not? While some art may be sexually arousing, this is not usually its stated aim, and when it is sexually explicit it is often asking us 'to look for meaning and significance beyond the erotic'.[21] Porn may transgress social and cultural taboos,[22] but when art appropriates pornographic themes or styles it is often seen as offering 'glimpses of an existence unconfined by rules and constraints',[23] or questioning elite definitions and boundaries of art. At the same time pornography itself has become 'a site for the exploration of sexual fantasy and identity to an ever-wider demographic' and is used by artists as a tool in the 'negotiation of access to public space and public discourse'.[24]

Indeed, there are similarities between some examples of pornography and art, and many artists have experimented with sexual themes and aesthetics in their work. Andy Warhol's film *Blow Job* (1964) focuses on a man's face as he (apparently) receives a blow job. Cosey Fanni Tutti worked as a softcore porn model and striptease performer in the 1970s, appearing in magazines like *Fiesta* and *Playbirds*. She turned images of herself in these roles into artworks in her *Magazine Actions* work, exploring sex in relation to commerce and self-image and experimenting with the aesthetics of different kinds of sex magazine.[25]

Robert Mapplethorpe documented promiscuous gay and BDSM subcultures in New York in the 1970s and his work has been described as 'art, porn and documentary all at the same time'.[26] Jeff Koons used erotic images of himself with his wife, the porn

October 19th - 26th 1976

SEXUAL TRANSGRESSIONS NO. 5

PROSTITUTION

Figure 4.2 Cosey Fanni Tutti's work at the ICA, 1976, as part of the group COUM Transmissions, who were called 'wreckers of civilization' by a Conservative MP. (By permission of Cosey F. Tutti.)

performer, Ilona Staller, in his work *Made in Heaven* (1991). Jemima Stehli's photographic series *Strip* (1999) used images of herself stripping in front of men designated as 'Critic', 'Writer', 'Curator' or 'Dealer' in order to question power and voyeurism in the art world. Anna Biller's film *Viva* (2007) recreated the style of a 1970s sexploitation movie in which suburban couples experiment with sex and drugs in 1970s Los Angeles in order to explore women's experiences of the sexual revolution.[27]

Sex continues to be a strong theme in art, but it is most frequently controversial when it features children. US photographer Sally Mann's *Immediate Family* (1992), a collection of photographs of her children, sometimes naked, was highly acclaimed by many but called child pornography by others. In 2007, Nan Goldin's photograph 'Klara and Edda Belly Dancing', which shows a naked girl, was removed from the Baltic Centre for Contemporary Art in the UK. In 2008 a number of Bill Henson's photographs featuring young naked models and presenting adolescence as 'a time which is neither childhood nor adulthood'[28] were removed from a gallery in Sydney, following claims that they were 'child pornography, child exploitation and . . . a crime'.[29]

In 2009, Richard Prince's work 'Spiritual America' (1983), featuring the naked and heavily made up ten-year-old actress Brooke Shields, was removed from the 'Pop Life' exhibition at Tate Modern, London after a visit by the Obscene Publications Unit of the Metropolitan Police. The work is 'a photograph of a photograph'. The original was taken by a commercial photographer for the Playboy publication *Sugar'n' Spice* in 1976. Shields later attempted to suppress the picture but was unsuccessful. Prince used the photograph in his artwork, placed in a gilt frame and displayed in a shopfront in a street in the Lower East Side, New York. 'Spiritual America' had been successfully exhibited as an artwork until it became part of the 'Pop Life' exhibition. Removed from Tate Modern, the image was swiftly replaced by another of Prince's works, made in collaboration with Shields, 'Spiritual America IV' (2005), featuring Shields in the same pose as the original, though this time aged forty and dressed in a bikini.

Clearly, the meaning of an image changes as it passes through different locations and contexts. 'Spiritual America' began its life as a commercial image in a publication which we would understand as pornographic today, but which was not seen as such at the time. Rephotographed by an artist and displayed in new spaces it became a work of art, a tasteful object carrying more cultural capital because it commented on the original image. But categorizations of images are open to reinterpretation and redefinition, especially in the current context where there is increased concern about the representation of children. When artistic images like this are circulated publicly they are more likely to become temporarily 'unhinged from the art system' and risk being seen as pornography.[30]

Sexual Forms and Styles

Although it is possible to describe pornographic style in a general way by comparing it with other media forms, there is a problem with assuming that all pornographies conform to this style. The terms *softcore* and *hardcore* are often used to further distinguish the style and content of pornography, usually referring to how explicit it is. Hardcore porn often adopts a 'principle of *maximum visibility*', using 'close-ups of body parts' and 'sexual positions that show the most of bodies and organs'.[31] Softcore may show nudity or simulated sex, or focus on some sex acts (for example, masturbation) but not others (for example, anal sex). Alternatively the distinction may simply be about the level of detail in which these acts are shown – whether there are close ups of genitals, for example. The explicit style of pornography is also often contrasted with texts that are considered to be *erotic*.

The word *erotica* became common in the 1950s and 1960s to describe books that featured sex 'in a safe and classy way',[32] combining 'the aesthetic (or literary) and the sexual (or pornographic)'.[33] While it is still usually seen as second-rate within the wider hierarchy of cultural representations, it is understood as more tasteful and respectable than pornography because of its 'classiness' and its claim to show the complex nature of desire rather than providing a 'quick masturbatory fix'.[34] For example, the filmmaker Candida Royalle made work with high production values[35] and a focus on 'story lines' and 'good original music'.[36] Andrew Blake, the award-winning erotic artist, produces films and photographs that have been described as 'decadent, lush, opulent . . . moneyed and sophisticated'.[37] The Swedish porn project, *Dirty Diaries* (2009), by Mia Engberg, has been described as 'stylistically intriguing', and a 'counterweight to "porn" and pornified media'.[38] The project is made up of thirteen short films which are all quite different: *Dildoman* uses animation to show a woman inserting a man inside her vagina, *Flasher Girl On Tour* features a woman exposing herself to men in Paris, and *On Your Back Woman!* shows women wrestling.

Figure 4.3   *Dirty Diaries*, a diverse collection of Swedish feminist porn films, premiered in 2009, with a manifesto that challenges sexism, censorship, homophobia and transphobia.

While porn is more likely to focus on 'showing and telling the details of sexual acts and bodily sensations', erotica may also be interested in representing 'motivation, desire', 'sexual build-up'[39] and sex in the context of relationships. The difference between the two has been described as that between 'depicting sexual pleasures in the rhetoric of the scratch' and 'prolonging the tension in the rhetoric of the itch'.[40]

Another way of thinking about this is to say that porn and erotica are realistic in different ways. The realism of porn often depends on its recording of the details of bodies and acts, while erotica has more of an 'emotional and sensual realism'.[41] It has been argued that erotic films and mainstream films that depict sex are more likely to use 'subtle effects of line, color, light' and to feature actors who show 'subtleties of sexual performance',[42] perhaps drawing on 'stylised, expressionistic and allegorical forms to reveal the emotional, experiential and social realities of sex and sexuality'.[43] In contrast, porn tends to create a sense of 'transparency and immediacy', while at the same time presenting 'escapist, fantasy-based and idealistic' sex.[44]

Erotica has also been associated with the representation of sex as loving, dignified and equal, offering 'sexually suggestive or arousing material that is free of sexism, racism, and homophobia and is respectful of all human beings ... portrayed'.[45] For example, *Dirty Diaries* is accompanied by a manifesto which challenges sexism, censorship, homophobia and transphobia.[46] Porn made by women for women is often described in this way – as showing sex which is 'pleasurable, intimate and caring between women and men we can relate to', 'characterized by warmth and respect, and a mutual sense of adoration and affirmation',[47] though clearly not all porn made by or for women does this. The term *domesticated pornographies* has been used to describe the types of sexual materials that were more accessible to women in the past, including erotic fiction and porn videos aimed at couples, as well as sexual self-help books, cable programmes focused on women's fantasies and desires, and lingerie catalogues for women, such as those produced by the Victoria's Secret company. Like erotica these claim to have aesthetic or psychological value,[48] and they display their tastefulness by drawing on visual styles used in art or fashion.[49] They may also emphasize the relation of the erotic to everyday life and identity through 'a much more *located* sense of sexual practice' than is found in hardcore porn.[50]

From Pornography to Pornographies

If we want to understand pornography we need to look at particular pornographies[51] of 'myriad types, texts and subgenres'.[52] As with other kinds of media there are a number of ways of distinguishing between these. For example, we can categorize pornographies by *medium* – whether they take the form of a photograph, film, video, written story, GIF, drawing or animation. In addition we can see that particular porn studios, directors and performers attract strong followings, which account for their success and their distinction within the market. We can identify pornographies in terms of their target audiences; for example, whether they are produced for straight or gay men and women.[53]

We can also categorize them in terms of the styles they employ;[54] for example, the elements of fantasy and melodrama in films such as *The Devil in Miss Jones* (1973), or the characteristics of parody, reworking and adaptation in films like *Edward Penishands* (1991), *Sex Files: A Dark XXX Parody* (2009), *Man of Steel XXX* (2013) and *Fifty Shades of Grey: A XXX Adaptation* (2012).[55] There are 'niche' films focusing on particular themes such as bondage.[56] Others have characteristics that relate them to more mainstream films; for example, *Pirates* (2005), a high-budget adult film that references the popular adventure film *Pirates of the Caribbean* (2003), integrating sex into the narrative and using 'visual effects typical of contemporary Hollywood blockbusters'.[57]

The distinctions between pornographies have become more pronounced online, where there is more space for 'a plurality of products[58] and new ways of displaying these 'in menus, links, and listings',[59] for example on porn tube sites which display a range of 'orientations, tastes, preferences, and body aesthetics'. These categories include *content features*, which on tube sites may include the apparent age of performers and their race, nationality, or body type; bodily functions; specific practices, scenarios or communities; combinations of performers or combinations of situation and characters. Other kinds of porn producers may use different kinds of categories.

The distinctions within pornography become more apparent as soon as we start to compare pornographies such as drawn pornography, gonzo porn and various types of amateur porn.

Drawn Pornography

Drawn pornography and erotica have a long history. The *Kama Sutra*, an illustrated Indian guide to living which includes advice on sexual practices, dates from between 400BCE and 200CE. Erotic art is found in many cultures around the world. *Shunga* paintings, scrolls and books produced in Japan from 1600 onwards showed erotic scenes set in 'lush landscapes or richly layered interiors' and depicted characters who were usually fully clothed

Figure 4.4 Pornhub categories display a range of tastes, preferences and bodily aesthetics.

with exaggerated genitalia.[60] *Tijuana Bibles* were American porn parodies of existing comic strips,[61] appearing in the 1920s, while early animated pornography from around the same time was humorous, featuring 'hyperbolically exaggerated body parts and wildly impossible sexual positions'.[62] Porn and erotic comics and drawings of all kinds have been produced since then,[63] and drawn and animated porn is now included on most porn tube sites.

New types of drawn pornography have also emerged; for example, *monstertoon* porn focuses on fantastic scenarios featuring elves, demons, monsters, celebrity lookalikes and game characters where 'huge bodies penetrate tiny ones and human-like bodies sprout novel sexual organs'.[64] Contemporary Japanese *ero manga* and *anime* are perhaps the most well-known forms of drawn pornography today, often going beyond the sexual 'in terms of plots, themes and settings'.[65] They include *loli-con*, featuring little girl characters and using a 'cute' aesthetic (known as *kawaii*);[66] boys' love (BL) or *yaoi*, developed by female artists for

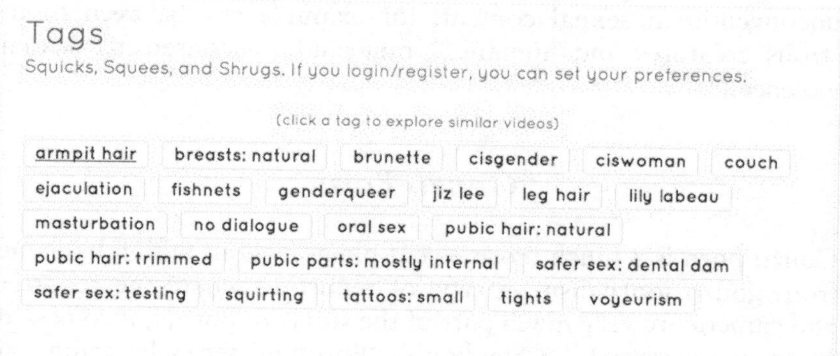

Tags

Squicks, Squees, and Shrugs. If you login/register, you can set your preferences.

(click a tag to explore similar videos)

armpit hair | breasts: natural | brunette | cisgender | ciswoman | couch
ejaculation | fishnets | genderqueer | jiz lee | leg hair | lily labeau
masturbation | no dialogue | oral sex | pubic hair: natural
pubic hair: trimmed | pubic parts: mostly internal | safer sex: dental dam
safer sex: testing | squirting | tattoos: small | tights | voyeurism

Figure 4.5 The Trenchcoat 'curated smut' site has a different way of tagging content.

Figure 4.6 A romantic boys' love image (Wikimedia Commons).

a female audience and focused on the depiction of love and sex between 'beautiful boys';[67] *ladies comics* written by women and popular with female readers, focusing on women pursuing their own sexual pleasure;[68] and *hentai*, a genre featuring extreme or unconventional sexual content, for example sex between monstrous creatures and humans,[69] rape and nonconsensual sexual violence.[70]

Gonzo Porn

Gonzo porn is a much more recent phenomenon, taking its name from gonzo journalism, a type of reporting where the reporter and camera are very much part of the story. In porn, gonzo is said to originate from John Stagliano's 'Buttman' series beginning in 1989, featuring Stagliano himself and depicting 'the adventures of a freelance video cameraman who is obsessed with the derrieres of beautiful women'.[71]

This type of porn uses a documentary style, filming in real time with a focus on 'live' performance and sex as a 'spectacle'. The continuous filming, lack of editing, point-of-view shots and handheld cameras emphasize the 'realness' of the sex. Viewers are invited to 'look at the sex' through the eyes of the camera operator or performer, while the female performer often appears to look directly at the viewer.

Gonzo has been criticized as 'degrading' and 'body-punishing' because of the way it is intensified by a performance style of 'expressive enthusiasm' and 'athletic' sexual numbers.[72] Rocco Siffredi, the well-known gonzo performer, is famous for his athletic, emotionally intense and often rough style, while female stars such as Asa Akira and Eva Angelina perform in a way that suggests a 'discovery of limits', and presents 'sex as endurance sport', 'suggestive of the physicality of all-in wrestling'.[73]

This performance style is particularly well suited to presenting the spectacle of 'a body caught in the grip of intense sensation or emotion';[74] it is often noisy, energetic and focused on bodily convulsions, with extreme demands made on the bodies of performers – particularly female performers.[75] It emphasizes the difference between 'ordinary' sex and a particular kind of professional activity that shows spectacular and extraordinary 'skill, ability and threshold'.[76]

Figure 4.7 Performer, director and producer Rocco Siffredi, famed for an intense and athletic performance style.

Gonzo performers are 'sexual athletes' whose performances involve 'pushing the boundaries of that which bodies are considered able to do'.[77] Gonzo also depicts sex which focuses on oral and anal practices rather than genitals, and is uninterested in a 'linear' goal-focused model of sex which ends with orgasm and in conventional depictions of sexual pleasure.[78]

Amateur Porn

Another type of pornography that has become particularly widespread is amateur pornography. The term is used in a variety of ways.[79] ProAm performers are 'people working in porn semi-professionally outside the large production companies',[80] but 'amateur' is also used to describe the reality-porn genres which draw heavily on the look of amateur porn; for example, Bangbus,[81] in which women are apparently picked up on the street and persuaded to have sex in the back of the 'bang bus'.

Amateur porn also refers to images and films made by non-performers and circulated for others to watch. The term *realcore*[82] was coined for the low-fi sexual images made by amateurs that appeared online in the late 1990s, part of a broader interest in public displays of 'the ordinary' which can also be seen in a range of reality genres. Amateur porn has become extremely widespread. Often circulated for free as part of a gift economy on sites such as Voyeurweb, it is also performed for money. SellYourSexTape, for example, is a commercial site featuring videos shot and submitted by amateur filmmakers and claiming to show the domestic lives of the performers and their 'real emotional intimacy'.[83]

Another kind of amateur production takes place in fan cultures such as slash communities who produce 'transformative works'.[84] Fans create erotic and pornographic images depicting homoerotic encounters between characters from TV shows, fiction and film series like *Harry Potter* (2001–11) or *Lord of the Rings* (2001–3) and share these online. Like slash writers, fans of Japanese animation, comics and gaming (ACG) also produce their own works, dubbing or subtitling Japanese, Korean and Chinese texts – making 'scanlations', 'fandubs' and 'fansubs',[85] as well as *dōjinshi* (amateur manga).

Homoerotic versions of manga texts have been produced by female fans since the late 1970s in much the same way that women in Western cultures have 'slashed' male characters from popular culture. This kind of fan culture is now international with its own commercial publications popular throughout Asia and the US.[86]

It has been argued that 'a new vocabulary is needed for addressing the complex meanings of amateur and commercial porn'.[87] New forms of 'pro-am' work[88] have been seen as part of a broader trend towards what has been called *participatory culture* where there is no longer a clear distinction between producer and consumer and people may be both *prosumer* and *produser*.[89]

In fact, although the distinctions and categories that we use to describe pornographies are useful in drawing attention to their particular characteristics, it's also possible to see a range of correspondences and similarities between different kinds of porn. Gonzo shares with some kinds of drawn porn a fascination with the excessive, but it also emphasizes the real, as does amateur porn. At the same time it is quite distinct from amateur porn in its use of athletic performers with extraordinary powers of endurance which distinguish them from performers in more everyday sexual images. As a stylistic model, gonzo is less varied than the much broader categories of drawn and amateur porn that I've described here. Drawn pornography includes a wide range of materials with a variety of histories, styles, content and audiences. Amateur porn takes in a range of practices which include sexual performances and media recreations and appears in a number of different communities, cultures and subcultures.

Cine-erotica

Pornography is not the only place where sex is depicted in media. In fact, there are a number of genres which specialize in the representation of sex. Exploitation films that were 'designed to create a fast profit by . . . exploiting contemporary cultural anxieties' often included nudity, striptease and suggestions of sexual deviance. The films were made in a way that suggested they were warnings to viewers, but their style celebrated – or 'exploited' the problem 'as much as critiquing it'.[90] While early exploitation films focused on sexual themes, they were different from the pornography of the time. Porn films showed 'actual, non-simulated sexual acts' aimed at heterosexual men in private spaces. Exploitation films, in contrast, were 'shown in theaters or other public places' and 'did not limit their appeal to a strictly heterosexual audience'.[91]

There were a wide range of exploitation subgenres with sexual themes. The sex hygiene film focused on issues such as venereal disease, homosexuality and transvestism.[92] Nudist camp films focused on naturism. After the Second World War, glamour films showed women in 'swimsuits, bikinis, lingerie, underwear, or other provocative outfits',[93] while late 1940s burlesque films featured women who 'strutted, pranced, swung their arms, bumped their hips, poured out of and stripped off their costumes in what appeared to be a flood of uncontained sexual display'.[94] Nudie-cutie films such as Russ Meyer's *The Immoral Mr Teas* (1959) were erotic feature films often featuring women with large breasts. Roughies contained scenes of rape, abduction and abuse, while kinkies also incorporated sadomasochistic practices. Other

Figure 4.8   The poster for *Faster, Pussycat! Kill! Kill!*, a 1965 American sexploitation film directed by Russ Meyer (Wikimedia Commons).

sexploitation films included both documentary and dramatic exposés of social problems such as prostitution and teenage promiscuity, and sex education films, also known as 'whitecoaters'.[95]

In addition there were sex and death and sex-horror films, often incorporating horror themes such as zombies and cannibals. For example Joe D'Amato's films *Porno Holocaust* (1979) and *Erotic Nights of the Living Dead* (1980) combined 'outrageous doses of sex and horror'.[96] This tradition has continued elsewhere. So-called snuff movies have been the subject of fascination for decades, following the sensationalist and false claim of the film *Snuff* (1975) to offer the spectacle of real death for entertainment and arousal.[97] Sex and horror are frequently combined in sex-horror fiction and horror film and porn films also use horror themes. More recently, zombie sex has become the focus of a variety of media.[98]

Another term used to describe particular kinds of sex media is the *cine-erotic*, which refers to taboo sexual imagery in 'a wide range of cult cycles that transcend soft and hard-core pornographic divisions'. These include 1950s American burlesque dramas, '1970s full-length explicit epics', and 'direct to video genres and cycles, which often parody and reflect current trends in mainstream film and TV production'.[99]

Often these types of film have blended together and there is plenty of cross-fertilization, both in cult and more mainstream types of media. British sex comedies such as *Confessions of a Window Cleaner* (1974), for example, combined simulated sex scenes with saucy humour in the tradition of the low-budget British *Carry On* films.[100] Feature-length softcore films such as *Emmanuelle* (1974) were 'situated . . . between hardcore and theatrical Hollywood'[101] and 'punctuated by . . . simulated, nonexplicit sexual spectacle'. They showed female nudity, 'striptease numbers, tub or shower sequences, modeling scenes, voyeur numbers, girl-girl segments, threesomes, orgies, and the like'.[102] They often focused on a woman's awakening sexuality,[103] emphasizing female desire.[104]

The softcore film has links to art cinema,[105] but is usually dismissed as 'a feminized, upper-middle-brow form of sexploitation'.[106] Other mainstream films which focus on sex, such as *Fatal Attraction* (1987), *Basic Instinct* (1992) and *Stoker* (2013), take the form of erotic thrillers, making use of 'softcore sexual display in the context of noirish plots'.[107] These focus on sexual intrigue, criminality and duplicity, with sex that 'always remains just mainstream . . . but only just'.[108]

Porno-chic and Mainstream Entertainment

In considering the many styles, forms and genres of particular kinds of sex media we should also take into account the range of representations that have been referred to as forms of 'porno-chic', or as 'pornified' or 'sexualized' media materials. These are mainstream media texts that are said to 'borrow from, refer to, or pastiche the styles and iconography of the pornographic'. For example, 'open, moist and lipstick-red lips, half-closed eyelids or hands suggestively placed on a bare bosom or stomach are staple elements in pornography, but also in music videos, cosmetics ads and fashion photography'.[109] However, unlike hardcore porn which tends to be understood as anonymous, 'real', intense, 'dirty' and unrefined, porno-chic texts may also feature celebrities, often in an ironic, sophisticated, glossy format.[110]

Madonna is 'the figure who more than any other can plausibly be said to have made porno "chic"',[111] particularly in the works she produced between 1989 and 1992. These included 'Justify My Love' (1990), a black-and-white music video set in a series of hotel rooms where dancers and actors dressed in fetish gear perform in a range of romantic and sexual scenarios, and *Sex* (1992), a book which contained scenes of 'masturbation, group sex, sado-masochism, lesbianism, and even simulated rape, all framed as the product of the star's sexual fantasies'. Both worked to 'appropriate the transgressive qualities of porn in a mass market context'.[112]

Porno-chic has continued to be associated with a range of music performers and especially with music video.[113] Christina Aguilera's 'Dirrty' (2002) features table dancing and furries; Rihanna performs in 'S&M' (2011) as a dominatrix; and in 'Wrecking Ball' (2013) Miley Cyrus, naked except for a pair of boots, swings on a wrecking ball and licks a sledgehammer seductively.

Porno-chic texts like these are often playful and seductive, working with the language of pastiche, parody and humour. But they can also be pedagogic: 'about' rather than 'in the style' of porn. For example, some mainstream films are about the business of adult entertainment, such as *Boogie Nights* (1997), *The People*

Figure 4.9 Madonna, 'Justify My Love', 1990. The music video was banned from a number of TV networks.

Versus Larry Flynt (1996) and *The Look of Love* (2013). Others are metaphorical, rather than playful or pedagogical, using explicit sex and pornography to represent something else. For example, in *A Serbian Film* (2010), which features scenes that show the decapitation of a restrained woman during sex and a man raping his unconscious wife and son, the world of pornography is used to represent horror. The film's director Srdjan Spasojević said that 'pornography was the only possible metaphor' he could use to depict the 'almost indescribable and exploitative chaos' that had defined his life.[114]

Porn as Culture

'The differences between pornography and other forms of culture are less meaningful than their similarities.'

It is often claimed that in these kinds of porno-chic texts mainstream media 'borrows' from pornography. Yet another approach to their

103

relationship suggests that porn simply shares many characteristics with other popular forms. For example, some have argued that porn shares the characteristics of early twentieth-century cinema, a cinema of 'attractions' that focused on spectacular images and on making a sensual impact on the viewer.[115] The structure of some kinds of pornography has also been compared to the musical film genre because it choreographs bodies engaged in sex in a similar way to the plotting of song and dance numbers within the narrative of a musical. Porn has been described as 'carnivalesque' because, like other forms of low culture such as dirty jokes and 'smutty folklore', it turns the usual order of things on its head, celebrating those things that are usually despised – the physical instead of the intellectual and the ordinary instead of the elite.[116]

From this point of view it can be argued that 'the differences between pornography and other forms of culture are less meaningful than their similarities'.[117] In particular, porn shares characteristics with forms of popular entertainment in general, being commercial and vulgar rather than artistic or worthy. As a form of popular entertainment, it emphasizes seriality[118] (using the same characters, situations and structures across many texts) and adaptation (taking characters or stories from one medium and transferring them to another). It provokes an emotional response, prefers happy endings and satisfying resolutions, and celebrates pleasure and sensation. Like entertainment it is interactive (becoming part of the sexual lives of its consumers) and spectacular (often with an emphasis on the amazing or the fascination of watching people having sex).[119]

The more we look at types of sex media – pornographic and otherwise – the more we can see that there are points of overlap and similarity between these and other examples of media and culture, as well as many distinctions and differences. In addition, in order to understand them fully we need to consider them not simply as types of texts, but as forms that are connected to particular spaces.[120] The ways we communicate and interact can also be seen in this way.[121] As media become increasingly interactive and communication technologies are embedded in our lives, an ever wider range of applications, platforms, zones, spaces, interactions and experiences become part of sex media.

Sex Zones and Media Spaces

The internet has become an important new space for sex.

Particular spaces and zones are often associated with sex.[122] In the past, technologies for travel became particularly important – the railway station became a place for cruising, as did the metro and tube in later times.[123] The development of cities also increased 'interconnectivity' between people,[124] and 'the ... density and busy-ness of city life' offered new possibilities for sexual encounters and experiments, providing 'a theatre for sexual display'.[125]

Specific kinds of space have been linked to particular kinds of sexual encounters. Commercial sex takes place in spaces such as brothels and red light districts, while cities like Amsterdam have become associated with sex tourism and countries such as Thailand have become famous for offering sex-reassignment surgeries.

While the bedroom is associated with sex in relationships – regardless of where people actually have sex – other spaces such as toilets, locker rooms and outdoor cruising and dogging areas are also used for sex,[126] with some spaces such as 'streets, sex clubs, and parks' particularly important for gay men.[127] The development of specific public spaces has also been important for sexual communities;[128] gay quarters such as Greenwich Village and Harlem in New York in the early twentieth century provided places for gay men to be visible to each other.[129] BDSM clubs and LGBT pride marches have become important for their communities in the same kinds of ways.[130]

But these kinds of spaces also become sites where sex is regulated.[131] For example, having sex in public is in many places a criminal offence. Adult entertainment and 'red light' zones are often set at a distance from other parts of cities, and especially from 'family sites'.[132] As living in urban centres has become more expensive and desirable, public and commercial sex in such areas has become increasingly restricted. For example, the 42nd Street area of New York was once the home of peep shows, porn theatres, adult video stores and sex movie houses where gay men had sex, but has now been 'cleaned up'.[133]

Prostitutes who work outside ('streetwalkers') have been driven out of many public places, while more glamorous gentlemen's clubs and sex boutiques for women have become more visible[134] as part of a process of gentrification.[135] Attacks on sex workers and traders become a way of closing down public – usually gay – sexual cultures and of forcing public forms of sex back into private spaces.[136] Meanwhile, a concern around migration and border crossings has emerged, with migrant workers in the sex industry often wrongly characterized as trafficked victims in need of 'rescue'.[137]

Technology and space have also been refigured for sex in other ways.[138] While buying and watching porn films was once carried out in designated shops and cinemas within urban sex zones, this kind of consumption has moved into people's homes through video, cable TV and the internet. The internet has become an important new space for sex in other ways – seen as a 'sexual playground' by some and a 'perilous vortex of danger' by others.[139] It has become a new zone for paid sex work, cam sites, erotic performances, sex-worker advertising sites, forums for sex workers and their clients, sex education and sex shops.[140]

Specialist, independent and amateur producers have created spaces for engaging with a range of sex media, including amateur porn, erotica and slash fiction, while swinger sites, sex chatrooms, sex-cam sites and various online communities provide new places to meet and interact. The internet has been especially important in allowing new groups of people to access sexual representations and services; for example, it has become much easier for women to become porn producers and consumers.[141]

New applications, platforms and technologies quickly become used in sexual ways – in Reddit posts and links, in GIFs, or on Skype, Chatroulette, Vine, Tumblr, Instagram, Pinterest and Snapchat.[142] There are also porn versions of social networking sites – Fuckbook, Pornostagram and Pinsex, which allow users to share, curate and create content.[143]

New spaces have made it possible to experiment with what sex is. In 1991 it was predicted that within thirty years people would be able to 'have sexual experiences with other people, at a distance'.[144] They would climb into a padded chamber and use 3D glasses and a bodysuit with intelligent sensor-effectors that could 'receive and transmit a realistic sense of tactile presence'.[145] It would be possible to 'experience erotic frissons or deep physical, social, emotional communion with another person'.[146] Sex could become 'virtual'.

Increasing attention is being paid to the impact of technologies on sex,[147] often in the form of predictions about its future. These predictions include new forms of 'sex tourism' which will draw together sex work, pornography and entertainment and which could include cybersex with a 'sensorama celebrity',[148] an avatar based on celebrities of the present and the past. It has been suggested that the storage and playback of a person's sexual pleasures through a pleasure chip might become possible.[149]

A common thread in predictions of this sort is towards increasing 'total immersion' through forms of virtual reality sex, implanted chips to produce bionic orgasms, and artificial body parts linked wirelessly to the brain.[150] It has been claimed that new combinations of sex and technology may 'blur the lines of fundamental concepts like gender, fidelity, privacy and beauty', whilst

Figure 4.10 New kinds of pornography such as virtual reality porn emphasize interactive experiences.

providing 'variety and novelty . . . more ways to share pleasure . . . an outlet for personal expression and mutual connection unlike anything the world has ever seen'.[151]

Sex Media Interactions

Cybersex was an early form of online sexual interaction, initially carried out entirely through dialogue in text,[152] and quickly becoming 'taken for granted' by its users, while at the same time 'shaking the ways in which human sexualities are taking place'.[153] An early practitioner of cybersex described how she felt it gave her the 'freedom to be and do anything'; 'I had all sorts of sex in every new way I could think of.'[154] People who have cybersex have described their encounters as a kind of 'self-game', carried out for 'sheer amusement or pleasure',[155] and as a source of 'desire, expression, intimacy, play, experimentation, arousal and/or orgasm'.[156]

But cybersex has a range of meanings for those who take part in it – just as other forms of sex have. It may be part of the routine that two or more partners develop in their sex lives. It may be an adventure, a space for experimenting with sexual identity,[157] a form of 'communication play',[158] or a way to learn new sexual techniques and experience forms of arousal that might not be possible in face-to-face encounters with others.[159] Researchers have been fascinated by the possibility that it might provide a way of experimenting with and reflecting on gender and sexual identities,[160] challenging the 'divisions of animal, spirit and machine',[161] and providing 'a kind of missing link between fantasies, desires for intimacy, the traditional role of text in representing these, and sexuality'.[162]

A variety of virtual sex experiments have been carried out as new technologies have made them possible.[163] 'Teledildonic' or 'remote controlled sex toys'[164] operated via the internet have emerged. Internet-enabled sex toys have been integrated with instant messaging,[165] phones and webcams, and are marketed for solo use and as a way of connecting to a sexual partner.[166] Some sex toys such as Hello Touch Lovely are 'wearable'.[167] Personalized sex toys can be made using 3D printing and casting.[168]

108

Figure 4.11 The virtual world Second Life makes possible all kinds of sexual activities between avatars (wikimedia commons).

Other developments have combined sex toys with different kinds of devices. For example, the OhMiBod is a vibrator that syncs with an iPod to vibrate to whatever music is being played – a new type of 'acsexsory'[169] that combines sex with other forms of leisure. New kinds of pornography also emphasize interactive experiences. Rift technology – using devices like the Oculus Rift – makes possible virtual reality porn and allows porn to be integrated with sex toys.[170]

Cybersex has also moved into animated platforms and games.[171] Multi-player online sex games such as Sociolotron have appeared, while games such as Luxuria Superbia use touch screens to allow players to interact with abstract representations of sexual pleasure.[172] Virtual worlds such as Red Light Center and Second Life allow users to interact as avatars who are 'creative self-(re) presentations' to engage in 'dramatic play'.[173]

Sex in Second Life allows residents to use text or voice chat in their avatar sex, while 'poseballs', animation sets and erotic furniture allow avatars to be animated for sexual activity. Residents can buy sex toys as well as male, female, hermaphrodite and animal genitalia. Second Life has also become home to a wide range of sexual communities such as furries and other non-human avatars, exotic dancers and sex workers, and it makes possible forms of sexual activity which may be beyond what is possible offline – for example, sex between whale and horse avatars.[174] For some people sex in Second Life may be experienced as a 'tightly bound combination' of their 'first' and 'second' lives.[175]

This move towards more vivid, immersive and interactive experiences is part of a wider trend of mixing representation, communication, performance and sexual activities. These are part of a range of technosexualities in which bodies are combined with objects, images and technologies.

The development of mobile networking has also altered the ways that sex, space and technology can be related. Communication is no longer tied to fixed points such as static computers,[176] and apps embed the 'virtual' in physical space in new ways.[177] Geosocial hook-up apps allow users to pinpoint each other using GPS technology and connect people and places on and offline in new ways, drawing together virtual and physical experience.[178] Geolocation is particularly important for LGBTQ people – who in the past relied on the safety provided by physical spaces such as gay villages – enabling them to 'see' other LGBTQ people in their spaces.[179]

Mobility becomes especially important in these kinds of encounters. Temporary spaces and connections can be created through digital nods, smiles and winks as people pass each other by.[180] Apps like Grindr and Tinder also collapse the division between interaction and representation in new ways; the nude images and erotic chat circulated on apps become a kind of amateur porn that can be stored by others.[181] Active pornographic spaces are created across the physical and virtual spaces of particular neighbourhoods where porn is screened in bars, clubs and the windows of sex shops and where both professional and amateur porn performers circulate information about their lives across social media platforms, making new forms of public sex culture.[182]

Increasingly then, sexual interactions involve a 'commingling of practices enabled by various systems of communication and technologies'.[183] For example, some gay men use online hook-up devices to arrange 'chemsex' parties which involve taking drugs. These arrangements draw together online chat, looking at pornography and browsing profiles, and lead up to 'intensive sex partying',[184] which combines chilling, chatting, taking drugs and having sex.[185] Dogging makes use of mobile phones, text messaging, camera and video phones, internet sites and cars, bringing people together in particular ways and spaces and regimes of 'techno-sex'.[186] More generally, technologies are now firmly part of the way people connect for sex and romance, whether as part of established relationships, for flirting, hooking up or online dating.

Media and other technologies play an important role in the ways we understand sex today and are increasingly part of everyday sex lives. To understand this properly we need to put them in a broader context by thinking about the ways that our ideas about work and leisure, public and private, health and well-being are changing. The next and final chapter considers these in more detail.

Summary

- Sex media tend to be placed low down in a cultural hierarchy which is suspicious of body genres and of media forms that invite the viewer's involvement.

- There is a wide range of sex media, each with differing and distinctive conventions.

- Sex media share characteristics with other forms of popular entertainment.

- Media provide new means of sexual visibility and connection, and media, space, representation, communication and interaction are increasingly intertwined.

5

Sex Media, Culture and Society

This chapter covers:

- The relation of sex to labour, play and leisure.

- The relation of sex to changing intimacies, relationships and cultures.

- The ways in which media and other technologies have impacted on how we experience and understand sex, bodies and life, and have worked to produce 'media-bodies' and 'cyborgs'.

- Developing ideas around sex and sexuality education and sexual ethics, sexual health, healthy sexual development and sexual citizenship.

- Media literacy, the role of media in sexuality education, and the importance of media and cultural studies in understanding sex media and its significance.

Sex Today

People have used media for sexual purposes for centuries. Sex has a long history of provoking attention and evoking anxiety. Today public attention frequently focuses very directly on sex media – on sexualized images, pornography and sexting – often expressing concern about their changing significance and our relation to them. Public debates and discussion frequently sensationalize this relation and encourage us to join in a 'public account' in which the relations between sex, media and technology are presented as simple and obvious, and often as risky and harmful.

But research suggests that in countries such as the UK, the US and Australia, people's own sexual experiences are not so simply characterized and are actually very diverse. They take place in a swiftly changing context where we live longer, more of us live alone, and the number of marriages has declined. Families are extended and recombined as people enter into new relationships. Ideas about gender, sex and sexuality have shifted, sometimes quite dramatically. There has been a growth in the diversity of sexual and gender communities.

A greater acceptance of some kinds of same-sex relationships is reflected in the introduction of civil partnerships and same-sex marriage. The sexual double standard that allowed sexual freedoms for men but not women persists, but it is increasingly challenged.[1] What is considered to be sexually 'normal' has also shifted in some ways, and the idea that sex is 'plastic'[2] – flexible and fluid, forged in new and diverse forms – is more common-place. Sex is understood and practised in a multitude of new ways, as part of a 'long, convoluted, messy, unfinished but profound revolution' taking place in our intimate lives.[3]

Yet alongside this transformation of attitudes towards gender and sexuality there is also an 'entrenchment around traditional roles, practices, and values',[4] as well as calls for a return to more conservative sexual norms. Other concerns focus on the way that sex has become a commodity or lifestyle,[5] a set of individual pleasures and freedoms that ignore the fact that we are part of communities or society.

From these kinds of perspectives the combination of sex with media is simply part of a 'general commodification of sex'.[6] Sex is seen as becoming too much like other leisure practices or too much like work; not private enough or private in the wrong sorts of ways. But these objections and concerns do not capture the complexity of the place of sex in contemporary life, the roles that media and technologies play in our understandings and experiences of sex, or the ways that sex, gender and sexuality 'are in the midst of a major transformation'.[7] In order to really understand the shifting relations between sex and media we need to consider them 'in conjunction with changes in other realms, such as the economy, labour, leisure, commodity, culture, and the self'.[8]

Sex and Labour

Sex is bound up with many people's paid work. To understand the place of sex in contemporary life we need to think about how it is connected to changes in the way that work and leisure are organized and how these relate to commerce and to our intimate lives. Sex work – the most visible way in which intimacy and commerce are combined – is part of a much broader sphere of *intimate labour* that is performed in Western societies.[9] These kinds of work are not necessarily new but they have grown in societies where work that was previously carried out by unpaid family members at home has become paid work performed in the service industries for those who can afford it.[10] They include childcare and domestic duties, as well as hairdressing, massage, home health support, personal training, counselling and therapy.[11]

Sex work is a huge and diverse sector.[12] It includes 'massage; erotic conversation ... dance ... bondage and domination ... attentive company at dinners and events; nude services like table waiting and telegram delivery', 'acting in sexual cinema and videos' and 'the sale of sex toys, clothes and gear, erotic literature, videos and DVDs'.[13] It takes place in a range of spaces, including 'strip clubs, peep shows, gentlemen's clubs ... pornographic film studios, pornographic photography studios, live-sex websites, escort agencies, spas, saunas, massage parlors, brothels, phone-sex services, Internet chat rooms, bathhouses, and BDSM dungeons'.[14] It includes workers who provide a 'girlfriend experience' or operate as a 'weekend boyfriend' and who charge for their performance of those roles.[15] Those who work in services that support sex work include 'parking attendants, waiters, guards, drivers, cashiers, cleaners, cooks, barmen and laundry workers', while many others, such as 'investors in property, entertainment and tourism; business owners and entrepreneurs; lawyers; accountants; airlines, limousine and taxi services; telephone communications businesses' also participate in the sex industries.[16]

Although sex work is marginalized and stigmatized as a form of labour, it is economically, socially and culturally significant. It is related to 'wider patterns in leisure, consumption, travel, and the hedonistic search for relaxation and pleasure' and to services that sell escapism, adventure and fantasy.[17] It reflects the importance of sexuality as central to 'late-capitalist consumer culture'.[18] The significance of sex as a form of work can also be seen in the many other forms of employment that involve or focus on sex – journalists who write about it, academics who research it, sex-advice givers and sex therapists,[19] as well as sex educators, authors of erotica, performers in 'raunchy' music videos and so on. These workers also include those in the 'rescue industry', enabling workers to leave sex work behind, those who treat sex addiction, and many others who make their livings from opposing or regulating aspects of sexual culture such as pornography.

So sex is bound up with many people's paid work and, as with other kinds of labour, these forms of work involve a range of experiences and carry a range of meanings. For some people sex work may be dangerous, alienating, a form of survival or the best of a bad set of choices. For others it may be fulfilling, a source of pleasure and creativity, or part of a set of political aims. It may involve valued relationships with other workers or with clients, or be experienced as an expression of 'personal and real sexuality'.[20] As with other forms of labour, work is rarely 'just' work, but likely to overlap with other important aspects of a person's life. Work often joins together different aspects of people's public and private lives, and in the same way forms of intimacy are entangled with commerce in a range of ways.

The term 'bounded authenticity' has been used to describe types of sex work which make possible 'the sale and purchase of authentic emotional and physical connection'.[21] Intimate connections and

	Early modern capitalism	Modern-industrial capitalism	Late capitalism
Work:	Domestic production	Wage labour	Service work: 'creative' and 'flexible' jobs
Kinship:	Extended kin networks	Nuclear	Recombinant families/isolable families
Sexual ethic:	Procreative	Companionate/ promiscuous (gendered double standard)	Bounded authenticity

Table 5.1 Different periods are characterized by different forms of work, kinship and 'sexual ethic'. In contemporary Western societies there has been a move to flexible work, different family forms and an ethic of 'bounded authenticity' in which authenticity and intimacy are bound up with commerce (Bernstein, 2007).

commerce are also becoming joined together in new ways. For example, the pornographic labour that has developed out of participatory online cultures[22] has led to amateur porn becoming the fastest growing type of pornography, while the rise of pornographic tube sites such as YouPorn and XTube have provided spaces where both amateur and commercial material can be shared.[23]

Alongside porn stars, professional 'amateur' performers and other more casual porn labourers, some people are working – sometimes paid, sometimes not – towards the 'reclaiming of porn culture',[24] linking together artistic production, sex-work education and political activism. For others still, making amateur porn may be part of their sexual self-expression or the way they create links with particular networks and communities. At the same time, while their labour may be freely given in the creation of user-generated content it also becomes part of the way that profit is generated online, and users may have very little control over what they produce.[25]

Sex within non-work relationships involves labour too. It may involve 'comparing notes, using some imagination, trying way-out or new experiences'.[26] It may need effort, practice and dedication to a set of 'techniques that provide personal meaning and pleasure',[27] or help to develop a 'repertoire of "skills" and improve performance'.[28] Being a 'sexpert' has also come to depend on a broader range of attributes such as developing a particular 'look' or the ability to perform 'confident sexual agency'. All of these practices involve sex as work that requires 'constant labour and reskilling'.[29] In addition, for some people, working at sex may involve bringing 'feelings more into line with how they suspect sex "ought to be" experienced',[30] faking pleasure or working at changing their responses to sexual practices.[31]

Sex advice often promotes a work ethic around sex, while sexual health has come to be seen as a kind of work that an individual is responsible for,[32] a duty even when it is experienced as pleasurable.[33] Becoming knowledgeable and good at sex may require the use of tools and toys,[34] paid experts and producers of 'training, instruction, counsel ... recipes, drugs and gadgets'.[35] This blurring of boundaries between sex and work has been seen as part of a broader corporatization of intimacy,[36] and the work we are encouraged to perform on ourselves as a kind of self-branding,[37] a form of 'cultural participation' which is at the same time a kind of 'commercial practice'.[38]

Sex and Leisure

Sex is also increasingly linked to leisure.[39] One sign of this is the steady development and visibility of toys, machines and other products for recreational sex,[40] with sex toys for women particularly visible and often considered a growth area.[41] Vibrators such as 'The Rabbit' are presented as fashionable and feminine, a trend often traced to its featuring in an episode of *Sex and the City* in 1998.

Figure 5.1 Sex toys feature in *Sex and the City*, 1998.

Toys may be marketed as fashion accessories with 'feminine' colours and stylish finishes, surfaces and textures,[42] or as luxury items such as the gold-plated 'pleasure objects' from Swedish designers Lelo,[43] who specialize in 'intimate lifestyle products'. The market for sex products has also diversified. Bad Dragon[44] makes 'fantasy-themed' sex toys modelled as the genitalia of dragons and gryphons, while Divine Interventions[45] makes religious-themed dildos such as the Jackhammer Jesus. Meanwhile amateur inventors make sex machines in suburban garages,[46] and a similar style of DIY production can be seen at the Homemade Sex Toys site,[47] which demonstrates how to carry out a variety of projects, including vibrators made out of fruit and vegetables, laser swords, dildos and flashlights. More elaborate equipment is featured at sites such as House of Gord,[48] 'the home of ultra bondage', which shows videos that make use of swing sets, sprinklers, pony carts, tables, stands, walkers, trailers, punishment boxes and treadmills. Sex scenes featuring machines such as Fuckzilla, Sybian, Titan, The Fucksall and The Octapussy are the focus of specialist sites such as FuckingMachines.[49]

Furniture designed for sex, such as Liberator Shapes, is described

Figure 5.2 A silicone sex doll at Real Doll.

as 'bedroom adventure gear' and allows people to 'create a playground'.[50] Sex is increasingly discussed in magazines and sex-advice books as a set of playful practices which might include massage, dressing up, stripping, dancing, games such as porn charades and strip poker, fantasy and role play, as well as technologies such as phones, email, texts, photography and video, and media forms such as pornography and erotica.[51]

This fascination with sex products and performances can also be seen in the developments within sex doll and sex robot construction. Inflatable dolls used for sex have been mass produced since the second half of the twentieth century, but today much more sophisticated sex dolls are available. Customers can choose body type, skin, eye and hair colour.[52]

For some, a relationship with a doll of this kind is a form of 'synthetic love' and one way of identifying as a 'technosexual'.[53] Another is interacting sexually with humanoid robots. The True Companion company claims to have designed the world's first sex robot which can 'talk, listen, carry on a conversation, feel your touch', 'be your true friend' and 'have an orgasm when you touch them!',[54] while Sinthetics offer manikins with fantasy options including elf ears and fangs.[55] It has been argued that in the future robots will serve as companions, lovers and life partners, providing 'great sex on tap for everyone 24/7'.[56]

As well as being linked to love and romance, sex offers types of sociability that are created through play.[57] The idea of sex as play or as a game is not new.[58] Sexual play in childhood has been described as a way of exploring and learning about sexuality. Sexual subcultures often use the term to describe their practices, while therapists prescribe forms of sexual play to people in long-term relationships.[59] Media representations and games are increasingly being used to open up 'different dimensions of what is typically conceived of as sex and sexuality',[60] while social media and other communication technologies are new spaces where people can play with sex.[61]

The expansion of social networking technologies for sex has made sex-as-play much more visible and accessible. Adult Friend Finder, a site for people looking for 'sex dates, adult matches, hookups and fuck friends', claims to have over 70 million members worldwide.[62] Other sites offer parties for recreational or 'leisure sex',[63] while some kinds of cybersex encounter take the form of 'casual, distant and noncommittal' game playing.[64] These kinds of 'party and friend sex' often have a 'theatrical element' that may be different from 'lovemaking with a committed partner',[65] while 'intensive sex partying'[66] or sex as a form of 'extreme sport' can be ways of 'testing the body's limits', 'creating new and exciting forms of intimacy', acquiring new kinds of skills or engaging in the pleasures of 'thrill seeking and risk-taking'.[67]

In all these examples sex can be seen as a form of 'playful exploration through which the boundaries of norms and bodily capacities may be reworked, and possibly expanded'.[68] Sexual play may be about exploring identities, attachments and tastes, and linked to sexual fantasies that also offer possibilities for exploring and reimagining desire and the self.[69] For some, sex may be a kind of 'serious leisure', experienced as 'important to the well-

120

Figure 5.3 Adult Friend Finder, the world's largest sex and swinger community.

being of the individual' and 'a vehicle for the . . . reaffirmation of communities as places in which the individual recognises relations of belonging'.[70]

Intimacies

In our use of media, we reinvent what intimacy means.

The changing relationships between sex, work and leisure are part of a number of broader shifts in the way we organize public and private life and build intimacies with others. While the older relations of sex to reproduction and to romantic ideals of binding love remain important, for some people sexual relationships are now less likely to be bound by duty than they were in the past and are only continued if those involved feel that it is satisfying enough to stay in them.[71] In this kind of 'pure' relationship, 'the relationship is its own reward'[72] rather than a means to something else, and sex becomes a way of maintaining it,[73] as well as making a monogamous and long-term relationship more sexually exciting.[74]

At the same time it has become more acceptable – at least in some cultures – to pursue an 'episodic' sex life through affairs, one-night stands, hook-ups and other forms of casual encounter.[75] Both 'pure' and 'episodic' relationships have become more 'easy to enter and to exit',[76] though of course people continue be bound together in all kinds of ways. Contemporary sexual relationships can also be understood in terms of the relationship to the self: as part of an 'adventure' which might be focused on experimentation, exploration and journeys of self-discovery.[77]

But it would be wrong to see contemporary sex lives as experienced only in terms of monogamy or episodic encounters. Many people are not in sexual relationships at all, are in relationships where sex plays little or no part, or identify as asexual.[78] Others explore different ways of being in sexual relationships. Some couples have affairs, while others are non-monogamous – in open relationships where individuals have multiple sexual relationships outside the couple, or in polyamorous relationships where people have multiple love relationships which may also be sexual.[79]

One way to think about these changes, alongside the new relations of sex to labour and leisure, is in terms of multiple sexual cultures and ways of life, the ways that different individuals and groups see sex and sexuality, how they negotiate it in their lives, and how they engage with others in ways that involve sex.

Shared lifestyles and collective identities can be formed around sexual fantasies, types of sex media, or spaces and zones associated with sex, sexual politics, or sexual 'orientations . . . fashions or performances'.[80] Gay, lesbian or bisexual communities and sexual subcultures such as swinging or BDSM provide experiences that enhance participants' quality of life.[81] For example, Fetlife is a social network for the BDSM and fetish community, while AVEN is an online asexual community and archive of resources on asexuality. Sex may offer sources of group identity, as 'a means for people to express their differences from the mainstream, and allow communities to create culture'.[82] More generally, the internet is displacing family, friendship groups, school and work as places through which to meet romantic and sexual partners for many, regardless of their sexual preferences or identities.[83]

These developments can be seen as part of the shift not only in the way we think about work and leisure, but also in what we class as private and public. Although sex is often seen as a private part of life, it is very public in other ways,[84] as part of the process of debate, policy-making, campaigning or regulation. This is one aspect of a wider public interest in people's lifestyles in which 'private' matters of the body, intimacy, pleasure and desire have become more public,[85] and in forms of 'striptease culture' that make possible new forms of 'public intimacy'.[86]

These changing intimacies depend heavily on the way we use media and communication technologies today. While older forms of representation such as writing and reading were associated with 'physical isolation' and with silence,[87] photography and the internet have made it possible to document our lives in new ways and to understand self-representation as a form of creative activity that involves others.[88] Representation and communication have increasingly overlapped in social media,[89] creating 'networked publics'.[90]

Media provide us with new ways of interacting. How we circulate and interpret images has become a way of expressing our identities, intentions and desires. Images may work as 'a kind of visual gossip',[91] as part of the way we create bonds.[92] Technology has become 'personal, affective and intimate'[93] and about making connections which are 'sensory, material, embodied, and energetic'.[94] Media provide us with spaces for 'imagined worlds co-created and maintained by persons and groups spread around the globe',[95] and with new ways of belonging to communities and to the social world.[96]

In our use of media, we reinvent 'what intimacy means'.[97] We might use games or music to carve out some solitude[98] in public spaces, or social media to create 'a public space of privacy' with others.[99] We may develop a 'public private self' – a 'public version of the private self'.[100] Forms of 'connected privacy' merge the private and public, linking 'individuals, groups, families, and communities' in new and different ways.[101]

Media Lives, Media-Bodies

We are 'living in, *rather than* with *media' in spaces where the material world is fused together with media.*

While human societies have 'always been technical',[102] technologies are much more central in our lives today, often in hybrid forms, as phones, cameras and clocks merge with television, radio, music and digital networks. They are also more embedded in the way we live, so much so that they may become invisible to us.[103] They are part of the way we live our relationships and take up our place in cultural, social, public and political worlds.[104]

Through processes of 'mediatization'[105] in which media, communications, culture and society are increasingly interrelated,[106] 'we have . . . entered a time in which we can see ourselves live'[107] and become part of an 'incessant recording . . . of lived experience' in ways that make us 'part of a larger media system'.[108] And as media have become mobile they have produced new forms of space, overlaying the physical world with 'layer upon layer of information supplied by governments, organizations, companies, communities and individuals'.[109] In many ways we are 'living *in*, rather than *with* media',[110] in spaces where the material world is fused together with media.[111]

As a result, relations between media and bodies have become more complex. We live in a culture which is fascinated with how people look, with looking at bodies, with the idea of 'body image',[112] and with forms of body work such as exercise, dieting, grooming and makeovers. Our use of images to represent who we are – for example in online profiles or avatars – indicates 'a change in circumstances of the relationship between images of human bodies and actual human bodies'.[113] Bodies are no longer separate from media; in many ways we have 'media-bodies'[114] which are constantly in a process of transformation or 'always-becoming'.[115] Cosmetic procedures, Photoshopping and other forms of body work operate as technologies of transformation[116] and as a way 'to live in a world where realities are multiple',[117] offering 'new ways of being'.[118]

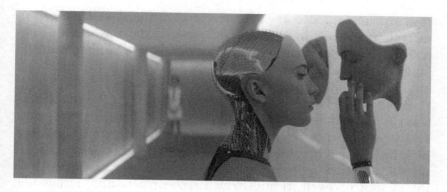

Figure 5.4   Ex_Machina features an intelligent humanoid robot, Ava (Flickr).

Cyborgs

Technologies and bodies are increasingly connected in sexual ways.

Like sex, technology has been a source of fascination in media, especially when it is joined to human bodies. Hybrid creatures may be objects of horror and pity like Frankenstein's monster,[119] recognizably human and heroic as in *Terminator 2* (1991), cartoon-sexy like the fembots from the *Austin Powers* film series (1997–2002), or a more complex mixture of these characteristics like the replicants in *Blade Runner* (1982), or the more recent cyborgs in *Humans* (2014) and *Ex_Machina* (2015).

Combining human and machine as 'humachines'[120] like this raises questions about our future as humans and what human life is.[121] While modifying and enhancing bodies is not new – practices such as tattooing, body piercing and surgery have been around for a long time[122] – we live in a 'world that is ever more mediated and determined by communication technologies, biomedicine, and information'. We are increasingly 'hybrids of machine and organism' or 'cyborgs'.[123] And there are more and more ways in which bodies and technologies connect.[124] Today's cyborgs include 'people with electronic pacemakers, artificial joints, drug implant systems, implanted corneal lenses, and artificial skin', those of us who are immunized against disease and those who use drugs to help us think, behave or feel differently.[125] We use media to 'amplify, accelerate, supercharge, enlarge, zoom in (or out), redact and bring life into focus',[126] extending our abilities.

Technologies and bodies are connected in specifically sexual ways too. Genital surgeries have become increasingly available. Cyborg penises can be created through phalloplasty, implants and prosthetics.[127] Procedures for women include labiaplasty, clitoral repositioning, G spot amplification (using collagen injected into the G spot to swell it) and hymen reconstruction.[128] Drugs like Viagra are used 'to construct, shape, and enhance bodies',[129] creating what some have called a 'Viagraborg'.[130] The increasing acceptance of 'sexual correction and enhancement through pills'[131] has meant that a 'hunt for pink Viagra' for women has followed.[132] Drug interventions like these tend to depend on an imaginary sexuality, an idea of what bodies 'ought to be' like, and often emphasize improving performance and appearance, rather than pleasure. It has been argued that these kinds of modifications draw on an idea of the body as a collection of parts,[133] as though it were a machine that needs maintenance,[134] and on an ideal of sexual desire as something that is predictable and uniform and therefore easy to reproduce.[135]

But technologies can also be used to refigure sex and gender, through practices of transitioning and transformation that involve surgery or hormones. They also impact on the way we imagine age and ageing. The development of drugs like Viagra means that physical features that were once seen as part of a 'normal' ageing process have begun to be presented 'as sexual dysfunctions that require treatment'.[136] Older bodies can resist the processes of ageing, being *re-sexed* through technological interventions[137] such as Viagra and surgical procedures. Media and communication technologies are also used in this way. Young people demonstrate and develop their maturity by engaging with media, with technology and with commerce,[138] and their growing sophistication as consumers is often seen as evidence that 'the worlds of the adult and the child are increasingly intermingled'.[139]

Living Dolls?

*Rather than seeing media and technologies as 'artificial',
it would be more accurate to say that they have become
a significant part of many kinds of sexual expression and
communication.*

For some people, these technological developments are simply
more evidence that culture has been 'pornified'. Part of the
concern expressed in debates about sexualization has to do with
the shifting relations between media and the different stages of
life – and in particular with the way these shifts complicate older
ideas about nature and authenticity.

Cultural and media practices that challenge older ideals of childhood have been criticized as a form of adultification, saturating
'young girls . . . with adult sexuality'. Fears about infantilization
can be seen in the claim that women are 'considered sexy only
when they appear young',[140] part of a wider move towards an
immature 'kidification' that makes culture 'soulless and empty',[141]
addictive and toxic.[142] When girls show interest in fashion, images
and media they are seen as 'not acting on authentic desire but . . .
responding to negative influences'.[143] The idea that pornography
might provide a cultural reference point for young people as they
develop their sexual identities – a kind of 'pornonormativity'[144] –
is often also presented as a concern about artificiality.

These concerns can also be seen when people associate sexualization with body practices such as pubic waxing, breast
enlargement and genital surgeries such as labiaplasty, and with
body aesthetics associated with glamour models and porn stars.
The idea that some women – 'strippers, porn stars, pinups – *aren't
even people*',[145] only 'living dolls',[146] is part of this broader concern
about authenticity. It can be seen as a form of sexism that presents
some groups of women as 'inferior copies' of 'real people',[147] and
some feminine styles and aesthetics as lacking in value.[148]

Rather than seeing media and technologies as 'artificial' in these
ways, it would be more accurate to say that they have become a

significant part of many kinds of sexual expression and communication.[149] Media now play an important part in our sex lives, and this complicates the idea that representation and reality are different and distinct. To compare a 'real', 'authentic' sexuality and an 'inferior copy' of this in porn and other forms of mediated sex misses the point about the relation of media and sex in contemporary culture. It assumes that mediated forms of sex have no meaning or that their meanings are simple, clear and obvious, that they lack value and variety, that when people engage in them they are simply repeating or copying rather than interacting and creating, and that their use by people in all kinds of different contexts means exactly the same thing in every instance.

Rather than trying to distinguish between authentic and inauthentic forms of sexual expression, we need to understand how identity, intimacy and particular sexual cultures[150] are intertwined with image-making, new media and digital culture[151] in a context where authenticity is not only experienced in terms of the 'pure, inner self of the individual' but as a 'relationship between individuals and commodity culture',[152] and with media and technologies.

Sexual Health and Well-being

Sexual health depends on 'a positive and respectful approach to sexuality and sexual relationships', experiences that are 'free of coercion, discrimination and violence', and 'the sexual rights of all persons'.

Health and well-being have become important issues in debates about sex. Critiques of the way sex is often subject to medicalization have shown how the pharmaceutical industry presents sexual problems as types of dysfunction. Focusing only on the body, it represents problems as 'simple medical matters' which require drugs as 'expensive magic fixes'.[153] However, sexual health is not just a physical issue – the World Health Organization defines it as 'a state of physical, emotional, mental and social wellbeing in rela-

Figure 5.5 The Fight the New Drug porn-addiction site contrasts people and love with pixels and porn.

tion to sexuality . . . not merely the absence of disease, dysfunction or infirmity'.[154]

In this kind of more holistic definition of sexual health, media and culture are increasingly the focus of attention. Some anti-porn campaigns have begun to present pornography as a public health issue.[155] Increasingly claims have been made that there is an 'epidemic' of porn addiction, or that internet pornography is a drug,[156] like 'crack cocaine'.[157] Porn addiction sites such as Your Brain on Porn recommend a practice that they describe as 'rebooting' the brain to overcome addiction, which involves avoiding any *artificial* sexual stimulation' including 'pixels, audio and literature'.[158]

In these approaches, sex and sexuality are presented as existing outside culture, while media and technology are seen in entirely negative terms. Set against an idea of 'healthy sex' that is related to 'love, respect, or connection to another human being',[159] that is 'private' and 'an expression of love',[160] some therapists and campaigners condemn the relationship of sex and media, calling this 'porn sex' 'debased, dehumanized, formulaic, and generic' and 'the result of an industrial product'.[161]

From this point of view, the key issues are not ethical ones, such as whether sexual practices and representations involve consent, but are based on normative views of sex. Criticisms that representations of consensual sexual practices such as anal sex, ejaculation onto a woman's body, or two or more men having sex with one women are 'degrading' operate in this way too.[162] So too do claims that pornography that includes consensual hair pulling, slapping, spanking and bondage is showing 'sexual violence' or that people who engage with porn and have casual or experimental sex are engaging in problematic and harmful behaviour. These views of 'unhealthy' sex depend on a moralistic view of good sex as monogamous, heterosexual and romantic, and bad sex as casual, experimental or kinky.[163]

Another place for the discussion of healthy sex is school sex education, but this has been widely criticized for being too focused on biology, on the 'mechanics' of sex,[164] and on how to delay sexual intercourse and avoid pregnancy and STIs. It has also been criticized for being highly heteronormative, with little consideration of other sexualities or sexual desire and pleasure.[165] Research with students suggests that they want to learn more about making sex enjoyable, about sexual desire and diversity, and the skills needed to engage in sexual intimacy.[166] But the issues that students feel are important, such as understanding the emotional and relational side of sex and sexual pleasure, are not usually addressed in formal sex education, which also often presents sex as dangerous and risky, a view which tends not to match students' own experiences.[167]

A different rights-based model of sexual health and education is suggested by the World Health Organization,[168] which calls for 'a positive and respectful approach to sexuality and sexual relationships', experiences that are 'free of coercion, discrimination and violence', and 'the sexual rights of all persons'. Another, put together by a group of academics, suggests that healthy sexual development should involve a range of rights, as well as the development of various kinds of knowledge, awareness, understanding, skills and accomplishments (Box 5.1).[169]

These rights-based models are more concerned with sexual ethics, less inclined to see media as inherently problematic, and far less conservative in their acceptance of the types of sex that people might want to engage in. They see entertainment, media

Box 5.1: Australian researchers involved in studying children's sexual development identify fifteen domains of healthy sexual development:

freedom from unwanted activity

an understanding of consent

education about biological aspects of sex

understanding of safety

relationship skills

agency

lifelong learning

resilience

open communication

sexual development should not be 'aggressive, coercive or joyless'

self-acceptance

awareness and acceptance that sex is pleasurable

understanding of parental and societal values

awareness of public/private boundaries

being competent in mediated sexuality

and communication technologies as an important aspect of sexuality education.[170] They are interested in the ways that media can be used to support sexual health and knowledge, and in the ways that educators such as Scarleteen, Oh Joy Sex Toy, BISH and Laci Green are already doing this.

Unlike biologically focused 'sex education' or moral approaches to sexual health, this kind of 'sexuality education' can focus more broadly on a range of knowledges and interests.[171] One

Figure 5.6   Scarleteen is an independent sexuality and relationships education and support organization and website, founded in 1998 by Heather Corinna. It is visited by around five million people each year, most between the ages of fifteen and twenty-five.

Figure 5.7   Laci Green is a sex-education activist. Her series Sex Plus has over one million subscribers and viewers in 196 countries.

framework that has proved useful for this kind of education is that of ethical decision-making.[172] Ethical decision-making takes a different starting point from moral approaches which emphasize heteronormativity, 'duty'[173] and a view of sex as harmful or risky.[174] While moral approaches rely on rules, focus on 'good' and 'bad' behaviours and acts,[175] and appeal to abstract forms of authority and judgement, ethical decision-making questions abstract categories of good and evil, normal and abnormal,[176] and draws on the idea that it is possible to balance 'care for the self' and 'care for the other/others'.[177] It is able to celebrate gender and sexual diversity[178] and focuses on relations rather than acts, which means that it can take into account the different kinds of relationships that exist between individuals and groups and the implications of these for ethical behaviour.

Ethical decision-making involves negotiation and reflection[179] and sees consent as a series of ongoing processes rather than a set of rules, fixed agreements or contracts.[180] It also considers 'how we are situated in our lives and how age, ability, gender, sexuality, culture and faith . . . may impact on . . . the possibilities we are able to imagine'.[181] Rather than closing down debate, and rejecting diversity and experimentation as moral approaches do, ethical decision-making creates a space for 'a multiplicity of responses to working out what feels ethical for that person, at that time, in a particular context'.[182]

In addition, because this approach sees ethics as a social and political issue, it also emphasizes what groups and communities can do – for example, offering support to survivors of abuse, calling out unethical behaviour, acting as an 'ethical bystander' and taking political action.[183] The focus here is on ethical behaviour or 'civility',[184] not respectability, heteronormativity, cisnormativity or 'middle-class manners'. This approach recognizes ethical cultures that are rarely acknowledged by mainstream moralists,[185] such as those within BDSM cultures. It acknowledges 'kinds of intimacy that bear no necessary relation to domestic space, to kinship, to the couple form, to property, or to the nation'[186] and argues that 'non normative sexual communities' have a 'well-developed tradition of thinking about what constitutes civility in sexual engagements'[187] which may provide models for sexual ethics more generally.

This is at the heart of an inclusive form of sexual citizenship where 'experiments in living' are of public importance,[188] and of an intimate citizenship where questions of public and private, intimacy and community, ethics and politics come together in a consideration of 'how to live the personal and intimate life in a late modern and global world'.[189]

Demands for improved and up-to-date sex education increasingly call for discussions about media to be included. Similarly, an understanding of media and technologies is becoming central to the way that we understand sexual health and well-being. This interest in the role of media is intensifying as part of the continuing interest in the possible futures of sex in a context of technological development.[190] It is important that this understanding is based on critical and evidence-based research and not the kind of 'media literacy' that simply involves 'denigrating all forms of media', or that tries to 'inoculate' people against particular kinds of 'bad' media[191] or persuade them to give these up.

A more productive perspective encourages people to understand how media work and to develop aesthetic and ethical criteria for interpreting media.[192] It considers forms of popular culture to be a potentially valuable part of our lives and 'a tool for thinking'[193] about issues of sexuality. This kind of perspective begins from people's 'existing knowledge and experience of media'[194] and takes this to be important, not only within individual lives, but more widely in communities, societies and politics.

Critical studies of the relations between sex, media and technology have an important role to play in this, not only as academic subjects that are interesting and important in their own right, but as sources of expertise that can be drawn on in other educational, legal and health contexts.

Using these, it is possible to develop a critique of the inequalities and injustices that may be involved in forms of sex media production, while understanding these as types of significant and creative labour which are important for individuals and wider sexual cultures.[195] It is possible to develop an appreciation of media representation that goes well beyond the idea that there are 'good' and 'bad' images of sex. This takes seriously the ways that sex media, alongside other body genres, explore issues of corporeality and sensation in ways that expose the body, push it to extremes, focus on opening it up, make it into a spectacle, and put it on display.[196]

Neither can sex media be understood in terms of 'media effects' – the ways that people engage with them are complex

Figure 5.8   Many programmes and articles about sex and sex media draw on poor evidence. This Bad Sex Media Bingo card, produced by Sense About Sex, identifies the worst examples as a way of encouraging media workers to produce more innovative, useful and ethical work.
(By permission Meg John Barker and Justin Hancock.)

and diverse.[197] While moral discourses see a lack of distance from media as a problem,[198] audience research shows that it is an audience's involvement with media, their knowledge of genres and the communities that form around them, and their investment in all of these, that makes their understanding possible.

The most extreme images may challenge commonly held beliefs, moral certainties and value systems 'by pushing at the limits of the watchable and the tolerable', and may invite ethical reflection because they 'involve and implicate spectators in particular intensified ways . . . demanding critical interrogation and ethical and affective response'.[199] Other sexual representations may work as 'possible sexual stories that can be tried on for size', with 'potential as tools for teaching and learning about *changing* sexual practices and sexual subjectivities'.[200]

Critical studies of sex, media and technology take seriously the bodily and affective responses of audiences, the power of sex media 'to move their viewers and readers' in ways that are not only about pleasure, desire and arousal, but about 'curiosity and interest . . . shame and disgust – as well as numerous things in between'.[201] They also take seriously the ways that people engage with media and technologies to create spaces of self-imagining, to accentuate desire, to explore and think about 'a world of possibilities' or visit 'a distant realm of desires and activities'.[202]

Media and technologies are bound up with the ways that people experience and attend to their bodies, work out their understanding of sexuality and develop their sexual preferences, tastes and orientations. They play a role in the way that people come to make decisions about their bodies, conduct sexual relationships, build intimacies with others, interact and communicate, organize public and private life, and belong to groups, communities, publics and social movements.[203] Sex and sexuality are not outside of culture, but bound together with the technologies, media and commodities that we use to express ourselves and manage our private, intimate and public lives.

At their most helpful, critical media studies can be a starting point for facilitating 'lessons in civic engagement that enable participation and meaningful engagement in our increasingly semiotic and digitally mediated world'.[204] They can help us to develop new ways of making sense of sex, as a means of engaging with the body and its limits, as an imaginative and a communicative practice, as a cultural pursuit and an exercise of taste and appreciation, as an arena of learning and teaching, as a set of skills, techniques and performances, and as a means of creating different forms of intimacy, connection, relationship and belonging. They can also support the development of new cultural competencies and social skills around sex and sexuality.[205] In societies where sexuality has become such a prominent topic of public interest in considering 'how to live', where 'our intimate lives are lived in the throes of major changes and conflicts'[206] and sexual cultures are intertwined with media and technologies, there is a real need for both.

Summary

- Contemporary sex can be understood as a form of intimate labour – both in terms of paid sex work and of 'sex as work' performed on the self and within relationships.

- Sex is increasingly related to leisure, with particular types of sex seen as recreational, and a developing range of sex leisure products.

- The way that we experience and understand sex is linked to changing intimacies, relationship structures and sexual cultures.

- Media make possible new forms of public and private life and complicate ideas about what is natural and authentic about human life.

- An understanding of the place of media and technologies in contemporary life is important for developing ideas about healthy sexual development, sexual ethics, sex and sexuality education, and sexual citizenship.

Notes

Introduction

1 See Smith, 2010a.
2 See Smith et al., 2017.
3 Jenkins, 2004; Attwood and Hunter, 2009.
4 Smith and Attwood, 2014. See also Barker, 2013.

Chapter 1

1 Sedgwick, 1990: 27.
2 Jackson and Scott, 2010: 2.
3 Lorber and Moore, 2011: 4.
4 Jackson and Scott, 2010: 83.
5 Serano, 2013: 8.
6 Grosz, 1994: viii.
7 Sedgwick, 1990: 31; Richards and Barker, 2013: 51.
8 Sedgwick, 1990: 27.
9 Serano, 2013: 9.
10 See Rubin, 1992; Pascoe, 2005; Serano, 2013: 16–17.
11 Nestle, 1984; Rubin, 1992; Duggan and McHugh, 1996; Halberstam, 1998; Volcano and Halberstam, 1999; Volcano and Dahl, 2008; Halberstam, 2012a.
12 Pascoe, 2005: 330; Richardson, 2009: 5.
13 Serano, 2013: 12.
14 Rubin, 2006: 479.
15 Kuper et al., 2012.
16 See Barker, 2014 for a discussion.

Notes

17 Serano, 2013: 14.
18 Serano, 2007: 25; Hines, 2007; Callis, 2014.
19 See Cryle and Downing, 2010 for a discussion of the history of sexuality and the 'normal'.
20 Richards and Barker, 2013: 43. See also Topp, 2012; www.isna.org.
21 Collins English Dictionary, www.collinsdictionary.com/dictionary/english/sex_1 and www.collinsdictionary.com/dictionary/english/sexual-intercourse.
22 Gray, 2003. See Potts, 1998 for a discussion.
23 See Potts, 2002: 51–60 for a discussion.
24 Lyall, 2008.
25 Segal, 1997: 189.
26 Katz, 1995. See also Chauncey, 1994; Blank, 2012.
27 Vicinus, 1982: 135.
28 Williams, 1976: 285–6.
29 In an American medical dictionary of 1901, and in 1934 in Webster's dictionary. See Katz, 1995.
30 Barker, 2012: 63.
31 Berlant and Warner, 1998.
32 Berlant and Warner, 1998: 554.
33 Yep, 2002: 167.
34 See lists of cisgender and heterosexual privilege at http://itspronounced metrosexual.com.
35 See Barker, 2012.
36 The term 'diversity of sex development' is also used. Richards and Barker, 2013: 44. See also Topp, 2012.
37 American Psychiatric Association, 1994: 537; Heyes, 2003.
38 Bocock, 1997: 70.
39 Laqueur, 1990: 149.
40 Or 'scientia sexualis'. See Foucault, 1976.
41 Williams, 1989: 3.
42 Stenger et al., 2001. See also Laqueur, 2003.
43 Rubin, 1984.
44 See Rubin, 1984 for a discussion of these features.
45 See Rubin, 1984 for a discussion of the 'charmed circle' and 'outer limits' of sex.
46 Bocock, 1997: 72.
47 Kinsey et al., 1948, 1953.
48 Schaefer, 2014: 2.
49 Schaefer, 2014: 4.
50 By Hugh Hefner who founded the Playboy empire.
51 Written by Helen Gurley Brown, who went on to become editor of *Cosmopolitan* magazine. A film *Sex and the Single Girl* appeared in 1964, directed by Richard Quine.

Notes

52 Gilman, 1968. See Schaefer, 2014 for a discussion. See also Radner and Luckett, 1999.
53 See Allyn, 2000; Escoffier, 2003.
54 See Delacoste and Alexander, 1987; Nagle, 1997; Kempadoo and Doezema, 1998; Chateauvert, 2013; Grant, 2014; Network of Sex Work Projects, www.nswp.org.
55 Bronstein, 2011: 30.
56 See, for example, Millett, 1969.
57 Chapkis, 1997: 11–32.
58 See, for example, Jeffreys, 1993.
59 Gerhard, 2001: 152.
60 See Samois, 1981; Rubin, 1984; Dimen, 1984; see Duggan and Hunter, 2006 for a discussion.
61 See Millett, 1969. See Bronstein, 2011 for a discussion.
62 Gerhard, 2001: 177. See, for example, Dworkin, 1981.
63 Bronstein, 2011: 313. See also Brents, 2008; Bronstein and Strub, 2016.
64 See Vance, 1984.
65 Downing, 2012.
66 Queen and Comella, 2008.
67 Queen, 1997: 128. See also Fahs, 2014.
68 Queen and Comella, 2008: 278.
69 Chapkis, 1997.
70 Egan, 2006: 77–80.
71 See, for example, Foucault, 1976; Weeks, 1977; Plummer, 1981; Rubin, 1984; Butler, 1990; Sedgwick, 1991; Simon, 1996; Weeks, 2007. See Rubin, 2011 and Plummer, 2012 for a history.
72 Plummer, 2012.
73 See Crenshaw, 1989; Collins, 2000; Nash, 2008; Taylor et al., 2010.
74 Beasley, 2005: 117.
75 Halberstam, 2012b: xv.
76 Halberstam, 2012b: 16.
77 Serano, 2013: 152.
78 Serano, 2013: 136.
79 Serano, 2013: 15.
80 Serano, 2013: 14–15.
81 Serano, 2013: 114.
82 Serano, 2013: 114–15.
83 See Langdridge and Barker, 2007.
84 Dworkin, 1987: 209.
85 FACT brief in Kelly, 1988: 56.
86 For discussions see, for example, van Zoonen, 1994; Carter, 2012; Kearney, 2012.
87 See, for example, Russo, 1987; Dyer, 1992; Weiss, 1993; Gever et al., 1993;

Notes

Budge and Hamer, 1994; Burston, 1995; Doty, 1995; Gross and Woods, 1999.
88 McNair, 2002; Attwood, 2006; Paasonen et al., 2007.
89 Plummer, 2003b: 19.
90 Giddens, 1992: 58.
91 See Mulholland, 2011.
92 Gill, 2003.
93 Duggan, 2002: 179.
94 Warner, 1999; Duggan, 2002.
95 Cox, 1999.
96 Daedone, 2011.
97 Kingsley, 2011.
98 Hasler, 2012.
99 Viljoen, 2013.
100 Harris, 2011.
101 Anderson and Berman, 2012.
102 Gregoire, 2012.
103 See Gill, 2009; Barker et al., 2017.
104 Hooper, 1999: 123–4.
105 Carrellas, 2007.
106 Em and Lo, 2006.
107 Lotney, 2000.
108 Lotney, 2000.
109 Lotney, 2000.
110 Em and Lo, 2008.
111 Zopol, 2009.
112 Midori, 2001.
113 Blue, 2006.
114 Weeks, 2007: 110.
115 Attwood and Smith, 2013: 326.
116 See Barker, 2012: 55–73.
117 Attwood and Smith, 2013: 330.
118 Barker, 2012: 69.
119 See Richards and Barker, 2013.
120 Zelizer, 2005: 1.
121 See Agustín, 2012.
122 Light et al., 2008: 300.
123 Plummer, 2003a: 275.
124 Tiefer, 2006: 273–4.
125 Solomon-Godeau, 1991: 232–3.
126 Williams, 1999: 48.
127 Williams, 1989.
128 Gaines, 2004: 34.

141

129 Kendrick, 1996: 248.
130 Marvin, 1998.
131 Tang and Bailey, 1999: 167.
132 Lynn, 2007.
133 Kibby and Costello, 2001: 359.
134 Arvidsson, 2007: 74.
135 O'Brien and Shapiro, 2004: 115.
136 Klein, 1999: 2.
137 Maddison, 2004. See also Coopersmith, 2006; Barss, 2011; Perdue, 2011.
138 Coopersmith, 2006: 2.
139 See Rubin, 1984 for a discussion of these features.

Chapter 2

1 Petley, 2009: 3.
2 Petley, 2009: 4.
3 Petley, 2009: 2.
4 Petley, 2009: 5.
5 Petley, 2009: 6.
6 Ussher, 1997: 258.
7 Carpenter, 1912.
8 Ellis and Symonds, 1897.
9 See Sinfield, 1994; Glick, 2009.
10 Hall, 1928: 22, 59, 60, 81.
11 In the preface to Hall, 1928.
12 Dollimore, 2001: 99.
13 Sinfield, 1994: 71.
14 Bland, 1995: 289.
15 Souhami, 1998: 178. See also Doan, 2001; Jagose, 2001; Doan and Prosser, 2002.
16 Foucault, 1976: 101.
17 Reuhl, 1982.
18 See Hunt, 1993.
19 Coopersmith, 2000: 34.
20 Hunt, 1993: 12–13.
21 Webster's Dictionary. See Kendrick, 1996 for a discussion.
22 Gaimster, 2000.
23 Tang and Bailey, 1999: 35.
24 Kendrick, 1996: 1–2.
25 Mey, 2006: 2.
26 Mey, 2006: 6.

27 1857, 1959, 1964.
28 Obscene Publications Act, 1959.
29 *Miller v California*, 1973.
30 Obscene Publications Act, 1959, Section 4.
31 James Douglas, *Sunday Express*, 19 August 1928. See Doan and Prosser, 2002 for a discussion.
32 See Hilliard, 2013.
33 See Rolph, 1961; Ladenson, 2007.
34 BBFC History 1912–1949, www.bbfc.co.uk/education-resources/student-guide/bbfc-history/1912–1949.
35 Hays Production Code, see www.artsreformation.com/a001/hays-code.html.
36 Petley, 2009: 57.
37 Meyer, 2003.
38 See Needham, 2017 for a discussion of Mapplethorpe's work in relation to art and pornography.
39 Levinson, 1989. See also McLeod and MacKenzie, 1998.
40 Williams, 1999: 282.
41 Kendrick, 1996: x–xii.
42 Kendrick, 1996: xiii.
43 See Kendrick, 1996.
44 Kieran, 2002: 31.
45 Rubin, 1993: 37. See also Hester, 2014.
46 Examples collected by Barker, 2012.
47 Maddison, 2013: 183.
48 Osgerby, 2001.
49 Ehrenreich, 1983: 42–51.
50 Osgerby, 2001: 201.
51 Kat Banyard, quoted in Bidisha, 2011.
52 Dines, 2010b.
53 See, for example, Dines, 2010c.
54 Kipnis, 1996: 123.
55 Kipnis, 1996: 125.
56 Kipnis, 1996: 129–31.
57 Paasonen, 2010b: 67–8.
58 Maddison, 2009: 49.
59 The trial focused on five films: *Extreme Teen 24* (2002), *Cocktails 2* (2001), *Ass Clowns 3* (2001), *1001 Ways to Eat My Jizz* (2002) and *Forced Entry* (2002).
60 See Maddison, 2009; Brinkema, 2014; Olson, 2016.
61 *Pure Max 16: Euro Version* (2004), *Max Hardcore Fists of Fury 3* (2004), *Max Hardcore Extreme Schoolgirls 6: Euro Version* (2004), *Max Hardcore Golden Guzzlers 5* (2003) and *Max Hardcore Golden Guzzlers 6* (2004).

62 See Maddison, 2009: 178.
63 Cossman, 2007: 59.
64 Brown, 2004, quoted in Olson, 2016: 404.
65 Jones, 2017.
66 Jones, 2016.
67 Jones, 2016. See also Carline, 2011; Attwood, 2014; Hester 2014.
68 See Weait, 2007 for a discussion.
69 See Attwood and Smith, 2010 for a discussion.
70 Criminal Justice and Immigration Act, 2008.
71 Criminal Justice and Immigration Act, 2008.
72 Kennedy and Smith, 2012: 242.
73 Kennedy and Smith, 2012: 241.
74 Weait, 2007: 73.
75 Cowan, 2010: 138.
76 Strub, 2015.
77 See Strub, 2011; Wilkinson, 2011; Strub, 2013; Stardust, 2014; Alilunas, 2016.
78 Foucault, 1988: 6.
79 Marwick, 2008.
80 Mitchell et al., 2012: 17.
81 Lenhart, 2009.
82 Livingstone et al., 2011: 32.
83 Mitchell et al., 2014.
84 Barbieri, 2009.
85 Kranz, 2009; Karaian, 2012.
86 Ringrose et al., 2012; Ringrose et al., 2013; Ringrose and Harvey, 2015.
87 Lenhart, 2009: 1.
88 Willard, 2010: 4. See also Albury et al., 2013.
89 Australian Government, 2008, in Albury et al., 2013.
90 Coroners and Justice Act, 2009.
91 Angelides, 2013. See also Eraker, 2010.
92 The term is from Leary, 2007. See Hasinoff, 2014 for a discussion.
93 See Stone, 2011.
94 *Miller v Mitchell*, 2010.
95 See Karaian, 2012.
96 See Angelides, 2013.
97 See Eraker, 2010.
98 Ringrose et al., 2013: 305.
99 See Lerum, 2009.
100 Wolak et al., 2012: 9.
101 Mitchell et al., 2012: 5.
102 Angelides, 2013: 678. See also Albury and Crawford, 2012.
103 Angelides, 2013; 671. See also Dobson and Ringrose, 2016.
104 Waites, 2005: 218. See also Karaian, 2014; Dobson, 2015.

Notes

105 Simpson, 2013.
106 Soderlund, 2008: 71.
107 Julius and Petley, 2009: 51.
108 Scoular and Sanders, 2010: 3.
109 Scoular and Sanders, 2010: 5.
110 See Petley, 2009. See also Goldsmith and Wu, 2006; Deibert et al., 2008; Lumby et al., 2009.
111 Deflem, 2006: 7.
112 Hunt, 2003: 165.
113 Protection of Children Act, 1978.
114 Under the Criminal Justice and Public Order Act, 1994.
115 Under the Criminal Justice and Immigration Act, 2008.
116 Under the Coroners and Justice Act, 2009.
117 Under the Protection of Children Act, 1978.
118 Under the Criminal Justice Act, 1988.
119 Under the Sexual Offences Act, 2003.
120 Kipnis, 1996: 4.
121 See Galbraith, 2011; Gillespie, 2012; Stapleton, 2012.
122 Lyon, 2007; McLelland, 2016.
123 See Lyon, 1994; Chun, 2006; Lyon, 2007; Andrejevic, 2009.
124 See Bauman et al., 2014; Lyon, 2015. See also Jacobs, 2012.
125 MacAskill, 2016.
126 See www.openrightsgroup.org.
127 Petley, 2012: 263.
128 See Simpson, 2011; Stapleton, 2012.
129 Goldstein, 2009.
130 Hasinoff, 2014: 106–7.
131 McLelland, 2011, 2012; Wood, 2013; McLelland, 2015.
132 Marwick, 2008.
133 Gregory, 2015.
134 McLelland, 2016.
135 Petley, 2012: 263.

Chapter 3

1 See Attwood, 2006.
2 American Psychological Association, 2007; Australian Senate, 2008; Papadopoulos, 2010; Bailey, 2011.
3 Levin and Kilbourne, 2008.
4 Liebau, 2008.
5 Cameron, 2010.

Notes

6 Levin and Kilbourne, 2008: 7.
7 Rush and La Nauze, 2006; American Psychological Association, 2007; Durham, 2008; Oppliger, 2008; Hamilton, 2009.
8 Biddulph, 2009: 165.
9 Dines, 2011: 93.
10 Spanier, 1975: 34–5. See Duschinsky, 2013 for a discussion.
11 Liebau, 2008.
12 Liebau, 2008: 230.
13 Oppliger, 2008: 205.
14 Gill, 2007b: 255.
15 Gill, 2012: 741. See also Gill, 2003, 2007a, 2007b, 2008, 2009.
16 Papadopoulos, 2010: 24.
17 Papadopoulos, 2010: 27.
18 Papadopoulos, 2010: 37. See also the discussion in Smith and Attwood, 2011.
19 Bailey, 2011; Barker and Duschinsky, 2012: 303–10.
20 American Psychological Association, 2007: 2.
21 Lerum and Dworkin, 2009: 259.
22 Bailey, 2011: 15.
23 Bailey, 2011: 49.
24 See Barker and Duschinsky, 2012. See also Lerum and Dworkin, 2009; Smith and Attwood, 2011.
25 Ringrose, 2016.
26 Kleinhans, 2004: 71.
27 Rush, 2009: 42.
28 Egan and Hawkes, 2012. See also Egan and Hawkes, 2007, 2008, 2009, 2010; Dyhouse, 2013.
29 Barker and Petley, 1997: 6; McNair, 2002; Tsaliki, 2015.
30 Jenkins, 2004.
31 Edelman, 2004. See also Robinson, 2013.
32 Bernstein, 2011.
33 Klein, 2009.
34 Egan, 2013a.
35 McKee, 2010: 131–4.
36 Smith, 2010a: 105.
37 See Boynton, 2011.
38 Lerum and Dworkin, 2009: 253.
39 Lerum and Dworkin, 2009: 258.
40 See Phoenix, 2011: 7 for a discussion.
41 Smith, 2010b: 178.
42 Lerum and Dworkin, 2009: 257.
43 See Buckingham et al., 2010: 42–58; Bragg et al., 2011; Bragg and Buckingham, 2013.

44 Evans and Riley, 2014: 17.
45 See Lerum and Dworkin, 2009; Smith and Attwood, 2011; Barker and Duschinsky, 2012; Egan, 2013b; Hasinoff, 2014, 2015.
46 Egan, 2013a: 74.
47 Egan, 2013a: 133.
48 Cage et al., 2014. See also Human Rights Watch, www.hrw.org/topic/lgbt-rights; Amnesty International, www.amnesty.org/en/what-we-do/sexual-and-reproductive-rights; International Lesbian, Gay, Bisexual, Transand Intersex Association, http://ilga.org.
49 Grant et al., 2011.
50 King et al., 2008.
51 See, for example, METRO, 2014; National LGBTI Health Alliance, Australia, http://lgbtihealth.org.au/statistics; CDC, www.cdc.gov/healthy-youth/disparities/smy.htm; ACLUS, www.aclu.org/issues/lgbt-rights.
52 Jorm et al., 2002. See also Barker et al., 2012.
53 UNESCO Institute for Statistics, 2013.
54 UN, 2010.
55 Global Citizen, 2012.
56 The World Bank, 2012.
57 FRA, 2014.
58 WHO, 2016.
59 McNair, 2014.
60 American Psychological Association, 2007: 2.
61 43% of girls have had intercourse at least once by the time they are nineteen; in 2002 it was 51.1%. 11% have had sex before fifteen compared to 19% in 1995. Fortenberry et al., 2010; Guttmacher Institute, 2011. See Egan, 2013b: 39 for a discussion.
62 12% of boys and 10% of girls from an 'opposite sex' partner. Herbenick et al., 2010.
63 9% of boys and 11% of girls in the previous twelve months. Herbenick et al., 2010.
64 1% of boys and 4% of girls. Herbenick et al., 2010.
65 Guttmacher Institute, 2011.
66 From 46% in 1991 to 63% in 2011. In 2011, about 18% of students who had sexual intercourse in the past three months reported that they or their partner had used birth control pills before their last sexual intercourse, and 60% reported condom use. Childstats, 'Sexual Activity'.
67 Guttmacher Institute, 2011.
68 39 per 1000 in 1991, 22 per 1000 in 2007, to 15 per 1000 in 2011 for those aged fifteen to seventeen. Childstats, 'Adolescent Births'.
69 By 53% between 1990 and 2007. Finkelhor and Jones 2006, 2012.
70 By 52% between 1993 and 2005. Guttmacher Institute, 2011.

Notes

71 42 per 1,000 in 1993 to 8 per 1,000 in 2011. Childstats, 'Youth Victims of Serious Violent Crimes'.

72 52 crimes per 1,000 in 1993 to 6 crimes per 1,000 in 2011 in those aged twelve to seventeen. Childstats, 'Youth Perpetrators of Serious Violent Crimes'.

73 From 84% in 1980 to 91% in 2011 for those aged eighteen to twenty-four. Childstats, 'High School Completion'.

74 An increase from 47% to 65% for males and from 52% to 72% for females. Childstats, 'College Enrolment'.

75 5% since 2001. Childstats, 'Emotional and Behavioral Difficulties'.

76 9% in 2004 to 8% in 2011 for those aged twelve to seventeen. Childstats, 'Adolescent Depression'.

77 UNICEF, 2013.

78 Childstats, 'Youth Victims of Serious Violent Crimes'.

79 10 reports per 1,000 for females versus 9 for males. Childstats, 'Child Maltreatment'.

80 15 reports per 1,000 compared to 9 per 1,000 for white non-Hispanic children. Childstats, 'Child Maltreatment'.

81 7% of males compared to 4% of females aged fourteen to seventeen, Childstats, 'Adolescent Depression'.

82 12–13% for females, 4–5% for males. Childstats, 'Adolescent Depression'.

83 CDC, www.cdc.gov/violenceprevention/suicide.

84 Hasinoff, 2014: 108. See also Renold and Ringrose, 2013; Herriot and Hiseler, 2015; Renold et al., 2015.

85 Albury and Crawford, 2012: 467.

86 Albury et al., 2013: 4.

87 Renold et al., 2015: 1.

88 See, for example, Bale, 2011: 306.

89 Buckingham and Bragg, 2004.

90 Buckingham and Bragg, 2003: 7; Duits and van Zoonen, 2011; McKee, 2012a; Watson, 2017.

91 Duits and van Zoonen, 2011; Tsaliki, 2015.

92 Buckingham and Bragg, 2004; Mulholland, 2011.

93 Buckingham et al., 2011; Bragg et al., 2011.

94 Buckingham et al., 2011; Renold and Ringrose, 2011.

95 Buckingham and Bragg, 2004: 71–3.

96 Jackson and Westrupp, 2010.

97 Kehily, 2002: 207.

98 Attwood et al., 2015; Masanet and Buckingham, 2015.

99 Nielson et al., 2015.

100 Lenhart et al., 2015.

101 Livingstone et al., 2011.

102 Livingstone et al., 2011: 42.

Notes

103 See Rovolis and Tsaliki, 2012 for a discussion. See also Tsaliki et al., 2014.
104 Livingstone et al., 2011.
105 Rovolis and Tsaliki, 2012: 167.
106 Rovolis and Tsaliki, 2012: 174.
107 Allen, 2005: 44–5.
108 Parks, 2010.
109 Bale, 2011: 306–7.
110 Mulholland, 2013; Scarcelli, 2015.
111 Watson, 2017.
112 Smith et al., 2015a.
113 Smith et al., 2015a, 2015b.
114 Bale, 2011: 307; Spisak and Paasonen, 2016.
115 Attwood, 2006.
116 McNair, 1996: 23.
117 See McNair, 2002; Paasonen et al., 2007; Attwood, 2009; McNair, 2012.
118 Arthurs, 2004: 146.
119 Hann, 2013.
120 Church Gibson, 2014.
121 Richter, 2015; Iversen, 2016.
122 Jackson and Vares, 2015; Jackson, S. et al., 2016.
123 Kehily, 2012. See Canaan, 1986; Lees, 1993; Skeggs, 2004; Ringrose et al., 2013.
124 Bale, 2011: 309.
125 See Pilcher, 2010; Vares et al., 2011; Jackson et al., 2012.
126 See Duits and van Zoonen, 2007.
127 Gill, 2012: 739.
128 Gill, 2012: 742.
129 Duits and van Zoonen, 2007: 164.
130 Gill, 2012: 738. See also Lerum and Dworkin, 2009.

Chapter 4

1 McNair, 2012: 18.
2 For example those listed by Ziplow, 1977: masturbation, straight sex, lesbianism, oral sex, ménage à trois, orgies, anal sex, S/M. See Williams, 1989: 126–7.
3 McNair, 2012: 14–15.
4 Leavis and Thompson, 1933: 3.
5 Storey, 2001: 33, 2003: 4. See also Levine, 1988.
6 Felski, 2005: 33.
7 Bourdieu, 1984: 54.

8 McKee, 2013.
9 Kipnis, 1996: 174.
10 Williams, 1989: ix.
11 Dyer, 1992: 121–2.
12 Hunt, 1998: 8. See also Cartmell et al., 1997; Sconce, 2007; Hunter, 2013.
13 Dennis, 2009: 3–4.
14 Nead, 1992: 85.
15 Nead, 1992: 89.
16 Nead, 1992: 91.
17 Bourdieu, 1986. See also Bourdieu, 1984.
18 Thornton, 1997: 202–3.
19 De Genevieve, 2004.
20 Horeck and Kendall, 2011: 2–3. See also L. Coleman, 2015, Forshaw, 2015.
21 McNair, 2012: 133.
22 Kipnis, 1996: 163.
23 Julius, 2002: 21.
24 Dennis, 2009: 194. See also Needham, 2017; Maes, 2013.
25 Many of these were shown at her 'Prostitution' exhibition in 1976. See Sprott, 2010.
26 McNair, 2002: 184.
27 See Johnson, 2012.
28 Higonnet, 2009: 110.
29 Marr, 2008: 15.
30 MacNeill, 2010: 83.
31 Williams, 1999: 48–9.
32 Kendrick, 1996: 244.
33 Andrews, 2006: 25.
34 Juffer, 1998: 104–6.
35 Sabo, 2012: 53.
36 http://candidaroyalle.com.
37 Blue, 2008.
38 Sabo, 2012: 200.
39 Paasonen, 2010a: 151.
40 Williams, 2008: 142.
41 Paasonen, 2010a: 151.
42 Williams, 2008: 181.
43 Krzywinska, 2006: 43.
44 Krzywinska, 2006: 48. See also L. Coleman, 2015.
45 Russell, 1993: 3.
46 www.miaengberg.com/dd.
47 Sabo, 2012: 83.
48 Juffer, 1998: 113.
49 Juffer, 1998: 113.

50 Juffer, 1998: 107.
51 Williams, 1989: 29.
52 McClintock, 1992: 115.
53 On porn for women see Lust, 2008; Ryberg, 2012; Sabo, 2012; Comella, 2013; Ziv, 2015; Attwood, forthcoming a. On trans porn see Steinbock, 2017 On lesbian porn see Butler, 2004; Beirne, 2012; Hines, 2012; Ryberg, 2015. On gay men's porn see Waugh, 1985; Dyer, 1992; Cante and Restivo, 2004; Escoffier, 2009; Mercer, 2012, 2017.
54 Tibbals, 2010: 632–9.
55 On porn parodies see Hunter, 2006; Jones, 2013; Watson, 2013; Booth, 2014; Jeffries, 2016.
56 Tibbals, 2010: 642.
57 Hines, 2012: 136.
58 Biasin and Zecca, 2009: 135.
59 Paasonen, 2010a: 138. See also Chun, 2006.
60 Polchin, 2013. See also Munro, 2008; Buckland, 2010; Gerstle et al., 2013.
61 Adelman, 1997; Pilcher, 2008.
62 Penley, 1997: 318.
63 Sabin, 1993; Pilcher, 2008; Roberts, 2015.
64 Paasonen, forthcoming a.
65 Napier, 2005: 64. See also McLelland, 2006a; Zanghellini, 2009; Prough, 2011.
66 Galbraith, 2009. See also Kinsella, 2000.
67 See McLelland, 2005, 2006b, 2009; Nagaike and Suganuma, 2013.
68 Shamoon, 2004.
69 McLelland, 2006a. See also Carbone, 2013.
70 Ortega-Bena, 2009: 20.
71 See Maina and Zecca, 2016b.
72 Biasin and Zecca, 2009: 142–5. See also Brodesco, 2016; Maina and Zecca, 2016a.
73 Smith, 2011: 205.
74 Williams, 1991: 76.
75 Maddison, 2013: 180–2.
76 Paasonen, 2011: 105.
77 Tristan Taormino, quoted in Paasonen, 2011: 106.
78 See Maina and Zecca, 2016a. See also Lodder, 2016 for a discussion.
79 See Zecca, 2014.
80 Esch and Mayer, 2007: 102.
81 See www.bangbus.com.
82 See www.sergiomessina.com.
83 See Hofer, 2014a, 2014b.
84 Coppa, 2006; Hellekson and Busse, 2006; Stasi, 2006; Tosenberger, 2008; Wood, 2013; McLelland, 2016.

85 Donovan, 2008: 18–20. See also Jenkins, 1992; McLelland, 2006b.
86 Liu, 2009; McLelland 2009; Pagliasotti, 2009.
87 Paasonen, 2011: 92–3. See also Paasonen, 2010c; Attwood, forthcoming b.
88 Leadbeater and Miller, 2004: 20.
89 Bruns, 2008.
90 Mathijs, 2011. See also Cook, 2005 and Studlar, 1989.
91 Schaefer, 1999: 8. See also Fisher and Walker, 2016.
92 Schaefer, 1999: 166.
93 Schaefer, 1999: 302.
94 Schaefer, 2008: 193.
95 See Hunter, 2008, 2013.
96 Mendik, 2012: 95.
97 See Jackson, N. et al., 2016.
98 Jones, 2018. See also Jones and McGlotten, 2014.
99 Mendik, 2012: 2.
100 See Hunt, 1998; Hunter, 2012a, 2012b, 2013, 2016.
101 Andrews, 2006: 184.
102 Andrews, 2006: 2.
103 Andrews, 2006: 71.
104 Andrews, 2006: 46.
105 Krzywinska, 2006: 34.
106 Wimmer, 2013: 202.
107 Williams, 2005: ix.
108 Williams, 2005: x–1.
109 Paasonen et al., 2007: 1.
110 McNair, 2002: 64–8.
111 McNair, 2002: 65.
112 McNair, 2002: 66.
113 See Railton and Watson, 2011; Railton, 2017.
114 In Cox, 2010.
115 Gunning, 2006.
116 Penley, 1997: 89–112.
117 Kipnis, 1996: viii.
118 See also Schaschek, 2013.
119 McKee, 2012b. See also McKee, 2016.
120 Juffer, 1998: 28.
121 See Race, 2015.
122 See Hubbard, 2012; Maginn and Steinmetz, 2014.
123 Gordo López and Cleminson, 2004: 94–6.
124 Gordo López and Cleminson, 2004: 78–80.
125 Hubbard, 2012: xiii.
126 See Humphreys, 1975; Bell, 2006; Mowlabocus, 2010.
127 Berlant and Warner, 1998: 560.

128 Leap, 1999.
129 Chauncey, 1994.
130 Hubbard, 2012: xiii.
131 Hubbard, 2012: xiv.
132 Hubbard et al., 2008, 2009.
133 Delany, 1999.
134 Coulmont and Hubbard, 2010. See also Bernstein, 2007.
135 Crewe and Martin, 2016; Sanders-McDonagh et al., 2016.
136 Chateauvert, 2013: 118.
137 See Agustín, 2007.
138 See Attwood, 2013.
139 O'Brien and Shapiro, 2004: 116.
140 See Döring, 2009.
141 Juffer, 1998: 233–4. See also Jacobs, 2007.
142 See, for example, Clark-Flory 2012, 2013a, 2013b, 2013c; Hester et al., 2015.
143 See Perraudin, 2014.
144 Rheingold, 1991: 345.
145 Rheingold, 1991: 346.
146 Rheingold, 1991: 351.
147 See Dowsett, 2015.
148 Barber, 2004: 327.
149 Barber, 2004: 330.
150 Lynn, 2005: 209.
151 Lynn, 2005: 210.
152 Attwood, 2009.
153 Plummer, 2008: 19.
154 Odzer, 1997: 43.
155 Waskul, 2003: 21.
156 Waskul, 2006.
157 Waskul, 2003: 22.
158 Waskul, 2003: 23.
159 Waskul, 2003: 21–5.
160 Turkle, 1997: 210–13.
161 MacRae, 1997: 262.
162 Ross, 2005: 344.
163 Blue, 2005.
164 Machulis, 2008. See also www.metafetish.com.
165 Ray, 2007: 249.
166 See, for example, http://we-vibe.com; www.lovense.com; and www.kiiroo.com. See also Bardzell and Bardzell, 2011.
167 See www.jimmyjane.com.
168 See Bourdet, 2013; https://newyorktoycollective.com; www.makerlove.com.

169 See www.ohmibod.com.
170 See, for example, https://virtualrealporn.com.
171 Lynn, 2006. See also Brathwaite, 2006; Brown, 2008.
172 On sex and games see Krzywinska, 2012; Brathwaite, 2006; Brown, 2015; Wysocki and Lauteria, 2015; Brown, 2017.
173 Waskul and Martin, 2010: 304.
174 Ruberg, 2010.
175 Waskul and Martin, 2010: 300. See also Proctor, 2015.
176 Mowlabocus, 2010: 187.
177 Mowlabocus, 2010: 183.
178 Mowlabocus, 2010: 15. See Gudelunas, 2012; Roth, 2014.
179 See Albury and Byron, 2016; Gorman-Murray and Nash, 2016.
180 Mowlabocus, 2010: 194–7; Tziallas, 2015.
181 Tziallas, 2015. See also Roth, 2014; Blackwell et al., 2015.
182 Arroyo, 2016.
183 Bell, 2006: 387–8.
184 Hurley and Prestage, 2009.
185 Race, 2015.
186 Bell, 2006: 392.

Chapter 5

1 See Bernstein, 2007; Weeks, 2007; Plummer, 2008; Jackson and Scott, 2010; McDermott, 2011; Halberstam, 2012b.
2 Giddens, 1992: 58. See also Diamond, 2008; Dean, 2014; Ward, 2015, Albury, 2017.
3 Weeks, 2007: 3.
4 Brents and Sanders, 2010: 47.
5 See, for example, Heath, 1982; Evans, 1993.
6 See Gilbert, 2013: 6.
7 Brents and Sanders, 2010: 47.
8 Brents and Sanders, 2010: 47.
9 Boris and Parreñas, 2010; Wolkowitz et al., 2013.
10 Ehrenreich and Hochschild, 2002: 4; Bernstein, 2007: 175; Cobble, 2010.
11 Agustín, 2007. See also Wolkowitz et al., 2013.
12 Chateauvert, 2013: 123. See also Harcourt and Donovan, 2005: 205.
13 Agustín, 2007: 60.
14 Chateauvert, 2013: 123.
15 Chateauvert, 2013: 136.
16 Agustín, 2007: 65.
17 Brents and Sanders, 2010: 45.

18 See Brents et al., 2010; Brents and Sanders, 2010: 45; Grant, 2014.
19 Nixon and du Gay, 2002: 496.
20 Ray, 2007.
21 Bernstein, 2007: 175.
22 Jenkins, 2006; Attwood, 2007; Levin Russo, 2007; Magnet, 2007.
23 See Mowlabocus, 2010; van Doorn, 2010.
24 Jacobs, 2007: 77.
25 Terranova, 2000; Coté and Pybus, 2007: 90; Paasonen, 2010c. See also Lee and Sullivan, 2016; Ruberg, 2016.
26 Comfort, 2003: 8.
27 Bernstein, 2007: 175.
28 Harvey and Gill, 2011.
29 Harvey and Gill, 2011: 56. See also Frith, 2015.
30 Duncombe and Marsden, 1996: 220.
31 Cacchioni, 2007.
32 Hakim, 2011.
33 Bourdieu, 1984: 365–71. See also Attwood et. al., 2015; Barker et al., 2017.
34 Harvey and Gill, 2011.
35 Bauman, 1999: 24.
36 Gregg, 2011.
37 Banet-Weiser, 2012: 60.
38 Banet-Weiser, 2012: 89.
39 See Attwood, 2010; Attwood and Smith, 2013.
40 See Orrell and Scuderi, 2016.
41 Juffer, 1998; Comella, 2003; Storr, 2003; Attwood, 2005.
42 Smith, 2007: 180.
43 See www.lelo.com.
44 See http://bad-dragon.com.
45 See http://divine-interventions.com.
46 Archibald, 2006: 6.
47 See www.homemade-sex-toys.com.
48 See www.houseofgord.com.
49 See www.kink.com/channel/fuckingmachines.
50 See www.liberator.com.
51 See Attwood, 2010.
52 See, for example, www.realdoll.com.
53 Beck, 2013.
54 See www.truecompanion.com.
55 See http://sinthetics.com.
56 Levy, 2008: 310. See also Yeoman and Mars, 2012; Devlin, 2015.
57 Race, 2015.
58 Ferguson, 2010: 60; Ruberg, 2010; Krzywinska, 2012; Brown, 2017.
59 See Paasonen, forthcoming b.

60 Shigematsu, 1999: 128.
61 Gregory, 2015; McLelland, 2016.
62 See http://adultfriendfinder.com. See also Jacobs, 2007.
63 See, for example, www.feverparties.com; www.killingkittens.com.
64 Waskul and Vannini, 2008.
65 Lynn, 2008.
66 Hurley and Prestage, 2009; Albury, 2017.
67 Attwood and Smith, 2013: 330.
68 Paasonen, forthcoming b.
69 Barker, 2014.
70 Rojek, 2000: 18.
71 Giddens, 1992: 58.
72 Baym, 2010: 104. See also Giddens, 1992.
73 Attwood and Smith, 2013.
74 Barker, 2012: 59.
75 Illouz, 1999; Bogle, 2008. See also Waskul and Vannini, 2008.
76 Bauman, 2003: xii.
77 Illouz, 1999: 176.
78 Bogaert, 2012. See Carrigan et al., 2013.
79 See Barker and Langdridge, 2010; Schippers, 2016.
80 Berlant and Warner, 1998; Newmahr, 2010.
81 Newmahr, 2010.
82 Hurley and Prestage, 2009: 36.
83 Rosenfeld and Thomas, 2012. See also Degim et al., 2015.
84 McNair, 2002; Attwood, 2006; Paasonen et al., 2007.
85 Goode and McKee, 2013: 114.
86 McNair, 2002: 98.
87 Kitzmann, 2004: 27.
88 Kitzmann, 2004: 43–5.
89 Papacharissi, 2010.
90 Ito, 2008: 2.
91 Chalfen, 2009: 262.
92 Summers, 2012. See also Miller, 2008; Mowlabocus, 2010: 197.
93 Deuze, 2012: 27.
94 Paasonen, 2011: 8–9.
95 Deuze, 2012: 59.
96 See boyd, 2014.
97 Turkle, 2011: 172. See also Chambers, 2013; Attwood et al., 2017.
98 Baym, 2010: 5.
99 Kitzmann, 2004: 122.
100 Marshall, 2010: 44.
101 Kitzmann, 2004: 95.
102 Kember and Zylinska, 2012: 18.

103 Bausinger, 1984: 346.
104 See Wouters, 2004, 2007; Attwood, 2010.
105 Hjarvard, 2008: 113.
106 See Hjarvard, 2012; Hepp et al., 2015.
107 Deuze, 2012: 237.
108 Deuze, 2012: 227.
109 Deuze, 2012: 193.
110 Deuze, 2012: 18.
111 Deuze, 2012: 3.
112 Chalfen, 2009: 260.
113 Hillis, 2009: 44.
114 Jones, 2008b.
115 Jones, 2008a: 56. See also R. Coleman, 2009.
116 Attwood, 2015. See also R. Coleman, 2015.
117 Jones, 2012b: 205.
118 Jones, 2012a: 31.
119 In the novel by Mary Shelley, 1818, and many adaptations since then.
120 Poster, 2004: 318. See also Fuller, 2011; Braidotti, 2013.
121 Deuze, 2012: 22.
122 Gilman, 1999; Owings et al., 2013.
123 Haraway, 1991: 149.
124 Smith and Morra, 2006: 4.
125 Hayles, 1995: 322.
126 Deuze, 2012: 24.
127 Potts, 2005: 5.
128 Braun, 2005: 407.
129 Loe, 2001: 98.
130 Potts, 2005.
131 Tiefer, 2006: 287.
132 See Hartley, 2006; Tiefer, 2015.
133 Loe, 2001: 102.
134 See Martin, 1994; Loe, 2001: 110.
135 Croissant, 2006: 335.
136 Marshall, 2010: 214. See also Vares, 2009: 505.
137 Marshall, 2010: 212–19. See also Walz, 2002.
138 Durham, 2008: 21.
139 Lumby, 2001: 55.
140 American Psychological Association, 2007: 3.
141 Crawford, 2006: 181.
142 Crawford, 2006: 190, 199, 201.
143 Renner, 2012: 36.
144 van Doorn, 2010: 411–30. See also Slater, 1998: 91–117.
145 Levy, 2005: 196.

146 Walters, 2010.
147 Serano, 2013: 114–15.
148 See Attwood, 2015. See also Tyler and Bennett, 2010.
149 Attwood, 2013; Albury, forthcoming.
150 Mowlabocus, 2007: 63.
151 Coté and Pybus, 2007: 88–106; Mowlabocus, 2010: 69–87.
152 Banet-Weiser, 2012: 14.
153 See www.newviewcampaign.org. See also Tiefer, 2004 .
154 WHO, 2006.
155 For example, Morality in Media, http://endsexualexploitation.org and Culture Reframed, www.culturereframed.org. See Elgot, 2014.
156 See, for example, http://fightthenewdrug.org.
157 Singel, 2004.
158 See http://yourbrainonporn.com.
159 Dines, 2010a: xi.
160 Dines, 2010a: xi.
161 Dines, 2010a: x. See also Malz and Malz, 2008; Smith and Attwood, 2013.
162 See Weitzer, 2011 for a discussion.
163 See Irvine, 1995, 2005; Bale, 2010; McKee, 2013; Reay et al., 2013; McKee, 2015.
164 Carmody, 2009: 42.
165 Fine, 1988; Allen, 2004; Forrest et al., 2004; Ingham, 2005; Hirst, 2008; Spencer et al., 2008; Carmody, 2009.
166 Allen, 2003; Forrest et al., 2004; Allen, 2005, 2008; Carmody, 2009.
167 Buckingham and Bragg, 2004; Allen, 2005; Fine and McLelland, 2006; Allen, 2008; Spencer et al., 2008; Carmody, 2009; Parks, 2010; McKee, 2012a.
168 WHO, 2006. See Bale, 2010, 2011.
169 McKee et al., 2010.
170 Allen and Rasmussen, 2017.
171 Watson and McKee, 2013: 449.
172 Carmody, 2005, 2009.
173 Carmody, 2009: 84.
174 Carmody, 2009: 92.
175 Dunn, 2003: 146.
176 Connolly, 1993: 379.
177 Foucault, 1997. See Albury, 2009: 648.
178 Allen, 2005.
179 Foucault, 1997. See Carmody, 2009: 89.
180 Barker, 2013.
181 Carmody, 2009: 91.
182 Carmody, 2009: 92. See Albury, 2009.
183 Carmody, 2009; Barker, 2013.

Notes

184 Goode and McKee, 2013: 117.
185 Warner, 1999: viii. See, for example, Easton and Liszt, 1998.
186 Berlant and Warner, 1998: 558.
187 Goode and McKee, 2013: 117. See also Albury, 2002.
188 Weeks, 1998: 36–40.
189 Plummer, 2001: 237. See also Plummer, 2003b; Albury, 2016.
190 Durham, 2016; Witt, 2016; Nixon and Düsterhöft, 2017.
191 Kellner and Share, 2005.
192 Kellner and Share, 2005: 372; Albury, 2014. See also Comella and Tarrant, 2015; Sullivan and McKee, 2015; Tarrant, 2016.
193 Lumby, 2011: 97.
194 Buckingham, 2003: 13.
195 Berlant and Warner, 1998: 551, 563.
196 See Jones and Mowlabocus, 2009 for a discussion.
197 Tait, 2008.
198 Falk, 1993: 7–11.
199 Horeck and Kendall, 2011: 8.
200 Albury, 2009: 650.
201 Paasonen, 2010b: 75.
202 Barker, 2014: 13.
203 Califia, 1994: 103; Smith et al., 2015b.
204 Hoechsmann and Poyntz, 2012: 201.
205 Jenkins et al., 2006: 4; Deuze, 2012: 221.
206 Plummer, 2003b: 145.

References

Films, TV and Music Videos

1001 Ways to Eat My Jizz. 2002. Dir. August Arkham. USA.
9 Songs. 2003. Dir. Michael Winterbottom. UK.
A Serbian Film. 2010. Dir. Srdjan Spasojevic. Serbia.
Ass Clowns 3. 2001. Dir. Thomas Zupko. USA.
Austin Powers: International Man of Mystery. 1997. Dir. Jay Roach. USA.
Baise Moi. 2000. Dirs. Virginie Despentes, Coralie Trinh Thi. France.
Basic Instinct. 1992. Dir. Paul Verhoeven. France.
Blade Runner. 1982. Dir. Ridley Scott. USA.
Blow Job. 1963. Dir. Andy Warhol. USA.
Blue is the Warmest Color. 2013. Dir. Abdellatif Kechiche. France.
Boogie Nights. 1997. Dir. Paul Thomas Anderson. USA.
Buttman series. 1989–. Dir. John Stagliano. USA.
Carry On series. 1958–92. UK.
Cocktails 2. 2001. Dirs. Robert Black, Lizzy Borden. USA.
Confessions of a Window Cleaner. 1974. Dir. Val Guest. UK.
Dildoman. 2009. Dir. Åsa Sandzén. Sweden.
Dirrty. 2002. Christina Aguilera. Dir. David LaChapelle. USA.
Edward Penishands. 1991. Dir. Paul Norman. USA.
Emmanuelle. 1974. Dir. Just Jaeckin. France.
Erotic Nights of the Living Dead. 1980. Dir. Joe D'Amato. Italy.
Ex_Machina. 2015. Dir. Alex Garland. UK.
Extreme Teen 24. 2002. Dirs. Robert Black, Stanley Ferrera. USA.
Faster Pussycat! Kill! Kill! 1965. Dir. Russ Meyer. USA.
Fatal Attraction. 1987. Dir. Adrian Lyne. USA.
Fifty Shades of Grey: A XXX Adaptation. 2012. Dir. Jim Powers. USA.
Flasher Girl on Tour. 2009. Dir. Joanna Rytel. Sweden.
Forced Entry. 2002. Dir. Lizzy Borden. USA.

References

Harry Potter series. 2001–11. UK.
Humans series. 2015–. UK
Intercourse with a Vampire. 1994. Dir. Paul Norman. USA.
In the Realm of the Senses. 1976. Dir. Nagisa Ôshima. Japan.
Intimacy. 2001. Dir. Patrice Chéreau. France.
Justify My Love. 1990. Madonna. Dir. Jean-Baptiste Mondino. USA.
Lord of the G Strings. 2002. Dir. Terry M. West. USA.
Lord of the Rings series. 2001–3. New Zealand.
Love. 2015. Dir. Gaspar Noe. France.
Man of Steel XXX. 2013. Dir. Axel Braun. USA.
Max Hardcore Extreme Schoolgirls 6: Euro Version. 2004. Dir. Max Hardcore. USA.
Max Hardcore Fists of Fury 3. 2004. Dir. Max Hardcore. USA.
Max Hardcore Golden Guzzlers 5. 2003. Dir. Max Hardcore. USA.
Max Hardcore Golden Guzzlers 6. 2004. Dir. Max Hardcore. USA.
Nymphomaniac. 2013. Dir. Lars von Trier. Denmark.
On Your Back Woman! 2009. Dir. Wolfe Madam. Sweden.
Pirates. 2005. Dir. Joone. USA.
Pirates of the Caribbean. 2003. Dir. Gore Verbinski. USA.
Porno Holocaust. 1979. Dir. Joe D'Amato. Italy.
Pure Max 16: Euro Version. 2004. Dir. Max Hardcore. USA.
Romance. 1999. Dir. Catherine Breillat. France.
S&M. 2011. Rihanna. Dir. Melina Matsoukas. USA.
Sex and the City series. 1998–2004. USA.
Sex and the Single Girl. 1964. Dir. Richard Quine. USA.
Sex Files: A Dark XXX Parody. Dir. Sam Hain. USA.
SpiderBabe. 2003. Dir. Johnny Crash. USA.
Stoker. 2013. Dir. Chan-wook Park. UK.
The Devil in Miss Jones. 1973. Dir. Gerard Damiano. USA.
The Immoral Mr Teas. 1959. Dir. Russ Meyer. USA.
The Look of Love. 2013. Dir. Michael Winterbottom. UK.
The People Versus Larry Flynt. 1996. Dir. Milos Forman. USA.
Terminator 2. 1991. Dir. James Cameron. USA.
Viva. 2007. Dir. Anna Biller. USA.
Wrecking Ball. 2013. Miley Cyrus. Dir. Terry Richardson. USA.

Online

Abby Winters	www.abbywinters.com
Adult Friend Finder	http://adultfriendfinder.com
AVEN	www.asexuality.org

References

Bad Dragon	http://bad-dragon.com
Bad Sex Media Bingo	https://badsexmediabingo.com
Bangbus	www.bangbus.com
Bish	www.bishuk.com
Candida Royalle	http://candidaroyalle.com
Culture Reframed	www.culturereframed.org
Dirty Diaries	www.miaengberg.com/dd
Divine Interventions	http://divine-interventions.com
Fetlife	https://fetlife.com
Fever Parties	www.feverparties.com
Fight The New Drug	http://fightthenewdrug.org
Fuckbook	www.fuckbook.com/en
FuckingMachines	www.kink.com/channel/fuckingmachines
Grindr	http://grindr.com
Homemade Sex Toys	www.homemade-sex-toys.com
House of Gord	www.houseofgord.com
ILGA	http://ilga.org
ISNA	www.isna.org
It's Pronounced Metrosexual	http://itspronouncedmetrosexual.com
Jimmyjane	www.jimmyjane.com
Kiiroo	www.kiiroo.com
Killing Kittens	www.killingkittens.com
Laci Green	www.youtube.com/user/lacigreen
Lelo	www.lelo.com
Liberator	www.liberator.com
Lovense	www.lovense.com
Luxuria Superbia	http://luxuria-superbia.com
MakerLove	www.makerlove.com
Morality in Media	http://endsexualexploitation.org
Network of Sex Projects	www.nswp.org
New View	www.newviewcampaign.org
New York Toy Collective	https://newyorktoycollective.com
Oh Joy Sex Toy	www.ohjoysextoy.com
OhMiBod	www.ohmibod.com
Open Rights Group	www.openrightsgroup.org
Pinsex	http://pinsex.tumblr.com
Pornhub	www.pornhub.com
Ratemynaughty	www.ratemynaughty.com
Real Doll	www.realdoll.com
Red Light Center	www.redlightcenter.com
Rocco Siffredi	www.roccosiffredi.com
Scarleteen	www.scarleteen.com
Second Life	http://secondlife.com

References

Sell Your Sex Tape	www.sellyoursextape.com
Sergio Messina	www.sergiomessina.com
Sinthetics	http://sinthetics.com
Slashdong	www.metafetish.com
Sociolotron	www.sociolotron.com
Tinder	www.gotinder.com
Trenchcoat	https://trenchcoatx.com
True Companion	www.truecompanion.com
VirtualRealPorn	https://virtualrealporn.com
Voyeurweb	www.voyeurweb.com
WeVibe	http://we-vibe.com
XTube	www.xtube.com
Your Brain on Porn	http://yourbrainonporn.com

Publications

Adelman, B. 1997. *Tijuana Bibles: Art and Wit in America's Forbidden Funnies, 1930s–1950s*. New York: Simon and Schuster.

Agustín, L. 2007. *Sex at the Margins: Migration, Labour Markets and the Rescue Industry*. London: Zed Books.

Agustín, L. 2012. Sex as work and sex work. *The Commoner 5*, www.commoner. org.uk/wp-content/uploads/2012/02/11-agustin.pdf.

Albury, K. 2002. *Yes Means Yes: Getting Explicit About Heterosex*. Sydney: Allen and Unwin.

Albury, K. 2009. Reading porn reparatively. *Sexualities* 12(5): 647–53.

Albury, K. 2014. Porn and sex education, porn as sex education. *Porn Studies* 1(1–2): 172–81.

Albury, K. 2016. Politics of sexting revisited. In McCosker, A., Vivienne, S. and Johns, A. (eds) *Negotiating Digital Citizenship: Control, Contest and Culture*. Lanham: Rowman and Littlefield, 213–30.

Albury, K. 2017. Heterosexual casual sex: from free love to Tinder. In Smith, C. and Attwood, F. (eds) *The Routledge Companion to Media, Sex and Sexuality*. Abingdon and New York: Routledge, 81–90.

Albury, K. forthcoming. Sexual expression in social media. In Burgess, J., Marwick, A. and Poell, T. (eds) *The SAGE Handbook of Social Media*. Thousand Oaks: Sage.

Albury, K. and Byron, P. 2016. Safe on my phone? Same-sex attracted young people's negotiations of intimacy, visibility, and risk on digital hook-up apps. *Social Media + Society* 2(4): 1–10.

Albury, K. and Crawford, K. 2012. Sexting, consent and young people's ethics: beyond Megan's Story. *Continuum* 26(3): 463–73.

References

Albury, K., Crawford, K., Byron, P. and Mathews, B. 2013. *Young People and Sexting in Australia: Ethics, Representation, and the Law.* Sydney: University of New South Wales, www.cci.edu.au/sites/default/files/Young_People_And_Sexting_Final.pdf.

Alilunas, P. 2016. *Smutty Little Movies: The Creation and Regulation of Adult Video.* Oakland: University of California Press.

Allen, L. 2003. Girls want sex, boys want love: young people negotiating (hetero) sex. *Sexualities* 6(2): 215–36.

Allen, L. 2004. Beyond the birds and the bees: constituting a discourse of erotics in sexuality education. *Gender and Education* 16(2): 151–67.

Allen, L. 2005. *Sexual Subjects: Young People, Sexuality and Education.* Basingstoke: Palgrave Macmillan.

Allen, L. 2008. 'They think you shouldn't be having sex anyway': young people's suggestions for improving sexuality education content. *Sexualities* 11(5): 573–94.

Allen, L. and Rasmussen, M.L. 2017. *The Palgrave Handbook of Sexuality Education.* Basingstoke: Palgrave Macmillan.

Allyn, D. 2000. *Make Love, Not War. The Sexual Revolution: An Unfettered History.* Boston: Little, Brown and Company.

American Psychiatric Association. 1994. *Diagnostic and Statistical Manual of Mental Disorders.* 4th edn. Washington: American Psychiatric Association.

American Psychological Association, Task Force on the Sexualization of Girls. 2007. *Report of the APA Task Force on the Sexualization of Girls,* www.apa.org/pi/women/programs/girls/report-full.pdf.

Anderson, D. and Berman, M. 2012. *Sex Tips For Straight Women from a Gay Man.* London: Thorsons.

Andrejevic, M. 2009. *iSpy: Surveillance and Power in the Interactive Era.* Topeka: University of Kansas Press.

Andrews, D. 2006. *Soft in the Middle: The Contemporary Softcore Feature in its Contexts.* Columbus: Ohio State University Press.

Angelides, S. 2013. 'Technology, hormones, and stupidity': the affective politics of teenage sexting. *Sexualities* 16(5–6): 665–89.

Archibald, T. 2006. *Sex Machines: Photographs and Interviews.* Los Angeles: Process Books.

Arroyo, B. 2016. Sexual affects and active pornographic space in the networked Gay Village. *Porn Studies* 3(1): 77–88.

Arthurs, J. 2004. *Television and Sexuality.* Maidenhead: Open University Press.

Arvidsson, A. 2007. Netporn: the work of fantasy in the information society. In Jacobs, K., Janssen, M. and Pasquinelli, M. (eds) *C'Lick Me: A Netporn Studies Reader.* Amsterdam: Institute of Network Cultures, 69–76.

Attwood, F. 2005. Fashion and passion: marketing sex to women. *Sexualities* 8(4): 395–409.

References

Attwood, F. 2006. Sexed up: theorizing the sexualization of culture. *Sexualities* 9(1): 77–94.

Attwood, F. 2007. No money shot? Commerce, pornography and new sex taste cultures. *Sexualities* 10(4): 441–56.

Attwood, F. 2009. 'Deepthroatfucker' and 'Discerning Adonis': men and cybersex. *International Journal of Cultural Studies* 12(3): 279–94.

Attwood, F. 2010. Sex and the citizens: erotic play and the new leisure culture. In Bramham, P. and Wagg, S. (eds) *The New Politics of Leisure and Pleasure*. Basingstoke: Palgrave Macmillan, 82–96.

Attwood, F. 2013. Cybersexuality and online culture. In Hartley, J., Burgess, J. and Bruns, A. (eds) *Companion to New Media Dynamics*. Malden: Wiley-Blackwell, 341–5.

Attwood, F. 2014. Immersion: 'extreme' texts, animated bodies and the media. *Media, Culture and Society* 36(8): 1186–95.

Attwood, F. 2015. The uncanny valley: transformations of the body and debates about sexualization. *International Journal of Cultural Studies* 18(3): 269–80.

Attwood, F. forthcoming a. Women's pornography. In Harrison, K. (ed) *Pornography*. Chester: University of Chester Press.

Attwood, F. forthcoming b. The politics of amateurism. In Burbridge, B. and Pollen, A. (eds) *Photography Reframed*. London: I.B. Tauris.

Attwood, F. and Hunter, I.Q. 2009. 'Not safe for work?' Teaching and researching the sexually explicit. *Sexualities* 12(5): 547–57.

Attwood, F. and Smith, C. 2010. Extreme concern: regulating 'dangerous pictures' in the United Kingdom. *Journal of Law and Society* 37(1): 171–88.

Attwood, F. and Smith, C. 2013. Leisure sex: more sex! Better Sex! Sex is f***ing brilliant! Sex, sex, sex, SEX. In Blackshaw, T. (ed.) *Routledge Handbook of Leisure Studies*. London: Routledge: 325–36.

Attwood, F., Bale, C. and Barker, M. 2013. *The Sexualization Report*, https://senseaboutsex.files.wordpress.com/2012/08/thesexualizationreport.pdf.

Attwood, F., Barker, M.J., Boynton, P. and Hancock, J. 2015. Sense about sex: media, sex advice, education and learning. *Sex Education* 15(5): 528–39.

Attwood, F., Hakim, J. and Winch, A. 2017. Mediated intimacies: bodies, technologies and relationships. *Journal of Gender Studies* 6(3): 249–54.

Australian Senate. 2008. Sexualisation of children in the contemporary media, www.aph.gov.au/binaries/senate/committee/eca_ctte/sexualisation_of_children/report/report.pdf.

Bailey, R. 2011. *Letting Children Be Children*. London: Department for Education, www.education.gov.uk/publications/eOrderingDownload/Bailey%20Review.pdf.

Bale, C. 2010. Sexualised culture and young people's sexual health: a cause for concern? *Sociology Compass* 4(10): 824–40.

Bale, C. 2011. Raunch or romance? Framing and interpreting the relationship between sexualized culture and young people's sexual health. *Sex Education* 11(3): 303–13.

Banet-Weiser, S. 2012. *Authentic*™: *The Politics of Ambivalence in a Brand Culture*. New York: New York University Press.

Barber, T. 2004. A pleasure prophesy: predictions for the sex tourist of the future. In Waskul, D.D. (ed.) *Net.seXXX: Readings on Sex, Pornography, and the Internet*. New York: Peter Lang, 323–36.

Barbieri, A. 2009. You don't know what sexting is? Texting explicit photographs has become a common part of courtship among teenagers. But the consequences can be tragic. *Guardian*, 7 August, www.guardian.co.uk/lifeand-style/2009/aug/07/sexting-teenagers-mobile-phones.

Bardzell, J. and Bardzell, S. 2011. 'Pleasure is your birthright': digitally enabled designer sex toys as a case of third-wave HCI. Proceedings of the SIGCHI Conference on Human Factors in Computing Systems. Vancouver, 257–66.

Barker, M. 2011. The problems of speaking about porn. Sex and Regulation event, Onscenity Network, British Academy.

Barker, M. 2012. *Rewriting the Rules: An Integrative Guide to Love, Sex and Relationships*. London: Routledge.

Barker, M. 2013. Consent is a grey area? A comparison of understandings of consent in *Fifty Shades of Grey* and on the BDSM blogosphere. *Sexualities* 16(8): 896–914.

Barker, M. 2014. The 'problem' of sexual fantasies. *Porn Studies* 1(1–2): 143–60.

Barker, M. and Duschinsky, R. 2012. Sexualisation's four faces. *Gender and Education* 24(3): 303–10.

Barker, M. and Langdridge, D. (eds) 2010. *Understanding Non-Monogamies*. London: Routledge.

Barker, M. and Petley, J. (eds) 1997. *Ill Effects: The Media/Violence Debate*. London: Routledge.

Barker, M.J. 2014. 57 genders (and none for me)? Reflections on the new Facebook gender categories, http://rewritingtherules.wordpress.com/2014/02/15/57-genders-and-none-for-me-reflections-on-the-new-facebook-gender-categories.

Barker, M.J. and Hancock, J. 2016. *Make Your Own Relationship User Guide*, https://sellfy.com/p/iCJZ.

Barker, M.J., Gill, R. and Harvey, L. 2017. *Mediated Intimacy: Sex Advice in Media Culture*. London: Polity.

Barker, M., Richards, C., Jones, R., Bowes-Catton, H. and Plowman, T. 2012. *The Bisexuality Report: Bisexual Inclusion in LGBT Equality and Diversity*. Milton Keynes: The Open University, www.open.ac.uk/ccig/files/ccig/The%20BisexualityReport%20Feb.2012.pdf.

Barss, P. 2011. *The Erotic Engine: How Pornography has Powered Mass Communication, from Gutenberg to Google*. Toronto: Anchor Canada.

Bauman, Z. 1999. On postmodern uses of sex. In Featherstone, F. (ed.) *Love and Eroticism*. London: Sage, 9–33.

References

Bauman, Z. 2003. *Liquid Love: On the Frailty of Human Bonds*. London: Polity.

Bauman, Z., Bigo, D., Esteves, P., Guild, E., Jabri, V., Lyon, D. and Walker, R.B. 2014. After Snowden: rethinking the impact of surveillance. *International Political Sociology* 8(2): 121–44.

Bausinger, H. 1984. Media, technology and everyday life. *Media, Culture and Society* 6(4): 343–51.

Baym, N. 2010. *Personal Connections in the Digital Age*. Cambridge: Polity.

Beasley, C. 2005. *Gender and Sexuality Studies: Critical Theories, Critical Thinkers*. Thousand Oaks: Sage.

Beck, J. 2013. Married to a doll: why one man advocates synthetic love. *The Atlantic*, 6 September, www.theatlantic.com/health/archive/2013/09/married-to-a-doll-why-one-man-advocates-synthetic-love/279361.

Beirne, R., 2012. Interrogating lesbian pornography: gender, sexual iconography and spectatorship. In Hines, C. and Kerr, D. (eds) *Hard to Swallow: Hard-Core Pornography on Screen*. London and New York: Wallflower Press, 237–8.

Bell, D. 2006. Bodies, technologies, spaces: on 'dogging'. *Sexualities* 9(4): 387–407.

Berlant, L. and Warner, M. 1998. Sex in public. *Critical Inquiry* 24(2): 547–66.

Bernstein, E. 2007. *Temporarily Yours: Intimacy, Authenticity, and the Commerce of Sex*. Chicago: University of Chicago Press.

Bernstein, R. 2011. *Racial Innocence: Performing American Childhood from Slavery to Civil Rights*. New York: New York University Press.

Biasin, E. and Zecca, F. 2009. Contemporary audiovisual pornography: branding strategy and gonzo film style. *Cinéma and Cie* 9(1): 133–50.

Biddulph, S. 2009. How girlhood was trashed and what we can do to get it back; a father's view. In Tankard Reist, M. (ed.) *Getting Real: Challenging the Sexualisation of Girls*. North Melbourne: Spinifex, 163–9.

Bidisha. 2011. 'Eff Off Hef!': Feminists fight the reopening of London Playboy Club, http://bidisha-online.blogspot.co.uk/2011/05/eff-off-hef-feminists-fight-reopening.html.

Blackwell, C., Birnholtz, J. and Abbott, C. 2015. Seeing and being seen: co-situation and impression formation using Grindr, a location-aware gay dating app. *New Media and Society* 17(7): 1117–36.

Bland, L. 1995. *Banishing the Beast: English Feminism and Sexual Morality, 1885–1914*. London: Penguin.

Blank, H. 2012. *Straight: The Surprisingly Short History of Heterosexuality*. Boston: Beacon Press.

Blue, V. 2005. Teledildonics products and teledildonic devices, *Tiny Nibbles*, www.tinynibbles.com/teledildonics.

Blue, V. 2006. *The Smart Girl's Guide to Porn*. San Francisco: Cleis Press.

Blue, V. 2008. The Helmut Newton of porn: Violet Blue interviews erotic film-making legend Andrew Blake, *SFGate*, 18 December, www.sfgate.com/living/article/The-Helmut-Newton-of-Porn-Violet-Blue-2531318.php.

References

Bocock, R. 1997. Choice and regulation: sexual moralities. In K. Thompson (ed.) *Media and Cultural Regulation*. London: Sage, 69–104.

Bogaert, A.F. 2012. *Understanding Asexuality*. Lanham: Rowman and Littlefield.

Bogle, K. 2008. *Hooking Up: Sex, Dating and Relationships on Campus*. New York: New York University Press.

Booth, P. 2014. Slash and porn: media subversion, hyper-articulation, and parody. *Continuum* 28(3): 396–409.

Boris, E. and Salazar Parreñas, R. 2010. *Intimate Labors: Cultures, Technologies, and the Politics of Care*. Stanford: Stanford Social Sciences.

Bourdet, K. 2013. Scanning the future of 3D-printed sex toys, www.vice.com/en_us/article/scanning-the-future-of-3d-printed-sex-toys.

Bourdieu, P. 1984. *Distinction: A Social Critique of the Judgment of Taste*. Boston: Harvard University Press.

Bourdieu, P. 1986. The forms of capital. In Richardson, J. (ed.) *Handbook of Theory and Research for the Sociology of Education*. New York: Greenwood, 241–58.

boyd, d. 2014. *It's Complicated: The Social Lives of Networked Teens*. New Haven: Yale University Press.

Boynton, P. 2011. Unpacking the Bailey Review on commercialisation and sexualisation of childhood, www.drpetra.co.uk/blog/unpacking-the-bailey-review-on-commercialisation-and-sexualisation-of-childhood.

Bragg, S. and Buckingham, D. 2013. Global concerns, local negotiations and moral selves: contemporary parenting and the 'sexualisation of childhood' debate. *Feminist Media Studies* 13(4): 643–59.

Bragg, S., Buckingham, D., Russell, R. and Willett, R. 2011. Too much, too soon? Children, 'sexualization' and consumer culture. *Sex Education* 11(3): 279–92.

Braidotti, R. 2013. *The Posthuman*. Cambridge: Polity Press.

Brathwaite, B. 2006. *Sex in Video Games*. Boston: Charles River Media.

Braun, V. 2005. In search of (better) sexual pleasure: female genital 'cosmetic' surgery. *Sexualities* 8(4): 407–24.

Brents, B.G. 2008. Sexual politics from Barnard to Las Vegas. *The Communication Review* 11(3): 237–46.

Brents, B.G. and Sanders, T. 2010. Mainstreaming the sex industry: economic inclusion and social ambivalence. *Journal of Law and Society* 37(1): 40–60.

Brents, B.G., Jackson, C. and Hausbeck, K. 2010. *The State of Sex: Tourism, Sex and Sin in the New American Heartland*. New York: Routledge.

Brinkema, E. 2014. Rough sex. In Dean, T., Ruszczycky, S. and Squires, D. (eds) *Porn Archives*. Durham: Duke University Press, 262–83.

Brodesco, A. 2016. POV to the people: online discourses about gonzo pornography. *Porn Studies* 3(4): 362–72.

Brodie, R.J. 1845. *The Secret Companion: A Medical Work on Onanism or Self-Pollution*. London: Brodie.

Bronstein, C. and Strub, W. (eds) 2016. *Porno Chic and the Sex Wars: American*

References

Sexual Representation in the 1970s. Amherst: University of Massachusetts Press.

Bronstein, C.B. 2011. *Battling Pornography: The American Feminist Anti-pornography Movement, 1976–1986*. Cambridge: Cambridge University Press.

Brown, A.M.L. 2015. *Sexuality in Role-playing Games*. London: Routledge.

Brown, A.M.L. 2017. Videogames and sex. In Smith, C. and Attwood, F. (eds) *The Routledge Companion to Media, Sex and Sexuality*. Abingdon and New York: Routledge, 239–47.

Brown, D. 2008. *Porn and Pong: How Grand Theft Auto, Tomb Raider, and Other Sexy Games Changed Our Culture*. Los Angeles: Feral House.

Brown, T. 2004. Flynt and Black each make one last response in debate on obscenity. *Adult Video News*, 15 April, http://business.avn.com/articles/video/Flyntand-Black-Each-Make-One-Last-Response-in-Debate-on-Obscenity-38282.html.

Bruns, A., 2008. *Blogs, Wikipedia, Second Life, and Beyond: From Production to Produsage*. New York: Peter Lang.

Buckingham, D. 2003. *Media Education: Literacy, Learning and Contemporary Culture*. Cambridge: Polity.

Buckingham, D. and Bragg, S. 2003. Young people, media and personal relationships, http://downloads.bbc.co.uk/guidelines/editorialguidelines/research/young-people.pdf.

Buckingham, D. and Bragg, S. 2004. *Young People, Sex and the Media: The Facts of Life?* Basingstoke and New York: Palgrave Macmillan.

Buckingham, D., Willett, R., Bragg, S., Russell, R. and Dorrer, N. 2010. *Sexualised Goods Aimed at Children*, Report to the Scottish Parliament, http://oro.open.ac.uk/25843/2/sexualised_goods_report.pdf

Buckland, R. 2010. *Shunga: Erotic Art in Japan*. London: British Museum Press.

Budge, B. and Hamer, D. (eds) 1994. *The Good, the Bad and the Gorgeous: Popular Culture's Romance with Lesbianism*. London: Pandora.

Burston, P. 1995. *What Are You Looking At? Queer Sex, Style, and Cinema*. London: Cassell.

Butler, H. 2004. What do you call a lesbian with long fingers? The development of lesbian and dyke pornography. In Williams, L. (ed.) *Porn Studies*. Durham: Duke University Press, 167–97.

Butler, J. 1990. *Gender Trouble: Feminism and the Subversion of Identity*. New York: Routledge.

Cacchioni, T. 2007. Heterosexuality and 'the labour of love': a contribution to recent debates on female sexual dysfunction. *Sexualities* 10(3): 299–320.

Cage, F., Herman, T. and Good, N. 2014. Lesbian, gay, bisexual and transgender rights around the world. *Guardian*, 16 May, www.theguardian.com/world/ng-interactive/2014/may/-sp-gay-rights-world-lesbian-bisexual-transgender.

Califia, P. 1994. *Public Sex: The Culture of Radical Sex*. San Francisco: Cleis Press.

References

Callis, A.S. 2014. Bisexual, pansexual, queer: non-binary identities and the sexual borderlands. *Sexualities* 17(1–2): 63–80.

Cameron, D. 2010. Too much, too young. *Daily Mail*, 19 February, www.dailymail.co.uk/debate/article-1252156/DAVID-CAMERON-Sexualisation-children-too-young.html.

Canaan, J. 1986. Why a 'slut' is a 'slut': cautionary tales of middle-class teenage girls' morality. In Varenne, H. (ed.) *Symbolizing America*. Lincoln: University of Nebraska Press, 184–208.

Cante, R.C. and Restivo, A. 2004. The cultural-aesthetic specificities of all-male moving image pornography. In Williams, L. (ed.) *Porn Studies*. Durham: Duke University Press, 142–66.

Carbone, M.B. 2013. *Tentacle Erotica: Horror, Seduction, Pornographic Imaginaries*. Milan: Mimesis International.

Carline, A. 2011. Criminal justice, extreme pornography and prostitution: Protecting women or promoting morality? *Sexualities* 14(3): 312–33.

Carmody, M. 2005. Ethical erotics: reconceptualizing anti-rape education. *Sexualities* 8(4): 469–85.

Carmody, M. 2009. *Sex and Ethics: Young People and Ethical Sex*. Melbourne: Palgrave Macmillan.

Carpenter, E. 1912. *The Intermediate Sex: A Study of Some Transitional Types of Men and Women*. New York: Mitchell Kennerley.

Carrellas, B. 2007. *Urban Tantra: Sacred Sex for the Twenty-first Century*. Berkeley: Ten Speed Press.

Carrigan, M., Gupta, K. and Morrison, T. 2013. Asexuality special theme issue editorial. *Psychology and Sexuality* 4(2): 111–20.

Carter, C. 2012. Sex/gender and the media: from sex roles to social construction and beyond. In Ross, K. (ed.) *The Handbook of Gender, Sex and Media*. Malden: Wiley-Blackwell, 365–82.

Cartmell, D., Hunter, I.Q. and Whelehan, I. (eds) 1997. *Trash Aesthetics: Popular Culture and its Audience*. London: Pluto Press.

Catinella Orrell, R. and Scuderi, J. 2016. *Objects of Desire: A Showcase of Modern Erotic Products and the Creative Minds Behind Them*. Atglen: Schiffer Publishing.

Chalfen, R. 2009. 'It's only a picture': sexting, 'smutty' snapshots and felony charges. *Visual Studies* 24(3): 258–68.

Chambers, D. 2013. *Social Media and Personal Relationships: Online Intimacies and Networked Friendship*. Basingstoke: Palgrave.

Chapkis, W. 1997. *Live Sex Acts: Women Performing Erotic Labor*. New York: Routledge.

Chateauvert, M. 2013. *Sex Workers Unite: A History of the Movement from Stonewall to Slutwalk*. Boston: Beacon Press.

Chauncey, G. 1994. *Gay New York: Gender, Urban Culture, and the Making of the Gay Male World, 1890–1940*. 3rd edn. New York: Basic Books.

References

Childstats. Adolescent Births, www.childstats.gov/americaschildren/family2.asp.

Childstats. Adolescent Depression, www.childstats.gov/americaschildren/health2.asp.

Childstats. Child Maltreatment, www.childstats.gov/americaschildren/family3.asp.

Childstats. College Enrolment, www.childstats.gov/americaschildren/edu6.asp.

Childstats. Emotional and Behavioral Difficulties, www.childstats.gov/americaschildren15/health3.asp.

Childstats. High School Completion, www.childstats.gov/americaschildren/edu2.asp. Childstats. Sexual Activity, www.childstats.gov/americaschildren/beh2.asp.

Childstats. Youth Perpetrators of Serious Violent Crimes, www.childstats.gov/americaschildren15/beh5.asp.

Childstats. Youth Victims of Serious Violent Crimes, www.childstats.gov/americaschildren15/phys6.asp.

Chun, W.H.K. 2006. *Control and Freedom: Power and Paranoia in the Age of Fiber Optics*. Cambridge: MIT Press.

Church Gibson, P. 2014. Pornostyle: sexualised dress and the fracturing of feminism. *Fashion Theory: The Journal of Dress, Body and Culture* 18(2): 189–206.

Clark-Flory, T. 2012. Better than actual porn!, *Salon*, 9 December, www.salon.com/2012/12/09/gif_porn_the_new_gonzo.

Clark-Flory, T. 2013a. The best of Tumblr porn, *Salon*, 26 May, www.salon.com/2013/05/26/the_best_of_tumblr_porn.

Clark-Flory, T. 2013b. The best of Reddit porn, *Salon*, 14 September, www.salon.com/2013/09/14/the_best_of_reddit_porn.

Clark-Flory, T. 2013c. Vine: the future of sex?, *Salon*, 31 January, www.salon.com/2013/01/31/vine_the_future_of_sex.

Cobble, D.S. 2010. More intimate unions. In Boris, E. and Salazar Parreñas, R. (eds) *Intimate Labors*. Stanford: Stanford University Press, 280–95.

Coleman, L. (ed.) 2015. *Sex and Storytelling in Modern Cinema: Explicit Sex, Performance and Cinematic Technique*. London: I.B. Tauris.

Coleman, R. 2009. *The Becoming of Bodies: Girls, Images, Experience*. Manchester: Manchester University Press.

Coleman, R. 2015. *Transforming Images: Screens, Affect, Futures*. London: Routledge.

Collins, P.H. 2000. *Black Feminist Thought*, 2nd edn. New York: Routledge.

Comella, L. 2003. (Safe) sex and the city: on vibrators, masturbation, and the myth of 'real' sex. *Feminist Media Studies* 3(1): 109–12.

Comella, L. 2013. From text to context: feminist porn and the making of a market. In Taormino, T., Parreñas Shimizu, C., Penley, C. and Miller-Young, M. (eds) *The Feminist Porn Book: The Politics of Producing Pleasure*. New York: The Feminist Press, 79–93.

171

References

Comella, L. and Tarrant, S. (eds) 2015. *New Views on Pornography: Sexuality, Politics, and the Law: Sexuality, Politics, and the Law.* Santa Barbara: Praeger.

Comfort, A. 1972. *The Joy of Sex: A Gourmet Guide to Lovemaking.* New York: Simon and Schuster.

Comfort, A. 2003. *The Joy of Sex.* London: Octopus.

Connolly, W. 1993. Beyond good and evil: the ethical sensibility of Michel Foucault. *Political Theory* 21(3): 365–89.

Cook, P. 2005. The pleasures and perils of exploitation films. In Cook, P. (ed.) *Screening the Past: Memory and Nostalgia in Cinema.* London and New York: Routledge, 52–64.

Coopersmith, J. 2000. Pornography, videotape and the internet. *IEEE Technology and Society Magazine* 19(1): 27–34.

Coopersmith, J. 2006. 'Does your mother know what you really do?' The changing nature and image of computer-based pornography. *History and Technology* 22(1): 1–25.

Coppa, F. 2006. A brief history of media fandom. In Hellekson, K. and Busse, K. (eds) *Fan Fiction and Fan Communities in the Age of the Internet: New Essays.* Jefferson: McFarland, 41–59.

Cossman, B. 2007. *Sexual Citizens: The Legal and Cultural Regulation of Sex and Belonging.* Stanford: Stanford University Press.

Coté, M. and Pybus, J. 2007. Learning to immaterial labour 2.0: MySpace and social networks. *Ephemera: Theory and Politics in Organization* 7(1): 88–106.

Coulmont, B. and Hubbard, P. 2010. Consuming sex: socio-legal shifts in the space and place of sex shops. *Journal of Law and Society* 37(1): 189–209.

Cowan, S. 2010. The pain of pleasure: consent and the criminalisation of sado-masochistic 'assaults'. In Chalmers, J., Leverick, F. and Farmer. L. (eds) *Essays in Criminal Law in Honour of Sir Gerald Gordon.* Edinburgh: Edinburgh University Press, 126–40.

Cox, T. 1999. *Hot Sex: How to Do It.* London: Corgi.

Cox, D. 2010. A Serbian film: when allegory gets nasty. *Guardian*, 13 December, www.theguardian.com/film/filmblog/2010/dec/13/a-serbian-film-allegorical-political

Crawford, K. 2006. *Adult Themes.* Sydney: Palgrave Macmillan.

Crenshaw, K. 1989. Demarginalizing the intersection of race and sex: a black feminist critique of antidiscrimination doctrine, feminist theory, and antiracist politics. *The University of Chicago Legal Forum* 1: 139–67.

Crewe, L. and Martin, A. 2016. Sex and the city: branding, gender and the commodification of sex consumption in contemporary retailing. *Urban Studies* 54 (3): 582–99.

Croissant, J.L. 2006. The new sexual technobody: Viagra in the hyperreal world. *Sexualities* 9(3): 333–44.

Cryle, P. and Downing, L. 2010. The natural and the normal in the history of sexuality. *Psychology and Sexuality* 1(3): 191–9.

References

Daedone, N. 2011. *Slow Sex: The Art and Craft of the Female Orgasm.* New York: Grand Central Publishing.

Dean, J.J. 2014. *Straights: Heterosexuality in Post-Closeted Culture.* New York: New York University Press.

Deflem, M. 2006. *Habermas, Modernity and Law.* London: Sage.

De Genevieve, B. (2004). No fisting, no squirting, no coffins. *Camerawork: A Journal of Photographic Arts,* Fall/Winter.

Degim, I. A., Johnson, J. and Fu, T. 2015. *Online Courtship: Interpersonal Interactions Across Borders.* Amsterdam: Institute of Network Cultures.

Deibert, R., Palfrey, J., Rohozinski, R. and Zittrain, J. 2008. *Access Denied: The Practice and Policy of Global Internet Filtering.* Cambridge: MIT Press.

Delacoste, F. and Alexander, P. 1987. *Sex Work: Writings by Women in the Sex Industry.* San Francisco: Cleis Press.

Delany, S.R. 1999. *Times Square Red, Times Square Blue.* New York: New York University Press.

Dennis, K. 2009. *Art/Porn: A History of Seeing and Touching.* Oxford: Berg.

Deuze, M. 2012. *Media Life.* Cambridge: Polity

Devlin, K. 2015. In defence of sex machines: why trying to ban sex robots is wrong, http://theconversation.com/in-defence-of-sex-machines-why-trying-to-ban-sex-robots-is-wrong-47641.

Diamond. L. 2008. *Sexual Fluidity: Understanding Women's Love and Desire.* Cambridge: Harvard University Press.

Dimen, M. 1984. Political correct? Political incorrect? In Vance, C.S. (ed.) *Pleasure and Danger: Exploring Female Sexuality.* London: Routledge, 138–48.

Dines, G. 2010a. *Pornland: How Porn Has Hijacked Our Sexuality.* Boston: Beacon Press.

Dines, G. 2010b. Not your father's Playboy. *Counterpunch,* 17 May, www.counterpunch.org/2010/05/17/not-your-father-s-playboy.

Dines, G. 2010c. Adventures in Pornland. *Huffington Post,* 6 July, www.huffingtonpost.com/gail-dines/adventures-in-pornland_b_636381.html.

Dines, G. 2011. How the hardcore porn industry is ruining young men's lives. *The Courier,* www.thecourier.com.au/story/89041/how-the-hardcore-porn-industry-is-ruining-young-mens-lives.

Doan, L. 2001. *Fashioning Sapphism: The Origins of a Modern English Lesbian Culture.* New York: Columbia University Press.

Doan, L. and Prosser, J. 2002. *Palatable Poison: Critical Perspectives on The Well of Loneliness.* New York: Columbia University Press.

Dobson, A.S. 2015. *Postfeminist Digital Cultures: Femininity, Social Media, and Self-Representation.* New York: Palgrave.

Dobson, A.S. and Ringrose, J. 2016. Sext education: pedagogies of sex, gender and shame in the schoolyards of Tagged and Exposed. *Sex Education* 16(1): 8–21.

Dollimore, J. 2001. *Sex, Literature and Censorship*. Cambridge: Polity.

Donovan, H. 2008: Gift versus capitalist economies: exchanging Anime and Manga in the US. In Levi, A., McHarry, M. and Pagliassotti, D. (eds) *Boys' Love Manga: Essays on the Sexual Ambiguity and Cross-Cultural Fandom of the Genre*. Jefferson: McFarland, 11–22.

Döring, N. 2009. The internet's impact on sexuality: a critical review of 15 years of research. *Computers in Human Behavior* 25: 1089–101.

Doty, A. (ed.) 1995. *Out in Culture: Gay, Lesbian, and Queer Essays on Popular Culture*. Durham: Duke University Press.

Downing, L. 2012. What is 'sex critical' and why should we care about it?, http://sexcritical.blogspot.co.uk/2012/07/what-is-sex-critical-and-why-should-we.html.

Dowsett, G. 2015. 'And next for your enjoyment!': sex, technology and the constitution of desire. *Culture, Health and Sexuality* 17(4): 527–39.

Duggan, L. 2002. *The twilight of equality? Neoliberalism, cultural politics, and the attack on democracy*. Boston: Beacon Press.

Duggan, L. and Hunter, N.D. (eds) 2006. *Sex Wars: Sexual Dissent and American Political Culture*. New York: Routledge.

Duggan, L. and McHugh, K. 1996. A fem(me)inist manifesto. *Women and Performance: a journal of feminist theory* 8(2): 153–9.

Duits, L. and van Zoonen, L. 2007. Headscarves and porno-chic: disciplining girls' bodies in the European multicultural society. *European Journal of Women's Studies* 13(2): 103–17.

Duits, L. and van Zoonen, L. 2011. Coming to terms with sexualization. *European Journal of Cultural Studies* 14(5): 491–506.

Duncombe, J. and Marsden, D. 1996. Whose orgasm is it anyway? 'Sex work' in long-term couple relationships. In Weeks, J. and Holland, J. (eds) *Sexual Cultures*. London: Macmillan, 220–38.

Dunn, A. 2003. Ethics impossible? Advertising and the infomercial. In Lumby, C. and Probyn, E. (eds) *Remote Control: New Media, New Ethics*. Cambridge: Cambridge University Press, 133–51.

Durham, M.G. 2008. *The Lolita Effect: The Media Sexualization of Girls and What We Can Do About It*. Woodstock: Overlook Press.

Durham, M.G. 2016. *Technosex: Precarious Corporealities, Mediated Sexualities and the Ethics of Embodied Technics*. London: Palgrave Macmillan.

Duschinsky, R. 2013. Childhood, responsibility and the liberal loophole: replaying the sex-wars in debates on sexualisation? *Sociological Research Online* 18(2), www.socresonline.org.uk/18/2/7.html.

Dworkin, A. 1981. *Pornography: Men Possessing Women*. London: Women's Press.

Dworkin, A. 1987. *Letters from a War Zone: Writings 1976–1987*. London: Secker and Warburg.

Dyer, R. 1992. Coming to terms: gay pornography. In *Only Entertainment*. London and New York: Routledge, 121–34.

References

Dyhouse, C. 2013. *Girl Trouble: Panic and Progress in the History of Young Women*. London: Zed Books.

Easton, D. and Liszt, C. A. 1998. *The Ethical Slut: A Guide to Infinite Sexual Possibilities*. San Francisco: Greenery Press.

Edelman, L. 2004. *No Future: Queer Theory and the Death Drive*. Durham: Duke University Press.

Egan, R.D. 2006. *Dancing for Dollars and Paying for Love: The Relationships Between Exotic Dancers and their Regulars*. New York: Palgrave Macmillan.

Egan, R.D. 2013a. Lost objects: feminism, sexualisation and melancholia. *Feminist Theory* 14: 265–74.

Egan, R.D. 2013b. *Becoming Sexual: A Critical Appraisal of the Sexualization of Girls*. Cambridge: Polity.

Egan, R.D. and Hawkes, G. 2007. Producing the prurient through the pedagogy of purity: childhood sexuality and the social purity movement. *Historical Sociology* 20(4): 443–61.

Egan, R.D. and Hawkes, G. 2008. Girls' sexuality and the strange carnalities of advertisements: deconstructing the discourse of corporate paedophilia. *Australian Feminist Studies* 23: 307–22.

Egan, R.D. and Hawkes, G. 2009. The problem with protection: or, why we need to move towards recognition and the sexual agency of children. *Continuum* 23: 389–400.

Egan, R.D. and Hawkes, G. 2010. *Theorizing the Sexual Child in Modernity*. Basingstoke: Palgrave Macmillan.

Egan, R.D. and Hawkes, G. 2012. Sexuality, youth and the perils of endangered innocence: how history can help us get past the panic. *Gender and Education* 23(4): 269–84.

Ehrenreich, B. 1983. *The Hearts of Men: American Dreams and the Flight from Commitment*. New York: Pluto.

Ehrenreich, B. and Hochschild, R.A. (2002) *Global Woman: Nannies, Maids and Sex Workers in the New Economy*. London: Granta Books.

Elgot, J. 2014. Extreme porn law must be put back on agenda, 'Stop Porn Culture' conference hears. *Huffington Post*, 15 March, www.huffingtonpost.co.uk/2014/03/15/stop-porn-culture_n_4970455.html.

Ellis, H. and Symonds, J.A. 1897. *Sexual Inversion*. London: Wilson and Macmillan.

Em and Lo. 2006. *RecSex: An A–Z Guide to Hooking Up*. San Francisco: Chronicle Books.

Em and Lo. 2008. *Sex: How To Do Everything*. New York: DK Publishing.

Eraker, E.C. 2010. Stemming sexting: sensible legal approaches to teenagers' exchange of self-produced pornography. *Berkeley Technology Law Journal* 25(1): 555–96.

Escoffier, J. (ed.) 2003. *Sexual Revolution*. New York: Thunder's Mouth Press.

References

Escoffier, J. 2009. *Bigger Than Life: The History of Gay Porn Cinema from Beefcake to Hardcore*. Philadelphia: Running Press.

Esch, K. and Mayer, V. 2007. How unprofessional: the profitable partnership of amateur porn and celebrity culture. In Paasonen, S. et al. (eds) *Pornification: Sex and Sexuality in Media Culture*. Oxford: Berg, 99–111.

Evans, A. and Riley, S. 2014. *Technologies of Sexiness: Sex, Identity and Consumer Culture*. New York: Oxford University Press.

Evans, D. 1993. *Sexual Citizenship: The Material Construction of Sexualities*. London: Routledge.

Fahs, B. 2014. 'Freedom to' and 'freedom from': a new vision for sex-positive politics, *Sexualities* 17(3): 267–90.

Falk, P. 1993. The representation of presence: outlining the anti-aesthetics of pornography. *Theory, Culture and Society* 10: 1–42.

Felski, R. 2005. The role of aesthetics in cultural studies. In Berube, M. (ed.) *The Aesthetics of Cultural Studies*. Malden: Blackwell, 28–43.

Ferguson, A. 2010. *Sex Doll: A History*. Jefferson: McFarland.

Fine, M. 1988. Sexuality, schooling, and adolescent females: the missing discourse of desire. *Harvard Educational Review* 58(1): 29–53.

Fine, M. and McLelland, S. 2006. Sexuality education and desire: still missing after all these years. *Harvard Educational Review* 76(3): 297–338.

Finkelhor, D. and Jones, L. 2006. Why have child maltreatment and child victimization declined? *Journal of Social Issues* 62(4): 685–716.

Finkelhor, D. and Jones, L. 2012. Have sexual abuse and physical abuse declined since the 1990s? Crimes Against Children Research Center, http://employees.achservices.org/images/stories/documents/havesapadeclined.pdf.

Fisher, A. and Walker, J. 2016. *Grindhouse: Cultural Exchange on 42nd Street, and Beyond*. London: Bloomsbury Academic.

Forrest, S.P., Strange, V., Oakley, A. and The RIPPLE study team. 2004. What do young people want from sex education? The results of a needs assessment from a peer-led sex education programme. *Culture Health and Sexuality* 6(4): 337–54.

Forshaw, B. 2015. *Sex and Film: The Erotic in British, American and World Cinema*. Basingstoke: Palgrave Macmillan.

Fortenberry, D., Schick, V., Herbenick, D., Sanders, S., Dodge, B. and Reece, M. 2010. Sexual behavior and condom use at last vaginal intercourse: a national sample of adolescents age 14–17. *International Society for Sexual Medicine* 7(5): 305–14.

Foucault, M. 1976. *The History of Sexuality: An Introduction*. London: Penguin.

Foucault, M. 1988. Sexual morality and the law. In *Politics, Philosophy, Culture: Interviews and Other Writings, 1977–1984*. New York: Routledge.

Foucault, M. 1997. *Ethics: Subjectivity and Truth*. New York: The New Press.

FRA 2014. Violence against women: an EU-wide survey. European Union

References

Agency for Fundamental Rights, http://fra.europa.eu/en/publication/2014/violence-against-women-eu-wide-survey-main-results-report.

Frith, H. 2015. *Orgasmic Bodies*. Basingstoke: Palgrave Macmillan.

Fuller, S. 2011. *Humanity 2.0: What it Means to be Human Past, Present and Future*. Basingstoke: Palgrave Macmillan.

Gaimster, D. 2000. Sex and sensibility at the British Museum. *History Today* 50(9), www.historytoday.com/david-gaimster/sex-and-sensibility-british-museum.

Gaines, J. 2004. Machines that make the body do things. In Church Gibson, P. (ed.) *More Dirty Looks: Gender, Pornography and Power*. London: BFI, 31–44.

Galbraith, P. 2009. Moe and the potential of fantasy in post-millennial Japan. *electronic journal of contemporary japanese studies*, 31 October, www.japanesestudies.org.uk/articles/2009/Galbraith.html.

Galbraith, P.W. 2011. Bishōjo games: 'techno-Intimacy' and the virtually human in Japan. *Game Studies* 11(2), http://gamestudies.org/1102/articles/galbraith.

Gerhard, J.F. 2001. *Desiring Revolution: Second-Wave Feminism and the Rewriting of American Sexual Thought, 1920 to 1982*. New York: Columbia University Press.

Gerstle, A., Clark, T., Ishigami, A. and Yano, A. (eds) 2013. *Shunga: Sex and Pleasure in Japanese Art*. London: British Museum Press.

Gever, M., Parmar, P. and Greyson, J. (eds) 1993. *Queer Looks: Perspectives on Lesbian and Gay Film and Video*. New York: Routledge.

Giddens, A. 1992. *The Transformation of Intimacy: Sexuality, Love and Eroticism in Modern Societies*. Cambridge: Polity Press.

Gilbert, J. 2013. What kind of a thing is neoliberalism? *New Formations* 80–1: 7–22.

Gill, R. 2003. From sexual objectification to sexual subjectification: the resexualisation of women's bodies in the media. *Feminist Media Studies* 3(1): 100–6.

Gill R. 2007a. Postfeminist media culture: elements of a sensibility. *European Journal of Cultural Studies* 10(2): 147–66.

Gill, R. 2007b. *Gender and the Media*. Cambridge: Polity.

Gill, R. 2008. Empowerment/sexism: figuring female sexual agency in contemporary advertising. *Feminism and Psychology* 18(1): 35–60.

Gill, R. 2009. Beyond the 'sexualization of culture' thesis: an intersection analysis of 'sixpacks,' 'midriffs' and 'hot lesbians'. *Sexualities* 12(2): 137–60.

Gill, R. 2012. Media, empowerment and the 'sexualization of culture' debates. *Sex Roles* 66: 736–45.

Gillespie, A.A. 2012. *Child Pornography: Law and Policy*. London: Routledge.

Gilman, R. 1968. There's a wave of pornography, obscenity, sexual expression. *New York Times Magazine*, 8 September.

Gilman, S.L. 1999. *Making the Body Beautiful: A Cultural History of Aesthetic Surgery*. Princeton: Princeton University Press.

Ginsburg, A. 1956. *Howl and Other Poems*. San Francisco: City Lights Books.

References

Glick, E. 2009. *Materializing Queer Desire: Oscar Wilde to Andy Warhol*. New York: SUNY Press.

Global Citizen. 2012. Introduction to the challenges for achieving gender equality, www.globalcitizen.org/en/content/introduction-to-the-challenges-of-achieving-gender.

Goldsmith, J. and Wu, T. 2006. *Who Controls the Internet? Illusions of a Borderless World*. Oxford: Oxford University Press.

Goldstein, L. 2009. Documenting and denial: discourses of sexual self-exploitation. *Jump Cut* 51, www.ejumpcut.org/archive/jc51.2009/goldstein/text.html.

Goode, L. and McKee, A. 2013. Conflict and seduction in the public sphere. *Media, Culture and Society* 35(1): 113–20.

Gordo-López, A.J. and Cleminson, R. 2004. *Techno-sexual Landscapes: Changing Relations Between Technology and Sexuality*. London: Free Association Books.

Gorman-Murray, A. and Nash, C. 2016. Transformations in LGBT consumer landscapes and leisure spaces in the neoliberal city. *Urban Studies* 54(3): 786–805.

Grant, J.M., Mottet, L.A. and Tanis, J. 2011. *Injustice at Every Turn: A Report of the National Transgender Discrimination Survey*. Washington: National Center for Transgender Equality and National Gay and Lesbian Task Force, www.thetaskforce.org/static_html/downloads/reports/reports/ntds_full.pdf.

Grant, M.G. 2014. *Playing the Whore: The Work of Sex Work*. London: Verso.

Gray, J. 2003. *Mars and Venus in the Bedroom: A Guide to Lasting Romance and Passion*. London: Vermilion.

Gregg, M. 2011. *Work's Intimacy*. Cambridge: Polity Press.

Gregoire, S.W. 2012. *The Good Girl's Guide to Great Sex (And You Thought Bad Girls Have All the Fun)*. Grand Rapids: Zondervan.

Gregory, T. 2015. Sexting and the politics of the image: when the invisible becomes visible in a consensus democracy. *Porn Studies* 2(4): 342–55.

Gross, L. and Woods, J.D. (eds) 1999. *The Columbia Reader on Lesbians and Gay Men in Media, Society and Politics*. New York: Columbia University Press.

Grosz, E.A. 1994. *Volatile Bodies: Toward a Corporeal Feminism*. 3rd edn. Bloomington: Indiana University Press.

Gudelunas, D. 2012. There's an app for that: the uses and gratifications of online social networks for gay men. *Sexuality and Culture* 16(4): 347–65.

Gunning, T. 2006. The cinema of attractions: early film, its spectator and the avant-garde. In Stauven, W. (ed.) *The Cinema of Attractions Reloaded*. Amsterdam: Amsterdam University Press, 381–8.

Gurley Brown, H. 1962. *Sex and the Single Girl*. New York: Bernard Geis Associates.

Guttmacher Institute. 2011. Facts on American teens' sexual and reproductive health, www.guttmacher.org/pubs/FBATSRH.html. Accessed 15 June 2013.

References

Hakim, C. 2011. *Honey Money: The Power of Erotic Capital*. London: Allen Lane.

Halberstam, J. 1998. *Female Masculinity*. Durham: Duke University Press.

Halberstam, J. 2012a. Global female masculinities. *Sexualities* 15(3–4): 336–54.

Halberstam, J. 2012b. *Gaga Feminism: Sex, Gender, and the End of Normal*. Boston: Beacon Press.

Hall, R. 1928. *The Well of Loneliness*. London: Jonathan Cape.

Hamilton, M. 2009. The seduction of girls: the human cost. In Tankard Reist, M. (ed.) *Getting Real: Challenging the Sexualization of Girls*. Melbourne: Spinifex Press, 55–66.

Hann, M. 2013. Miley Cyrus's new Wrecking Ball video says young women should be sexually available. *Guardian*, 10 September, www.theguardian.com/music/musicblog/2013/sep/10/miley-cyrus-wrecking-ball.

Haraway, D. 1991. *Simians, Cyborgs, and Women: The Reinvention of Nature*. London: Routledge.

Harcourt, C. and Donovan, B. 2005. The many faces of sex work. *Sexual Transmission International* 81: 201–6.

Harris, J. 2011. *The Thinking Man's Guide To Pleasuring A Woman: 6 Powerful Keys To Unlocking The Elusive Female Orgasm (Written by a Woman Who Knows)*. Kindle Edition.

Hartley, H. 2006. The 'pinking' of Viagra culture: drug industry efforts to create and repackage sex drugs for women. *Sexualities* 9(3): 363–78.

Harvey, L. and Gill, R. 2011. Spicing it up: sexual entrepreneurs and *The Sex Inspectors*. In Gill, R. and Scharff, C. (eds) *New Femininities: Postfeminism, Neoliberalism and Subjectivity*. Basingstoke: Palgrave Macmillan, 52–67.

Hasinoff, A.A. 2014. Blaming sexualization for sexting. *Girlhood Studies* 7(1): 102–20.

Hasinoff, A.A. 2015. *Sexting Panic: Rethinking Criminalization, Privacy, and Consent*. Illinois: University of Illinois Press.

Hasler, N. 2012. *Sex: A Book for Teens. An Uncensored Guide to your Body, Sex, and Safety*. San Francisco: Zest Books.

Hayles, K. 1995. The life of cyborgs: writing the posthuman. In Gray, C.H., Figueroa-Sarriera, H.J. and Mentor, S. (eds) *The Cyborg Handbook*. New York: Routledge, 321–35.

Heath, S. 1982. *The Sexual Fix*. London: Macmillan.

Hellekson, K. and Busse, K. (eds) 2006. *Fan Fiction and Fan Communities in the Age of the Internet: New Essays*. Jefferson: McFarland.

Hepp, A., Hjarvard, S. and Lundby, K. 2015. Mediatization: theorizing the interplay between media, culture and society. *Media, Culture and Society* 37(2): 314–32.

Herbenick, D., Reece, M., Schick, V., Sanders, S.A., Dodge, B. and Fortenberry, J.D. 2010. Sexual behavior in the United States: results from a national probability sample of men and women ages 14–94. *Journal of Sexual Medicine* 7 (Supplement 5): 255–65.

Herriot, L. and Hiseler, L.E. 2015. Documentaries on the sexualisation of girls: examining slut-shaming, victim-blaming, and what's being left off-screen. In Renold, E., Ringrose, J. and Egan, R.D. (eds) *Children, Sexuality and Sexualisation*. Basingstoke: Palgrave Macmillan, 289–304.

Hester, H. 2014. *Beyond Explicit: Pornography and the Displacement of Sex*. New York: SUNY Press.

Hester, H., Jones, B. and Taylor-Harman, S. 2015. Giffing a fuck: non-narrative pleasures in participatory porn cultures and female fandom. *Porn Studies* 2(4): 356–66.

Heyes, C.J. 2003. Feminist solidarity after queer theory: the case of transgender. *Signs: Journal of Women in Culture and Society* 28(4): 1093–1120.

Higonnet, A. 2009. Pretty Babies, Index on Censorship, www.indexoncensorship.org/wp-content/uploads/2009/03/higonnet_obscenity_spring09.pdf.

Hilliard, C. 2013. 'Is it a book that you would even wish your wife or your servants to read?' Obscenity law and the politics of reading in modern England. *The American Historical Review* 118(3): 653–78.

Hillis, K. 2009. *Online a Lot of the Time: Ritual, Fetish, Sign*. Durham: Duke University Press.

Hines, C. 2012. Playmates of the Caribbean: taking Hollywood, making hardcore. In Hines, C. and Kerr, D. (eds) *Hard to Swallow: Hard-Core Pornography on Screen*. London: Wallflower Press, 126–44.

Hines, S. 2007. *TransForming Gender: Transgender Practices of Identity, Intimacy and Care*. Bristol: Policy Press.

Hirst, J. 2008. Developing sexual competence: exploring strategies for the provision of effective sexualities and relationships education. *Sex Education* 8(4): 399–413.

Hjarvard, S. 2008. The mediatization of society: a theory of the media as agents of social and cultural change. *Nordicom Review* 29(2): 105–34.

Hjarvard, S. 2012. Doing the right thing: media and communication studies in a mediatized world. *Nordicom Review* 33 (Supplement 1): 27–34.

Hoechsmann, M. and Poyntz, S.R. 2012. *Media Literacies: A Critical Introduction*. Malden: Wiley-Blackwell.

Hofer, K.P. 2014a. Porning intimacy: homemade pornography on Sell Your Sex Tape. In Biasin, E., Maina, G. and Zecca, F. (eds) *Porn After Porn: Contemporary Alternative Pornographies*. Milan: Mimesis International, 305–20.

Hofer, K.P. 2014b. Pornographic domesticity: amateur couple porn, straight subjectivities, and sexual labour. *Porn Studies* 1(4): 334–45.

Hooper, A. 1999. *Great Sex Guide*. London: Dorling Kindersley.

Horeck, T. and Kendall, T. (eds) 2011. *The New Extremism in Cinema: From France to Europe*. Edinburgh: Edinburgh University Press.

Hubbard, P. 2012. *Cities and Sexualities*. London: Routledge.

References

Hubbard, P., Matthews, R. and Scoular, J. 2009. Legal geographies – controlling sexually oriented businesses: Law, Licensing, and the geographies of a controversial land use. *Urban Geography* 30: 185–205.

Hubbard, P., Matthews, R., Scoular, J. and Agustín, L. 2008. Away from prying eyes? The urban geographies of 'adult entertainment'. *Progress in Human Geography* 32(3): 363–81.

Humphreys, L. 1975. *Tearoom Trade: Impersonal Sex in Public Places.* Piscataway: Transaction Publishers.

Hunt, A. 2003. Risk and moralization in everyday life. In Ericson, R. and Doyle, A. (eds) *Risk and Morality.* Toronto: University of Toronto Press, 165–92.

Hunt, L. 1993. *The Invention of Pornography: Obscenity and the Origins of Modernity, 1500–1800.* New York: Zone Books.

Hunt, L. 1998. *British Low Culture: From Safari Suits to Sexploitation.* London: Routledge.

Hunter, I.Q. 2006. Tolkien dirty. In Mathijis, E. (ed.) *Lord of the Rings: Popular Culture in Global Context.* London: Wallflower Press, 321–38.

Hunter, I.Q. 2008. Take an easy ride: sexploitation in the 1970s. In Shail, R. (ed.) *Seventies British Cinema.* London: Palgrave Macmillan, 3–13.

Hunter, I.Q. 2012a. A clockwork orgy: a user's guide. In Mendik, X. (ed.) *Peep Shows: Cult Film and the Cine-Erotic.* London: Wallflower Press, 126–34.

Hunter, I.Q. 2012b. From window cleaner to potato man: confessions of a working-class stereotype. In Hunter, I.Q. and Porter, L. (eds) *British Comedy Cinema.* London: Routledge, 154–70.

Hunter, I.Q. 2013. *British Trash Cinema.* London: BFI/Palgrave.

Hunter, I.Q. 2016. *Cult Film as a Guide to Life: Fandom, Adaptation and Identity.* London: Bloomsbury Academic.

Hurley, M. and Prestage, G. 2009. Intensive sex partying amongst gay men in Sydney. *Culture, Health and Sexuality* 11(6): 597–610.

Illouz, E.1999. The lost innocence of love: romance as a postmodern condition. In Featherstone, M. (ed.) *Love and Eroticism.* Thousand Oaks: Sage/Theory, Culture and Society, 161–86.

Ingham, R. 2005. 'We didn't cover that at school': education against pleasure or education for pleasure? *Sex Education* 5(4): 375–88.

Irvine, J. 1995. Reinventing perversion: sex addiction and cultural anxieties. *Journal of the History of Sexuality* 5(3): 429–49.

Irvine, J. 2005. *Disorders of Desire: Sexuality and Gender in Modern American Sexology.* Philadelphia: Temple University Press.

Ito, M. 2008. Introduction. In Vernelis, K. (ed.) *Networked Publics.* Cambridge: MIT Press, 1–14.

Iversen, K. 2016. Miley Cyrus explains what it means to be pansexual, *Nylon,* 11 October, www.nylon.com/articles/miley-cyrus-pansexual.

Jackson, N., Kimber, S., Walker, J. and Watson, T.J. (eds) 2016. *Snuff: Real Death and Screen Media.* London: Bloomsbury Academic.

References

Jackson, S. and Scott, S. 2010. *Theorizing Sexuality*. Maidenhead: Open University Press.

Jackson, S. and Vares, T. 2015. 'Too many bad role models for us girls': girls, female pop celebrities and 'sexualisation'. *Sexualities* 18(4): 480–98.

Jackson, S. and Westrupp, E. 2010. Sex, popular culture and the pre-teen girl. *Sexualities* 13: 357–76.

Jackson, S., Goddard, S. and Cossens, S. 2016. The importance of [not] being Miley: girls making sense of Miley Cyrus. *European Journal of Cultural Studies* 19(6): 547–64.

Jackson, S., Vares, T. and Gill, R. 2012. 'The whole playboy mansion image': girls' fashioning and fashioned selves within a postfeminist culture. *Feminism and Psychology* 23(2): 143–62.

Jacobs, K. 2007. *Netporn: DIY Web Culture and Sexual Politics*. Lanham: Rowman and Littlefield.

Jacobs, K. 2012. *People's Pornography: Sex and Surveillance on the Chinese Internet*. Bristol: Intellect.

Jagose, A. 2001. The evolution of a lesbian icon. *Genders* 34: 1–32.

Jeffreys, S. 1993. *The Lesbian Heresy: A Feminist Perspective on the Lesbian Sexual Revolution*. Melbourne: Spinifex.

Jeffries, D. 2016. This looks like a blowjob for Superman: servicing fanboys with superhero porn parodies. *Porn Studies* 3(3): 276–94.

Jenkins, H. 1992. *Textual Poachers: Television Fans and Participatory Culture*. New York: Routledge.

Jenkins, H. 2004. So you want to teach pornography? In Church Gibson, P. (ed.) *More Dirty Looks: Gender, Pornography and Power*. London: BFI, 1–7.

Jenkins, H. 2006. *Fans, Bloggers, and Gamers: Exploring Participatory Culture*. New York: New York University Press.

Jenkins, J., Clinton, K., Purushotma, R., Robison, A.J. and Weigelet, M. 2006. *Confronting the Challenges of Participatory Culture: Media Education for the 21st Century*. Chicago: The MacArthur Foundation, http://files.eric.ed.gov/fulltext/ED536086.pdf.

Johnson, B. 2012. Semblance and the sexual revolution: a critical review of *Viva*. In Mendik, X. (ed.) *Peep Shows: Cult Film and the Cine-Erotic*. London: Wallflower Press, 264–74.

Jones, B. 2013. Slow evolution: first time pics and *The X-Files* porn parody. *Journal of Adaptation in Film and Performance* 6(3): 369–85.

Jones, M. 2008a. *Skintight: An Anatomy of Cosmetic Surgery*. Oxford: Berg.

Jones, M. 2008b. Media-bodies and screen-births: cosmetic surgery reality television. *Continuum* 22(4): 515–24.

Jones, M. 2012a. Media-bodies and Photoshop. In Attwood, F., Campbell, V., Hunter, I.Q. and Lockyer, S. (eds) *Controversial Images: Media Representations on the Edge*. Basingstoke: Palgrave Macmillan, 19–35.

182

References

Jones, M. 2012b. Cosmetic surgery and the fashionable face. *Fashion Theory: The Journal of Dress, Body and Culture* 16(2): 193–210.

Jones, S. 2016. 'Extreme' porn? The implications of a label. *Porn Studies* 3(3): 295–307.

Jones, S. 2017. Sex and horror. In Smith, C. and Attwood, F. (eds) *The Routledge Companion to Media, Sex and Sexuality*. Abingdon and New York: Routledge, 290–9.

Jones, S. and McGlotten, S. 2014. *Zombies and Sexuality: Essays on Desire and the Living Dead*. Jefferson: McFarland.

Jones, S. and Mowlabocus, S. 2009. Hard times and rough rides: the legal and ethical impossibilities of researching 'shock' pornographies. *Sexualities* 12(5): 613–28.

Jorm, A.F., Korten, A.E., Rodgers, B., Jacomb, P.A. and Christensen, H. 2002. Sexual orientation and mental health: results from a community survey of young and middle-aged adults. *The British Journal of Psychiatry* 180(5): 423–27.

Juffer, J. 1998. *At Home with Pornography: Women, Sex, and Everyday life*. New York: New York University Press.

Julius, A. 2002. *Transgressions: The Offences of Art*. Chicago: University of Chicago Press.

Julius, A. and Petley, J. 2009. Crimes of transgression. *Index on Censorship* 38(1): 50–9, www.indexoncensorship.org/wp-content/uploads/2009/03/julius_obscenity_sprring09.pdf.

Karaian, L. 2012. Lolita speaks: 'sexting', teenage girls and the law. *Crime, Media, Culture* 8.1: 57–73.

Karaian, L. 2014. Policing 'sexting': Responsibilization, respectability and sexual subjectivity in child protection/crime prevention responses to teenagers' digital sexual expression. *Theoretical Criminology* 18(3): 282–99.

Katz, J.N. 1995. *The Invention of Heterosexuality*. New York: Dutton Books.

Kearney, M. C. 2011. *The Gender and Media Reader*. New York: Routledge.

Kehily, M.J. 2002. *Sexuality, Gender and Schooling: Shifting Agendas in Social Learning*. London: Routledge.

Kehily, M.J. 2012. Contextualising the sexualisation of girls debate: innocence, experience and young female sexuality. *Gender and Education* 24(3): 255–68.

Kellner, D. and Share, J. 2005. Toward critical media literacy: core concepts, debates, organizations and policy. *Discourse: Studies in the Cultural Politics of Education* 26(3): 369–86.

Kelly, L. 1988. The US Ordinances: censorship or radical law reform. In Chester, G. and Dickey, J. (eds) *Feminism and Censorship: The Current Debate*. Bridport: Prism Press, 52–61.

Kember, S. and Zylinska, J. 2012. *Life After New Media: Mediation as a Vital Process*. Cambridge: MIT Press.

Kempadoo, K. and Doezema, J. (eds) 1998. *Global Sex Workers: Rights, Resistance, and Redefinition*. New York: Routledge.

Kendrick, W.M. 1996. *The Secret Museum: Pornography in Modern Culture*. Berkeley: University of California Press.

Kennedy, J. and Smith, C. 2012. 'His soul shatters at about 0:23': spankwire, self-scaring and hyberbolic shock. In Attwood, F., Campbell, V., Hunter, I.Q. and Lockyer, S. (eds) *Controversial Images: Media Representations on the Edge*. London: Palgrave Macmillan, 239–53.

Kibby, M. and Costello, B. 2001. Between the image and the act: interactive sex entertainment on the internet. *Sexualities* 4(3): 353–69.

Kieran, M. 2002. On obscenity: the thrill and repulsion of the morally prohibited. *Philosophy and Phenomenological Research* LXIV(1): 31–56.

King, M., Semlyen, J., Tai, S.S., Killaspy, H., Osborn, D., Popelyuk, D. and Nazareth, I. 2008. A systematic review of mental disorder, suicide, and deliberate self harm in lesbian, gay and bisexual people. *BMC Psychiatry* 28, www.ncbi.nlm.nih.gov/pmc/articles/PMC2533652.

Kingsley, E. 2011. *Just F*ck Me! What Women Want Men to Know About Taking Control in the Bedroom*. Secret Life Publishing.

Kinsella, S. 2000. *Adult Manga: Culture and Power in Contemporary Japanese Society*. Honolulu: University of Hawaii Press.

Kinsey, A., Pomeroy, W. and Martin, C. 1948. *Sexual Behavior in the Human Male*. Philadelphia: W.B. Saunders.

Kinsey, A., Pomeroy, W., Martin, C. and Gebhard, P. 1953. *Sexual Behavior in the Human Female*. Philadelphia: W.B. Saunders.

Kipnis, L. 1996. *Bound and Gagged: Pornography and the Politics of Fantasy in America*. New York: Grove Press.

Kitzmann, A. 2004. *Saved from Oblivion: Documenting the Daily from Diaries to Web Cams*. New York: Peter Lang.

Klein, M. 1999. The history and future of sex. *Electronic Journal of Human Sexuality* 2, www.ejhs.org/volume2/history.htm.

Klein, R. 2009. The harmful medicalization of sexualized girls. In Tankard Reist, M. (ed.) *Getting Real: Challenging the Sexualization of Girls*. Melbourne: Spinifex Press, 131–48.

Kleinhans, C. 2004. Virtual child porn: the law and the semiotics of the image. In Church Gibson, P. (ed.) *More Dirty Looks: Gender Pornography and Power*. London: BFI, 71–84.

Krafft-Ebing, R. von 1894. *Psychopathia Sexualis*. Stuttgart: Ferdinand Enke.

Kranz, C. 2009. Nude photo led to suicide: family wants to educate teens about dangers of sexting, http://news.cincinnati.com/article/20090322/NEWS01/903220312/Nude-photo-led-to-suicide. Accessed 24 October 2009.

Krzywinska, T. 2006. *Sex and the Cinema*. London and New York: Wallflower Press.

Krzywinska, T. 2012. The strange case of the misappearance of sex in videogames. In Fromme, J. and Unger, A. (eds) *Computer Games and New Media Cultures: A Handbook of Digital Games Studies*. Heidelberg: Springer, 143–60.

Kuper, L.E., Nussbaum, R. and Mustanski, B. 2012. Exploring the diversity of gender and sexual orientation identities in an online sample of transgender individuals. *Journal of Sex Research* 49(2–3): 244–54.

Ladenson, E. 2007. *Dirt for Art's Sake: Books on Trial from Madame Bovary to Lolita*. Ithaca: Cornell University Press.

Langdridge, D. and Barker, M. (eds) 2007. *Safe, Sane and Consensual: Contemporary Perspectives on Sadomasochism*. Basingstoke: Palgrave Macmillan.

Laqueur, T.W. 1990. *Making Sex: Body and Gender from the Greeks to Freud*. Cambridge: Harvard University Press.

Laqueur, T.W. 2003. *Solitary Sex: A Cultural History of Masturbation*. New York: Zone Books.

Lawrence, D.H. 1960 [1928]. *Lady Chatterley's Lover*. London: Penguin.

Leadbeater, C. and Miller, P. 2004. *The Pro-Am Revolution: How Enthusiasts are Changing Our Society and Economy*. London: Demos.

Leap, W. 1999. *Public Sex/Gay Space*. New York: Columbia University.

Leary, M. G. 2007. Self-produced child pornography: the appropriate societal response to juvenile self-sexual exploitation. *Virginia Journal of Social Policy & the Law* 15: 1–50

Leavis, F.R. and Thompson, D. 1933. *Culture and Environment: The Training of Critical Awareness*. London: Chatto and Windus.

Lee, J. and Sullivan, R. 2016. Porn and labour: the labour of porn studies. *Porn Studies* 3(2): 104–6.

Lees, S. 1993. *Sugar and Spice: Sexuality and Adolescent Girls*. Harmondsworth: Penguin.

Lenhart, A. 2009. Teens and sexting: how and why minor teens are sending sexually suggestive nude or nearly nude images via text messaging. Pew Research Center, www.pewinternet.org/2009/12/15/teens-and-sexting/http://www.ncdsv.org/images/pewinternet_teensandsexting_12-2009.pdf.

Lenhart, A., Smith, A. and Anderson, M. 2015. Teens, technology and romantic relationships. Pew Research Center, www.pewinternet.org/2015/10/01/teens-technology-and-romantic-relationships.

Lerum, K. 2009. The real problem with 'sexting': adult complicity in labelling teens 'perverts' and 'criminals', *The Society Pages*, 23 December http://thesocietypages.org/sexuality/2009/12/23/the-real-problem-with-sexting-adult-complicity-in-labeling-teens-sluts-perverts-and-criminals.

Lerum, K. and Dworkin, S. 2009. Bad girls rule: an interdisciplinary feminist commentary on the report of the APA Task Force on the sexualisation of girls. *Journal of Sex Research* 46(4): 250–63.

Levin, D. and Kilbourne, J. 2008. *So Sexy, So Soon: The New Sexualized*

Childhood and What Parents Can Do to Protect Their Kids. New York: Ballantine Books.

Levin Russo, J. 2007. 'The real thing': reframing queer pornography for virtual spaces. In Jacobs, K. Janssen, M. and Pasquinelli, M. (eds) *C'Lick Me: A Netporn Studies Reader*. Amsterdam: Institute of Network Cultures, 239–52.

Levine, L.W. 1988. *Highbrow/Lowbrow: The Emergence of Cultural Hierarchy in America*. Cambridge: Harvard University Press.

Levinson, D.A. 1989. Robert Mapplethorpe's extraordinary vision, *The Tech*, 110(31), http://tech.mit.edu/V110/N31/mapple.31a.html.

Levy, A. 2005. *Female Chauvinist Pigs: Women and the Rise of Raunch Culture*. New York and London: Free Press.

Levy, D. 2008. *Love and Sex with Robots*. London: Duckworth Overlook.

Liebau, C.P. 2008. *Prude: How the Sex-obsessed Culture Damages Girls (and America Too!)*. Nashville: FaithWords.

Light, B., Fletcher, G. and Adam, A. 2008. Gay men, Gaydar and the commodification of difference. *Information Technology and People* 21(3): 300–14.

Liu, T. 2009. Conflicting discourses of boys' love and subcultural tactics in mainland China and Hong Kong. *Intersections: Gender and Sexuality in Asia and the Pacific* 20, http://intersections.anu.edu.au/issue20/liu.htm.

Livingstone, S., Haddon, L., Görzig, A. and Ólafsson, K. 2011. *Risks and Safety on the Internet: The Perspective of European children*. London: EU Kids Online.

Lodder, M. 2016. Visual pleasure and gonzo pornography: Mason's challenge to convention in 'the hardest of hardcore'. *Porn Studies* 3(4): 373–85.

Loe, M. 2001. Fixing broken masculinity: Viagra and the production of gender and sexuality. *Sexuality and Culture* 5(3): 97–125.

Lorber, J. and Moore, L.J. 2011. *Gendered Bodies: Feminist Perspectives*. 2nd edn. Oxford: Oxford University Press.

Lotney, K. 2000. *The Ultimate Guide to Strap-on Sex for Women: A Complete Resource for Women and Men*. San Francisco: Cleis Press.

Lovelace, L. 1974. *Inside Linda Lovelace*. London: Heinrich Hanau Publications Ltd.

Lumby, C. 2001. Watching them watching us: the trouble with teenage girls. *Continuum* 15(1): 49–55.

Lumby, C. 2011. Past the post in feminist media studies. *Feminist Media Studies* 11(1): 95–100.

Lumby, C., Green, L. and Hartley, J. 2009. Untangling the net: the scope of content caught by mandatory internet filtering, www.ecu.edu.au/__data/assets/pdf_file/0003/32835/Untangling_The_Net.pdf.

Lust, E. 2008. *Good Porn: A Woman's Guide*. Santa Cruz: Editorial Melusina.

Lyall, S. 2008. Revising 'sex' for the 21st century. *New York Times*, 17 December, www.nytimes.com/2008/12/18/fashion/18joy.html

Lynn, R. 2005. *The Sexual Revolution 2.0*. Berkeley: Ulysses Press.

References

Lynn, R. 2006. Real sex, virtual worlds. *Wired*, 30 June, http://archive. wired.com/culture/lifestyle/commentary/sexdrive/2006/06/71284?currentPage =all.

Lynn, R. 2007. Web 2.0 leaves porn behind. *Wired*, 10 August, www.wired.com/culture/lifestyle/commentary/sexdrive/2007/08/sexdrive_0809?currentPage=all.

Lynn, R. 2008. Random musing on sex and 'play', www.reginalynn.com/archives/518. Accessed 10 November 2008.

Lyon, D. 1994. *The Electronic Eye: The Rise of Surveillance Society*. Minneapolis: University of Minnesota Press.

Lyon, D. 2007. *Surveillance Studies: An Overview*. Cambridge: Polity.

Lyon, D. 2015. The Snowden stakes: challenges for understanding surveillance today. *Surveillance & Society* 13(2): 139–52.

MacAskill, E. 2016. 'Extreme surveillance' becomes UK law with barely a whimper. *Guardian*, 19 November, www.theguardian.com/world/2016/nov/19/extreme-surveillance-becomes-uk-law-with-barely-a-whimper.

McClintock, A. 1992. Gonad the Barbarian and the Venus Flytrap: portraying the female and male orgasm. In Segal, L. and McIntosh, M. (eds) *Sex Exposed: Sexuality and the Pornography Debate*. London: Virago, 111–31.

McDermott, E. 2011. The world some have won: sexuality, class and inequality. *Sexualities* 14(1): 63–78.

Machulis, K. 2008. Really, really, really intimate interfaces, https://conferences.oreilly.com/et2008/public/schedule/detail/1366.

McKee, A. 2010. Everything is child abuse. *Media International Australia* 135(1): 131–40.

McKee, A. 2012a. The importance of entertainment for sexuality education. *Sex Education* 12(5): 499–509.

McKee, A. 2012b. Pornography as entertainment. *Continuum* 26(4): 541–52.

McKee, A. 2013. The power of art, the power of entertainment. *Media, Culture and Society* 35(6): 759–70.

McKee, A. 2015. Methodological issues in defining aggression for content analyses of sexually explicit material. *Archives of Sexual Behavior* 44(1): 81–7.

McKee, A. 2016. *Fun! What the Entertainment Industries Can Tell Us About Living a Good Life*. New York: Palgrave Macmillan.

McKee, A., Albury, K., Dunne, M., Grieshaber, S., Hartley, J., Lumby, C. and Mathews, B. 2010. Healthy sexual development: a multidisciplinary framework for research. *International Journal of Sexual Health* 22(1): 14–19.

McLelland, M. 2005. The world of yaoi: the internet, censorship and the global 'boys' love' fandom. *Australian Feminist Law Journal* 23(1): 61–77.

McLelland, M. 2006a. A short history of 'hentai'. *Intersections: Gender, History and Culture in the Asian Context* 12, http://intersections.anu.edu.au/issue12/mclelland.html.

McLelland, M. 2006b. Why are Japanese girls' comics full of boys bonking?

References

Refractory: A Journal of Entertainment Media, http://refractory.unimelb.edu.au/2006/12/04/why-are-japanese-girls%E2%80%99-comics-full-of-boys-bonking1-mark-mclelland.

McLelland, M. 2009. Japanese transnational fandoms and female consumers. *Intersections: Gender and Sexuality in Asia and the Pacific* 20, http://intersections.anu.edu.au/issue20_contents.htm.

McLelland, M. 2011. Thought policing or the protection of youth? Debate in Japan over the 'non-existent youth bill'. *International Journal of Comic Art* 13(1): 348–67.

McLelland, M. 2012. Australia's 'child-abuse material' legislation, internet regulation and the juridification of the imagination. *International Journal of Cultural Studies* 15(5): 467–83.

McLelland, M. 2015. Sex, censorship and media regulation in Japan: a historical overview. In McLelland, M. and Mackie, V. (eds) *Routledge Handbook of Sexuality Studies in East Asia*. Abingdon: Routledge, 402–13.

McLelland, M. (ed.) 2016. *The End of Cool Japan: Ethical, Legal, and Cultural Challenges to Japanese Popular Culture*. New York: Routledge.

McLeod, D. M and MacKenzie, J.A. 1998. Print media and public reaction to the controversy over NEA funding for Robert Mapplethorpe's 'The Perfect Moment' exhibit. *Journalism and Mass Communication Quarterly* 75(2): 278–91.

McNair, B. 1996. *Mediated Sex: Pornography and Postmodern Culture*. London and New York: Arnold.

McNair, B. 2002. *Striptease Culture: Sex, Media and the Democratization of Desire*. London: Routledge.

McNair, B. 2012. *Porno? Chic!: How Pornography Changed the World and Made it a Better Place*. London: Routledge.

McNair, B. 2014. Rethinking the effects paradigm in porn studies. *Porn Studies* 1(1–2): 161–71.

MacNeill, K. 2010. When subject becomes object: nakedness, art and the public sphere. *Media International Australia* 135(1): 82–93.

MacRae, S. 1997. Flesh made word: sex text and the virtual body. In Porter, D. (ed.) *Internet Culture*. London: Routledge, 73–86.

Maddison, S. 2004. From porno-topia to total information awareness, or what forces really govern access to porn? *New Formations* 52: 35–57.

Maddison, S. 2009. 'Choke on it, bitch!' Porn studies, extreme gonzo and the mainstreaming of hard-core. In Attwood, F. (ed.) *Mainstreaming Sex: The Sexualization of Western Culture*. London: I.B. Tauris, 37–53.

Maddison, S. 2013. 'It's gonna hurt a little bit. But that's okay – it makes my cock feel good': Max Hardcore and the myth of pleasure. In Attwood, F., Campbell, V., Hunter, I.Q and Lockyer, S. (eds) *Controversial Images: Media Representations on the Edge*. Basingstoke: Palgrave Macmillan, 170–85.

Madonna 1992. *Sex*. New York: Warner Books.

References

Maes, H.R.V. (ed.) 2013. *Pornographic Art and the Aesthetics of Pornography*. Basingstoke: Palgrave Macmillan.

Maginn, P.J. and Steinmetz, C. (eds) 2014. *(Sub)urban Sexscapes: Geographies and Regulation of the Sex Industry*. London: Routledge.

Magnet, S. 2007. Feminist sexualities, race and the internet: an investigation of suicidegirls.com. *New Media and Society* 9(4): 577–602.

Maina, G. and Zecca, F. 2016a. Harder than fiction: the stylistic model of gonzo pornography. *Porn Studies* 3(4): 337–50.

Maina, G. and Zecca, F. 2016b. John Stagliano interviewed by Giovanna Maina and Federico Zecca. *Porn Studies* 3(4): 420–26.

Malz, W. and Malz, L. 2008. *The Porn Trap: A Guide to Healing from Porn Addiction, for Sufferers and Their Loved Ones*. New York: William Morrow Paperbacks.

Marr, D. 2008. *The Henson Case*. Melbourne: text publishing.

Marshall, B.L. 2010. Science, medicine and virility surveillance: 'sexy seniors' in the pharmaceutical imagination. *Sociology of Health and Illness* 32(2): 211–24.

Marshall, P.D. 2010. The promotion and presentation of the self: celebrity as marker of presentational media. *Celebrity Studies* 1(1): 35–48.

Martin, E. 1994. *Flexible Bodies*. Boston: Beacon Press.

Marvin, C. 1998. *When Old Technologies Were New: Thinking About Electric Communication in the Nineteenth Century*. Oxford: Oxford University Press.

Marwick, A.E. 2008. To catch a predator? The MySpace moral panic. *First Monday* 13(6), http://firstmonday.org/htbin/cgiwrap/bin/ojs/index.php/fm/article/viewArticle/2152.

Masanet, M. and Buckingham, D. 2015. Advice on life? Online fan forums as a space for peer-to-peer sex and relationships education. *Sex Education* 15 (5): 486–99.

Mathijs, E. 2011. Exploitation film. Oxford Bibliographies Online, www.oxfordbibliographies.com/view/document/obo-9780199791286/obo-9780199791286-0096.xml.

Mendik, X. 2012. *Peep Shows: Cult Film and the Cine-Erotic*. London: Wallflower Press.

Mercer, J. 2012. Coming of age: problematizing gay porn and the eroticized older man. *Journal of Gender Studies* 21(3): 313–26.

Mercer, J. 2017. *Gay Pornography: Representations of Sexuality and Masculinity*. London: I.B. Tauris.

METRO, 2014. Mental health and wellbeing, www.metrocentreonline.org/mental-health.

Mey, K. 2006. *Art and Obscenity*. London: I.B. Tauris.

Meyer, R. 2003. The Jesse Helms Theory of Art. *October* 104: 131–148.

Midori 2001. *The Seductive Art of Japanese Bondage*. San Francisco: Greenery Press.

References

Miller, V. 2008. New media, networking and phatic culture. *Convergence* 14(4): 387–400.

Millett, K. 1969. *Sexual Politics*. New York: Granada Publishing.

Mowlabocus, S. 2007. Gay men and the pornification of everyday life. In Paasonen, S., Nikunen, K. and Saarenmaa, L. (eds) *Pornification: Sex and Sexuality in Media Culture*. Oxford: Berg, 61–71.

Mowlabocus, S. 2010. *Gaydar Culture: Gay Men, Technology and Embodiment in the Digital Age*. Farnham: Ashgate.

Mitchell, A., Patrick, K., Heywood, W., Blackman, P. and Pitts, M. 2014. *5th National Survey of Australian Secondary Students and Sexual Health 2013*. Melbourne: La Trobe University.

Mitchell, K.J., Finkelhor, D., Jones, L.M. and Wolak, J. 2012. Prevalence and characteristics of youth sexting: a national study. *Pediatrics* 129(1): 13–20.

Mulholland, M. 2011. When porno meets hetero: sexpo, heteronormativity and the pornification of the mainstream. *Australian Feminist Studies* 26(67): 119–35.

Mulholland, M. 2013. *Young People and Pornography: Negotiating Pornification*. New York: Palgrave.

Munro, M. 2008. *Understanding Shunga: A Guide to Japanese Erotic Art*. London: Erotic Review Books.

Nagaike, K. and Suganuma, K. 2013. Transnational boys' love fan studies. *Transformative Works and Cultures* 12, http://journal.transformativeworks. org/index.php/twc/article/view/504/394.

Nagle, J. (ed.) 1997. *Whores and Other Feminists*. New York: Routledge.

Napier, S. 2005. *Anime from Akira to Howl's Moving Castle*. New York: Palgrave Macmillan.

Nash, J.C. 2008. Re-thinking intersectionality. *Feminist Review* 89: 1–15.

Nead, L. 1992. *The Female Nude: Art, Obscenity and Sexuality*. London and New York: Routledge.

Needham, G. 2017. 'Not on public display': the art/porn debate. In Smith, C. and Attwood, F. (eds) *The Routledge Companion to Media, Sex and Sexuality*. Abingdon and New York: Routledge, 163–73.

Nestle, J. 1984. The fem question. In Vance, C.S. (ed.) *Pleasure and Danger: Exploring Female Sexuality*. London: Routledge, 232–41.

Newmahr, S. 2010. Rethinking kink: sadomasochism as serious leisure. *Qualitative Sociology* 33(3): 313–31.

Nielson, S., Paasonen, S. and Spisak, S. 2015. 'Pervy role-play and such': girls' experiences of sexual messaging online. *Sex Education* 15(5): 472–85.

Nixon, P. and Düsterhöft, I. (eds) 2017. *Sex in the Digital Age*. Farnham: Ashgate.

Nixon, S. and du Gay, P. 2002. Who needs cultural intermediaries?. *Cultural Studies* 16(4): 495–500.

O'Brien, J. and Shapiro, E. 2004. 'Doing it' on the Web: emerging discourses on internet sex. In Gauntlett, G. and Horsley, R. (eds) *Web Studies*. London: Arnold, 114–26.

Odzer, C. 1997. *Virtual Spaces: Sex and the Cyber Citizen*. New York: Berkley Books.

Olson, I. 2016. Too extreme: gonzo, snuff, and governmentality. *Porn Studies* 3(4): 398–410.

Oppliger, P. 2008. *Girls Gone Skank: The Sexualization of Girls in American Culture*. Jefferson: McFarland.

Ortega-Brena, M. 2009. Peek-a-boo, I see you: watching Japanese hard-core animation. *Sexuality and Culture* 13(1): 17–31.

Osgerby, B. 2001. *Playboys in Paradise: Masculinity, Youth and Leisure-style in Modern America*. Oxford and New York: Berg.

Paasonen, S. 2010a. Good amateurs: erotica writing and notions of quality. In Attwood, F. (ed.) *Porn.com: Making Sense of Online Pornography*. New York: Peter Lang, 138–54.

Paasonen, S. 2010b. Repetition and hyperbole: the gendered choreographies of heteroporn. In Boyle, K. (ed.) *Everyday Pornography*. London: Routledge, 63–76.

Paasonen, S. 2010c. Labors of love: netporn, Web 2.0, and the meanings of ama-teurism. *New Media and Society* 12(8): 1297–1312.

Paasonen, S. 2011. *Carnal Resonance: Affect and Online Pornography*. Cambridge: MIT Press.

Paasonen, S. forthcoming a. The affective and affectless bodies of Monster Toon Porn. In Nixon, P. and Düsterhöft, I. (eds) *Sex in the Digital Age*. Farnham: Ashgate.

Paasonen, S. forthcoming b. Many splendored things: sexuality, playfulness and play. *Sexualities*.

Paasonen, S., Nikunen, K. and Saarenmaa, L. (eds) 2007. *Pornification: Sex and Sexuality in Media Culture*. Oxford: Berg.

Pagliasotti, D. 2009. GloBLisation and hybridisation: publishers' strategies for bringing boys' love to the United States. *Intersections: Gender and Sexuality in Asia and the Pacific* 20, http://intersections.anu.edu.au/issue20/pagliassotti.htm.

Papacharissi, Z. 2010. *A Private Sphere: Democracy in a Digital Age*. Cambridge: Polity.

Papadopoulos, L. 2010. *Sexualisation of Young People Review*. London: Home Office, http://webarchive.nationalarchives.gov.uk/+/http:/www.homeoffice.gov.uk/documents/sexualisation-of-young-people.pdf.

Parks, L. 2010. Aussie youth play it safe when it comes to sex info. Family Planning New South Wales, www.fpnsw.org.au/851916_3.html. Accessed 12 August 2010.

Pascoe, C.J. 2005. 'Dude, you're a fag': adolescent masculinity and the fag dis-course. *Sexualities* 8(3): 329–46.

Penley, C. 1997. Crackers and whackers: the white trashing of porn. In Wray, M. and Newitz, A. (eds) *White Trash: Race and Class in America.* London and New York: Routledge, 89–112.

Perdue, L. 2011. EroticaBiz: how sex shaped the internet. In Waskul, D.D. (ed.) *Net.seXXX: Readings on Sex, Pornography, and the Internet.* New York: Peter Lang, 259–94.

Perraudin, F. 2014. Social porn: why people are sharing their sex lives online. *Guardian,* 18 March, www.theguardian.com/lifeandstyle/2014/mar/18/social-porn-sharing-sex-lives-online-porntube-pinsex-pornostagram-pornography.

Petley, J. 2009. *Censorship: A Beginner's Guide.* London: Oneworld.

Petley, J. 2012. Punishing the peep show: carnality and the Dangerous Images Acts. In Mendik, X. (ed.) *Peep Shows: Cult Film and the Cine-Erotic.* London: Wallflower Press, 251–63.

Phoenix, A. 2011. Review of recent literature for the Bailey Review of commercialisation and sexualisation of childhood: Childhood Wellbeing Research Centre, www.cwrc.ac.uk/projects/documents/CWRC_commercialisationsexualisation_review_final_WP_No_2.pdf.

Pilcher, J. 2010. What not to wear? Girls, clothing and 'showing' the body. *Children and Society* 24(6): 461–70.

Pilcher, T. 2008. *Erotic Comics: A Graphic History from Tijuana Bibles to Underground Comix.* New York: Abrams.

Plummer, K. 1981. Going gay: identities, life cycles and lifestyles in the male gay world. In Hart, J. and Richardson, D. (eds) *The Theory and Practice of Homosexuality.* London: Routledge and Kegan Paul, 93–110.

Plummer, K. 2001. The square of intimate citizenship. *Citizenship Studies* 5(3): 237–53.

Plummer, K. 2003a. Re-presenting sexualities in the media. *Sexualities* 6(3): 275–6.

Plummer, K. 2003b. *Intimate Citizenship: Private Decisions and Public Dialogues.* Seattle and London: University of Washington Press.

Plummer, K. 2008. Studying sexualities for a better world? Ten years of *Sexualities. Sexualities* 11(1–2): 7–22.

Plummer, K. 2012. Critical sexualities studies. In Ritzer, G. (ed.) *The Wiley-Blackwell Companion to Sociology.* Chichester: Wiley-Blackwell, 243–68.

Polchin, J. 2013. Culture shock. The Smart Set, 3 November, http://thesmartset.com/article11031301.

Poster, M. 2004. The information empire. *Comparative Literature Studies* 41(3): 317–34.

Potts, A. 1998. The science/fiction of sex: John Gray's 'Mars and Venus in the Bedroom'. *Sexualities* 1(2): 153–73.

Potts, A. 2002. *The Science/Fiction of Sex: Feminist Deconstruction and the Vocabularies of Heterosex.* London: Routledge.

References

Potts, A. 2005. Cyborg masculinity in the Viagra era. *Sexualities, Evolution and Gender* 7(1): 3–16.

Proctor, L. 2015. Troubling the margins between intimacy and anonymity: queer(y)ing the virtual sex industry in Second Life. In Laing, M., Pilcher, K. and Smith, N. (eds) *Queer Sex Work*. Abingdon: Routledge, 151–63.

Prough, J.S. 2011. *Straight from the Heart: Gender, Intimacy, and the Cultural Production of Shojo Manga*. Honolulu: University of Hawai'i Press.

Queen, C. 1997. Sex radical politics, sex-positive feminist thought, and whore stigma. In Nagle, J. (ed.) *Whores and Other Feminists*. New York: Routledge, 125–35.

Queen, C. and Comella, L. 2008. The necessary revolution: sex-positive feminism in the post-Barnard era. *The Communication Review* 11(3): 274–91.

Race, K. 2015. 'Party and play': online hook-up devices and the emergence of PNP practices among gay men. *Sexualities* 18(3): 253–75.

Radner, H. and Luckett, M. (eds) 1999. *Swinging Single: Representing Sexuality in the 1960s*. Minneapolis: University of Minnesota Press.

Railton, D. 2017. Sex and music video. In Smith, C. and Attwood, F. (eds) *The Routledge Companion to Media, Sex and Sexuality*. Abingdon and New York: Routledge, 259–7.

Railton, C. and Watson, P. 2011. *Music Video and the Politics of Representation*. Edinburgh: Edinburgh University Press.

Ray, A. 2007. *Naked on the Internet: Hookups, Downloads and Cashing in on Internet Sexploration*. Emeryville: Seal Press.

Reay, B., Attwood, N. and Gooder, C. 2013. Inventing sex: the short history of sex addiction. *Sexuality and Culture* 17(1): 1–19.

Renner, K.J. 2012. Monstrous schoolgirls: casual sex in the twenty-first-century horror film. *Red Feather: An International Journal of Children's Visual Culture* 3(2): 34–50.

Renold, E. and Ringrose, J. 2011. Schizoid subjectivities? Re-theorising teen-girls' sexual cultures in an era of 'sexualisation'. *Journal of Sociology* 47(4): 389–409.

Renold, E. and Ringrose, J. 2013. Introduction: feminisms re-figuring 'sexualisation', sexuality and 'the girl'. *Feminist Theory* 14(3): 247–54.

Renold, E., Ringrose, J. and Egan, R.D. (eds) 2015. *Children, Sexuality and Sexualisation*. Basingstoke: Palgrave Macmillan.

Reuhl, S. 1982. Inverts and experts: Radclyffe Hall and the lesbian identity. In Brunt, R. and Rowan, C. (eds) *Feminism, Culture and Politics*. London: Lawrence and Wishart, 15–36.

Rheingold, H. 1991. *Virtual Reality*. New York: Summit.

Richards, C. and Barker, M. 2013. *Sexuality and Gender for Mental Health Professionals: A Practical Guide*. London: Sage.

Richardson, N. 2009. Effeminophobia, misogyny and queer friendship: the cultural themes of Channel 4's *Playing it Straight*. *Sexualities* 12(4): 525–44.

References

Richter, L. 2015. Rebel girl and the wrecking ball: the cruel optimism of empowerment and the revival of feminism in contemporary popular music. *Multilingual Discourses* 2(1–2): 173–205.

Ringrose, J. 2016. Postfeminist media panics over girls' 'sexualisation': implications for UK sex and relationship guidance and curriculum. In Sundaram, V. and Sauntson, H. (eds) *Global Perspectives and Key Debates in Sex and Relationships Education: Addressing Issues of Gender, Sexuality, Plurality and Power*. Basingstoke: Palgrave Macmillan, 30–47.

Ringrose, J. and Harvey, L. 2015. Boobs, back-off, six packs and bits: mediated body parts, gendered reward, and sexual shame in teens' sexting images. *Continuum* 29(2): 205–17.

Ringrose, J., Gill, R., Livingstone, S. and Harvey L. 2012. *A Qualitative Study of Children, Young People and 'Sexting'*. London: National Society for the Prevention of Cruelty to Children, www.nspcc.org.uk/globalassets/documents/research-reports/qualitative-study-children-young-people-sexting-report.pdf.

Ringrose, J., Harvey, L., Gill, R. and Livingstone, S. 2013. Teen girls, sexual double standards and 'sexting': gendered value in digital image exchange. *Feminist Theory* 14(3): 305–23.

Roberts, J. 2015. Girly porno comics: contemporary US pornographic comics for women. *Journal of Graphic Novels and Comics* 6(3): 214–29.

Robinson, K. 2013. *Innocence, Knowledge, and the Construction of Childhood: The Contradictory Nature of Sexuality and Censorship in Children's Contemporary Lives*. London: Routledge.

Rojek, C. 2000. *Leisure and Culture*. Basingstoke: Palgrave Macmillan.

Rolph, C.H. 1990. *The Trial of Lady Chatterley: Regina v. Penguin Books Limited*. London: Penguin.

Rosenfeld, M.J. and Thomas, R.J. 2012. Searching for a mate: the rise of the internet as a social intermediary. *American Sociological Review* 77(4): 523–47.

Ross, M. 2005. Typing, doing, and being: sexuality and the internet. *Journal of Sex Research* 42(4): 342–52.

Roth, Y. 2014. Locating the 'scruff guy': theorizing body and space in gay geosocial media. *International Journal of Communication* 8: 2113–33.

Rovolis, A. and Tsaliki, L. 2012. Pornography. In Livingstone, S., Haddon, L. and Görzig, A. (eds) *Children, Risk and Safety on the Internet*. Bristol: Policy Press, 165–76.

Ruberg, B. 2010. Sex as game: playing with the erotic body in virtual worlds. *Rhizomes* 21, www.rhizomes.net/issue21/ruberg.html.

Ruberg, B. 2016. Doing it for free: digital labour and the fantasy of amateur online pornography. *Porn Studies* 3(2): 147–59.

Rubin, G. 1984. Thinking sex: notes for a radical theory of the politics of sex. In Vance, C.S. (ed.) *Pleasure and Danger: Exploring Female Sexuality*. London: Routledge, 275–96.

References

Rubin, G. 1993. Misguided, dangerous and wrong. In Assiter, A. and Carol, A. (eds) *Bad Girls and Dirty Pictures: The Challenge to Reclaim Feminism*. London: Pluto Press, 1–17.

Rubin, G. 2006. Of catamites and kings: reflections on butch, gender, and boundaries. In Stryker, S. and Whittle, S. (eds) *The Transgender Studies Reader*. New York: Routledge, 471–81.

Rubin, G. 2011. Introduction: sex, gender, politics. In *Deviations: A Gayle Rubin Reader*. Durham: Duke University Press, 1–32.

Rush, E. 2009. What are the risks of premature sexualisation for children? In Tankard Reist, M. (ed.) *Getting Real: Challenging the Sexualisation of Girls*. Melbourne: Spinifex Press, 41–54.

Rush, E. and La Nauze, A. 2006. *Corporate Paedophilia: Sexualisation of Children in Australia*. Deakin: Australian Institute, www.tai.org.au/documents/dp_fulltext/DP90.pdf.

Russell, D. (ed.) 1993. *Making Violence Sexy: Feminist Views on Pornography*. New York: Teacher's College Press.

Russo, V. 1987. *The Celluloid Closet: Homosexuality in the Movies*. New York: HarperPaperbacks.

Ryberg, I. 2012. *Imagining Safe Spaces: The Politics of Queer, Feminist and Lesbian Pornography*. Stockholm: Acta Universitatis Stockholmiensis.

Ryberg, I. 2015. Carnal fantasizing: embodied spectatorship of queer, feminist and lesbian pornography. *Porn Studies* 2(2–3): 161–73.

Sabin, R. 1993. *Adult Comics: An Introduction*. London: Routledge.

Sabo, A.G. 2012. *After Pornified: How Women are Transforming Pornography and Why it Matters*. Winchester and Washington: Zero Books.

Samois 1981. *Coming to Power: Writings and Graphics on Lesbian S/M*. Palo Alto: Up Press.

Sanders-McDonagh, E., Peyrefitte, M. and Ryalls, M. 2016. Sanitising the city: exploring hegemonic gentrification in London's Soho. *Sociological Research Online* 21(3), www.socresonline.org.uk/21/3/3.html.

Scarcelli, C.M. 2015. 'It is disgusting, but. . .': adolescent girls' relationship to internet pornography as gender performance'. *Porn Studies* 2(2–3): 237–49.

Schaefer, E. 1999. *Bold! Daring! Shocking! True!: A History of Exploitation Films, 1919–1959*. Durham: Duke University Press.

Schaefer, E. 2008. The obscene seen: spectacle and transgression in postwar burlesque films. In Mathijs, E. and Mendik, X. (eds) *The Cult Film Reader*. Maidenhead: Open University Press, 186–99.

Schaefer, E. (ed.) 2014. *Sex Scene: Media and the Sexual Revolution*. Durham: Duke University Press.

Schaschek, S. 2013. *Pornography and Seriality: The Culture of Producing Pleasure*. Basingstoke: Palgrave.

Schippers, M. 2016. *Beyond Monogamy: Polyamory and the Future of Polyqueer Sexualities*. New York: New York University Press.

References

Sconce, J. 2007. *Sleaze Artists: Cinema at the Margins of Taste, Style, and Politics*. Durham and London: Duke University Press.

Scoular, J. and Sanders, T. 2010. Introduction: The Changing Social and Legal Context of Sexual Commerce: Why Regulation Matters. *Journal of Law and Society* 37(1): 1–11.

Sedgwick, E.K. 1990. *Epistemology of the Closet*. Berkeley: University of California Press.

Sedgwick, E.K. 1991. How to bring your kids up gay. *Social Text* (29): 18–27.

Segal, L. 1997. Sexualities. In Woodward, K. (ed.) *Identity and Difference*. London: Sage, 183–228.

Selby Jr., H. 1964. *Last Exit to Brooklyn*. New York: Grove Press.

Serano, J. 2007. *Whipping Girl: A Transsexual Woman on Sexism and the Scapegoating of Femininity*. Berkeley: Avalon Publishing Group.

Serano, J. 2013. *Excluded: Making Feminist and Queer Movements More Inclusive*. Berkeley: Avalon Publishing Group.

Shamoon, D. 2004. Office sluts and rebel flowers: the pleasures of Japanese pornographic comics for women. In Williams, L. (ed.) *Porn Studies*. Durham: Duke University Press, 77–103.

Shelley, M. 1818. *Frankenstein, or, The Modern Prometheus*. London: Lackington, Hughes, Harding, Mavor and Jones.

Shigematsu, S. 1999. Dimensions of desire: sex, fantasy, and fetish in Japanese comics. In Lent, J.A. (ed.) *Themes in Asian Cartooning: Cute, Cheap, Mad, and Sexy*. Bowling Green: Bowling Green State University Popular Press, 127–63.

Simon, W. 1996. *Postmodern Sexualities*. London: Routledge.

Simpson B. 2011. Sexualizing the child: the strange case of Bill Henson, his 'absolutely revolting' images and the law of childhood innocence. *Sexualities* 14(3): 290–311.

Simpson, B. 2013. Challenging childhood, challenging children: children's rights and sexting. *Sexualities* 16 (5–6): 690–709.

Sinfield, A. 1994. *The Wilde Century: Oscar Wilde, Effeminacy and the Queer Moment*. New York: Columbia University Press.

Singel, R. 2004. Internet porn. Worse than crack? *Wired*, 19 November, http://archive.wired.com/science/discoveries/news/2004/11/65772.

Skeggs, B. 2004. *Class, Self, Culture*. London: Routledge.

Slater, D. 1998. Trading sexpics on IRC: embodiment and authenticity on the internet. *Body and Society* 4(4): 91–117.

Smith, C. 2007. Designed for pleasure: style, indulgence and accessorized sex. *European Journal of Cultural Studies* 10(2): 167–84.

Smith, C. 2010a. Pornographication: a discourse for all seasons. *International Journal of Media and Cultural Politics* 6(1): 103–8.

Smith, C. 2010b. Review: Papadopoulos, Linda: *Sexualisation of Young People Review*, London: Home Office, February 2010, *Participations* 7(1), www.participations.org/Volume%207/Issue%201/papadopoulos.pdf.

References

Smith, C. 2011. Reel intercourse: doing sex on camera. In Kerr, D. and Hines, C. (eds) *Hard to Swallow? Reading Pornography on Screen*. New York: Columbia University Press, 194–214.

Smith, C. and Attwood, F. 2011. Lamenting sexualization: research, rhetoric and the story of young people's 'sexualization' in the UK Home Office review. *Sex Education* 11(3): 327–37.

Smith, C. and Attwood, F. 2013. Emotional truths and thrilling sideshows: the resurgence of anti-porn feminism. In Taormino, T., Parreñas Shimizu, C., Penley, C. and Miller-Young, M. (eds) *The Feminist Porn Book: The Politics of Producing Pleasure*. New York: The Feminist Press, 41–57.

Smith, C. and Attwood, F. 2014. Anti/pro/critical porn studies. *Porn Studies* 1(1–2): 7–23.

Smith, C. and Attwood, F. 2017. *The Routledge Handbook of Media, Sex and Sexuality*. London: Routledge.

Smith, C., Barker, M. and Attwood, F. 2015a. Teenage kicks: Die Auseinandersetzung junger Menschen mit Pornografie, Ergebnisse des porn-research.org-Fragebogens. In Andergassen, L., Claasesen, T., Grawinkel, K., Meier, M. (eds) *Explicit! Neue Perspektiven zu Pornographie und Gesellschaft*. Berlin: Bertz + Fischer, 45–63.

Smith, C., Barker, M. and Attwood, F. 2015b. Why do people watch porn? In Comella, L. and Tarrant, S. (eds) *New Views on Pornography: Sexuality, Politics, and the Law*. Santa Barbara: Praeger, 267–86.

Smith, M. and Morra, J. 2006. *The Prosthetic Impulse: From a Posthuman Present to a Biocultural Future*. Cambridge: MIT Press.

Soderlund, G. 2008. Journalist or panderer? Framing underage webcam sites. *Sexuality Research and Social Policy* 5(4): 62–72.

Solomon-Godeau, A. 1991. *Photography at the Dock: Essays on Photographic History, Institutions, and Practices*. Minneapolis: University of Minnesota Press.

Souhami, D. 1998. *The Trials of Radclyffe Hall*. London: Weidenfeld and Nicolson.

Spanier, G.B. 1975. Sexualisation and premarital sexual behaviour. *The Family Coordinator* 24(1): 33–41.

Spencer, G., Maxwell, C. and Aggleton, P. 2008. What does 'empowerment' mean in school-based sex and relationship education? *Sex Education* 8(3): 345–56.

Spisak, S. and Paasonen, S. 2016. Bad education? Childhood recollections of pornography, sexual exploration, learning and agency in Finland. *Childhood* 24(1): 99–112.

Sprott, S. 2010. Cosey Fanni Tutti, *Vice*, 1 November, www.vice.com/en_uk/read/cosey-fanni-tutti-597-v17n11.

Stapleton, A. 2012. Border patrol: Trevor Brown, aesthetics and the protection of fictitious children. In Attwood, F., Campbell, V., Hunter, I.Q. and Lockyer,

References

S. (eds) *Controversial Images: Media Representations on the Edge*. London: Palgrave Macmillan, 115–30.

Stardust, Z. 2014. Fisting is not permitted: criminal intimacies, queer sexualities and feminist porn in the Australian legal context. *Porn Studies* 1(3): 242–59.

Stasi, M. 2006. The toy soldiers from Leeds. In Hellekson, K. and Busse, K. (eds) *Fan Fiction and Fan Communities in the Age of the Internet*. Jefferson: McFarland, 115–33.

Steinbock, E. 2017. Representing trans sexualities. In Smith, C. and Attwood, F. (eds) *The Routledge Companion to Media, Sex and Sexuality*. Abingdon and New York: Routledge, 27–37.

Stengers, J., Van Neck, A., Hoffmann, K.A. and Van, A. 2001. *Masturbation: The History of a Great Terror*. New York: Palgrave Macmillan.

Stone, N. 2011. The 'sexting' quagmire: criminal justice responses to adolescents' electronic transmission of indecent images in the UK and the USA. *Youth Justice* 11(3): 266–81.

Storey, J. 2001. 'Expecting rain': opera as popular culture?. In Collins, J. (ed.) *High-Pop: Making Culture into Popular Entertainment*. Oxford: Blackwell, 32–55.

Storey, J. 2003. *Inventing Popular Culture: From Folklore to Globalisation*. Oxford: Blackwell.

Storr, M. 2003. *Latex and Lingerie: Shopping for Pleasure at Ann Summers Parties*. Oxford: Berg.

Strub, W. 2011. *Perversion for Profit: The Politics of Pornography and the Rise of the New Right*. New York: Columbia University Press.

Strub, W. 2013. *Obscenity Rules: Roth v. United States and the Long Struggle Over Sexual Expression*. Lawrence: University Press of Kansas.

Strub, W. 2015. Queer smut, queer rights. In Comella, L. and Tarrant, S. (eds) *New Views on Pornography: Sexuality, Politics, and the Law*. Santa Barbara: Praeger, 147–64.

Studlar, G. 1989. Midnight s/excess: cult configurations of femininity and the perverse. *Journal of Popular Film and Television* 17(10): 2–14.

Sullivan, R. and McKee, A. 2015. *Pornography: Structures, Agency and Performance*. Cambridge: Polity.

Summers, F. 2012. What a body can do: from the frenzy of the communicative to the visual bond, http://eitherand.org/exhibitionism/what-can-body-do-frenzy-communicative-visual-bond.

Tait, S. 2008. Pornographies of violence? Internet spectatorship on body horror. *Critical Studies in Media Communication* 25(1): 91–111.

Tang, I. and Bailey, F. 1999. *Pornography: The Secret History of Civilization*. London: Channel 4 Books.

Tankard Reist, M. 2009. *Getting Real: Challenging the Sexualisation of Girls*. Melbourne: Spinifex Press.

References

Tarrant, S. 2016. *The Pornography Industry: What Everyone Needs to Know.* Oxford: Oxford University Press.

Taylor, Y., Hines, S. and Casey, M. 2010. *Theorizing Intersectionality and Sexuality.* Basingstoke: Palgrave Macmillan.

Terranova, T. 2000. Free labor: producing culture for the digital economy. *Social Text* 63 (18/2): 33–58.

Thornton, S. 1997. The social logic of subcultural capital. In Gelder, K. (ed.) *The Subcultures Reader.* London: Routledge, 200–9.

Tibbals, C.A. 2010. From The Devil in Miss Jones to DMJ6: power, inequality, and consistency in the content of US adult films. *Sexualities* 13(5): 625–44.

Tiefer, L. 2004. *Sex is Not a Natural Act, and Other Essays.* 2nd edn. Boulder: Westview Press.

Tiefer, L. 2006. The Viagra phenomenon. *Sexualities* 9(3): 273–94.

Tiefer, L. 2015. Women's sexual problems: is there a pill for that? In McHugh, M.C. and Chrisler, J.C. (eds) *The Wrong Prescription for Women: How Medicine and Media Create a 'Need' for Treatments, Drugs, and Surgery*: Santa Barbara: Praeger, 147–60.

Topp, S.S. 2013. Against the quiet revolution: the rhetorical construction of intersex individuals as disordered. *Sexualities* 16 (1–2): 180–94.

Tosenberger, C. 2008. Homosexuality at the online Hogwarts: Harry Potter slash fanfiction. *Children's Literature* 36: 185–207.

Tsaliki, L. 2015. Popular culture and moral panics about 'children at risk': revisiting the sexualisation-of-young-girls debate. *Sex Education* 15(5): 500–14.

Tsaliki, L., Chronaki, D. and Ólafsson, K. 2014. Experiences with sexual content: what we know from the research so far, www.lse.ac.uk/media@lse/research/EUKidsOnline/EU%20Kids%20III/Reports/SexualContent.pdf.

Turkle, S. 1997. *Life on the Screen: Identity in the Age of the Internet.* New York: Touchstone.

Turkle, S. 2011. *Alone Together: Why We Expect More from Technology and Less from Each Other.* New York: Basic Books.

Tyler, I. and Bennett, B. 2010. 'Celebrity chav': fame, femininity and social class. *European Journal of Cultural Studies* 13(3): 375–93.

Tziallas, E. 2015. Gamified eroticism: gay male 'social networking' applications and self-pornography. *Sexuality and Culture* 19(4): 759–75.

UN 2010. The world's women, http://unstats.un.org/unsd/demographic/products/Worldswomen/WW2010pub.htm.

UNESCO Institute for Statistics 2013. Adult and youth literacy, www.uis.unesco.org/literacy/Documents/fs26-2013-literacy-en.pdf.

UNICEF 2013. Child well-being in rich countries: a comparative overview, www.unicef-irc.org/publications/pdf/rc11_eng.pdf.

Ussher, J.M. 1997. *Fantasies of Femininity: Reframing the Boundaries of Sex.* London: Penguin.

References

Vance, C.S. (ed.) 1984. *Pleasure and Danger: Exploring Female Sexuality.* London: Routledge.

van Doorn, N. 2010. Keeping it real: user-generated pornography, gender reification, and visual pleasure. *Convergence* 16(4): 411–30.

van Zoonen, L. 1994. *Feminist Media Studies.* Thousand Oaks: SAGE.

Vares, T. 2009. Reading the 'sexy oldie': gender, age(ing) and embodiment. *Sexualities* 12(4): 503–24

Vares, T., Jackson, S. and Gill, R. 2011. Preteen girls read 'tween' popular culture. *International Journal of Media and Cultural Politics* 7(2): 139–54.

Vicinus, M. 1982. Sexuality and power: a review of current work in the history of sexuality. *Feminist Studies* 8(1): 133–56.

Viljoen, P.O. 2013. *He Never Saw Me Naked. Sex After 60: Enjoying Sex After Turning 60.* Kindle Edition.

Volcano, D.L. and Dahl, U. 2008. *Femmes of Power: Exploding Queer Femininities.* London: Serpent's Tail.

Volcano, D.L. and Halberstam, J.J. 1999. *The Drag King Book.* London: Serpent's Tail.

Waites, M. 2005. *The Age of Consent: Young People, Sexuality and Citizenship.* Basingstoke: Palgrave Macmillan.

Walters, N. 2010. *Living Dolls: The Return of Sexism.* London: Virago.

Walz, T. 2002. Crones, dirty old men, sexy seniors: representations of the sexuality of older persons. *Journal of Aging and Identity* 7(2): 99–112.

Warner, M. 1999. *The Trouble With Normal: Sex, Politics, and the Ethics of Queer Life.* 2nd edn. New York: Free Press.

Ward, J. 2015. *Not Gay: Sex Between Straight White Men.* New York: New York University Press.

Waskul, D.D. 2003. *Self-Games and Body-Play: Personhood in Online Chat and Cybersex.* New York: Peter Lang.

Waskul, D.D. 2006. Internet sex: the seductive 'freedom to'. In Seidman, S. Fischer, N. and Meeks, C. (eds) *Introducing the New Sexuality Studies.* London: Routledge, 281–9.

Waskul, D.D. and Martin, J. 2010. 'Now the orgy is over'. *Symbolic Interaction* 33(2): 297–318.

Waskul, D.D. and Vannini, P. 2008. Ludic and ludic(rous) relationships: sex, play, and the internet. In Holland, S. (ed.) *Remote Relationships in a Small World.* New York: Peter Lang, 241–61.

Watson, A.-F. and McKee, A. 2013. Masturbation and the media. *Sexuality and Culture* 17 (3): 449–75.

Watson, A.-F. 2017. Young people, sexuality education and the media. In Smith, C. and Attwood, F. (eds) *The Routledge Companion to Media, Sex and Sexuality.* Abingdon and New York: Routledge, 223–36.

Watson, T. 2013. There's something rotten in the state of Texas: genre,

References

adaptation and *The Texas Vibrator Massacre*. *Journal of Adaptation in Film and Performance* 6(3): 387–400.

Waugh, T. 1985. Men's pornography: gay vs. straight. *Jump Cut: A Review of Contemporary Media* 30: 30–5.

Weait, M. 2007. Sadomasochism and the law. In Langdridge, D. and Barker, M. (eds) *Safe, Sane and Consensual: Contemporary Perspectives on Sadomasochism*. Basingstoke: Palgrave Macmillan, 63–84.

Weeks, J. 1977. *Coming Out: Homosexual Politics in Britain, from the Nineteenth Century to the Present*. London: Quartet Books.

Weeks, J. 1998. The sexual citizen. *Theory, Culture and Society* 15(3–4): 35–52.

Weeks, J. 2007. *The World We Have Won: The Remaking of Erotic and Intimate Life*. London and New York: Routledge.

Weiss, A. 1993. *Vampires and Violets: Lesbians in Film*. New York: Penguin Books.

Weitzer, R. 2011. Pornography's effects: the need for solid evidence. *Violence Against Women* 17(5): 666–75.

WHO 2006. Defining sexual health: report of a technical consultation on sexual health. Geneva: World Health Organization, www.who.int/reproductivehealth/publications/sexual_health/defining_sexual_health.pdf.

WHO 2016. Violence against women, www.who.int/mediacentre/factsheets/fs239/en.

Wilkinson, E. 2011. 'Extreme pornography' and the contested spaces of virtual citizenship. *Social and Cultural Geography* 12(5): 493–508.

Willard, N. 2010. Sexting and youth: achieving a rational response. Centre for Safe and Responsible Internet Use, www.cyberbully.org/documents/sexting.pdf.

Williams, L. 1989. *Hard Core: Power, Pleasure and the 'Frenzy of the Visible'*. London: Pandora.

Williams, L. 1991. Film bodies: gender, genre, excess. *Film Quarterly* 44(4): 2–13.

Williams, L. 1999. *Hard Core: Power, Pleasure and the 'Frenzy of the Visible'*. Expanded edn. Berkeley: University of California Press.

Williams, L. 2004a. *Porn Studies*. Durham: Duke University Press.

Williams, L. 2004b. Second thoughts on hard core: American obscenity and the scapegoating of deviance. In Church Gibson, P. (ed.) *More Dirty Looks*. London: BFI, 165–75.

Williams, L. 2008. *Screening Sex*. Durham: Duke University Press.

Williams, L.R. 2005. *The Erotic Thriller in Contemporary Cinema*. Bloomington: Indiana University Press.

Williams, R. 1976. *Keywords: A Vocabulary of Culture and Society*. Oxford: Oxford University Press.

Wimmer, L. 2013. Forever *Emmanuelle*: Sylvia Kristel and soft-core cult

References

stardom. In Egan, K. and Thomas, S. (eds) 2013. *Cult Film Stardom: Offbeat Attractions and Processes of Cultification*. Basingstoke: Palgrave Macmillan, 197–211.

Witt, E. 2016. *Future Sex*. New York: Farrar, Straus and Giroux.

Wolak, J., Finkelhor, D. and Mitchell, K.J. 2012. How often are teens arrested for sexting? Data from a national sample of police cases. *Podiatrics* 129(1): 4–12.

Wolkowitz, C., Cohen, R.L., Sanders, T. and Hardy, K. (eds) 2013. *Body/Sex/ Work: Intimate, Embodied and Sexualised Labour*. Basingstoke: Palgrave Macmillan.

Wood, A. 2013. Boys' love anime and queer desires in convergence culture: transnational fandom, censorship and resistance. *Journal of Graphic Novels and Comics* 4(1): 44–63.

The World Bank 2012. Gender equality and development, https://openknowl edge.worldbank.org/handle/10986/4391.

Wouters, C. 2004. *Sex and Manners: Female Emancipation in the West 1890–2000*. London: Sage.

Wouters, C. 2007. *Informalization: Manners and Emotions Since 1890*. London: Sage.

Wysocki, M. and Lauteria, E.W. 2015. *Rated M for Mature: Sex and Sexuality in Video Games*. London: Bloomsbury Academic

Yeoman, I. and Mars, M. 2012. Robots, men and sex tourism. *Futures* 44: 365–71.

Yep, G.A. 2002. From homophobia and heterosexism to heteronormativity: toward the development of a model of queer interventions in the university classroom. *Journal of Lesbian Studies* 6(3–4): 163–76.

Zanghellini, A. 2009. Underage sex and romance in Japanese homoerotic manga and anime. *Social and Legal Studies* 18(2): 159–77.

Zecca, F. 2014. Porn sweet home: a survey of amateur pornography. In Biasin, E., Maina, G. and Zecca, F. (eds) *Porn After Porn: Contemporary Alternative Pornographies*. Milan: Mimesis International, 321–38.

Zelizer, V.R.A. 2005. *The Purchase of Intimacy*. Princeton: Princeton University Press.

Ziplow, S. 1977. *Film Maker's Guide to Pornography*. New York: Drake Publishers.

Ziv, A. 2015. *Explicit Utopias: Rewriting the Sexual in Women's Pornography*. New York: SUNY Press.

Zopol, F. 2009. *The Sex Instruction Manual: Essential Information and Techniques for Optimum Performance*. Philadelphia: Quirk Books.

Index

adultification, 127
aesthetics, 78, 82–3, 87
agender, 10
amateur porn, 97–9, 110, 116
androgyny, 10
animated pornography, 94
animation, comics and gaming (ACG), 58, 98
anime, 94
art cinema, 101
artificiality, 127
asexuality, 7, 8, 9, 122
authenticity, 115–16, 127–8

BDSM, 9, 20, 51, 87, 105, 122, 133
benign sexual variation, 15, 31
binaries, 2, 9, 10, 11, 24, 31
biological differentiation, 7
bisexuality, 7, 8, 9, 70, 122
body genres, 84, 111, 132
body image, 64, 67, 124
body work, 124
bounded authenticity, 115–16
boys' love/BL, 94–5

carnivalesque, 104
charmed circle of sex, 16, 17, 25
child, the figure of 65, 66, 69, 75, 81
cine-erotic, 99, 101
cisgender, 10, 14, 24
cisnormativity, 14, 133
cissexism, 23
comics, 58, 94, 95, 98
commerce, 16, 20, 29, 114–16
consent, 52, 54, 55, 64, 129, 131, 133
consumption, 26, 46, 68, 83, 106

content, media, 80, 83–4, 86, 87, 90, 93
context, media, 76, 80, 83, 85, 87, 89
corporatization of intimacy, 117
counterculture, 18
critical sexuality studies, 22–3
cult film, 101
cultural capital, 86, 89
cultural hierarchy, 84, 111
cultural value, 41, 45, 86
cybersex, 107–9, 120
cyborgs, 125

dogging, 105, 111
dōjinshi, 98
domesticated pornographies, 92
drawn pornography, 93–6, 99

entertainment, 78, 84, 104
episodic sex, 121
ero manga, 94
erotic thriller, 86, 101
erotica, 4, 86, 90, 91
ethical decision-making, 132–3
essence, biological, 8, 13
excess, 3, 45, 47, 60, 98
exploitation and film, 99–100
extreme pornography, 50

fan cultures, 98
feminism, 19, 20–4, 59, 63
free speech, 45

gay liberation, 19
gender, 7, 8, 10, 11
    and sexual diversity (GSD), 9, 24, 133
    and sexual equalities, 70–1

203

Index

#CARLOS'S
PLACES

#travels#trips#tips#food#fashion#art#hotels#cities#friends

Cover photo: © Pablo Arroyo

© 2014 Assouline Publishing
601 West 26th Street, 18th Floor
New York, NY 10001, USA
Tel.: 212 989-6810 Fax: 212 647-0005
assouline.com
ISBN: 9781614282440
Design by Cécilia Maurin.
Printed in China.

CARLOS SOUZA

#CARLOS'S PLACES

#travels#trips#tips#food#fashion#art#hotels#cities#friends

ASSOULINE

#MOMA

The MoMA is one of my favorite
spots in New York City—so many
memorable exhibitions, like the recent
Richard Serra show, and the garden
is absolutely wonderful.

#FOREWORD

Carlos Souza is a preternaturally sunny, globe-trotting Brazilian of arresting style who, for more years than either of us would probably care to remember, calibrated the exacting calendar of Valentino Garavani, the legendarily social Roman couturier and one of the planet's most inexhaustible bon viveurs. As consigliere to this evergreen testament to jet-set living, and being an inveterate sun-seeker, Carlos has long traversed a world awash with loveliness and beautiful people, recording an astonishing degree of hedonistic activity and general good times along the way. Utilizing only the camera of his cellphone and his insatiable eye, he has redacted all this into a helter-skelter mosaic of international sights and sensations that run from Old World pavements to New World penthouses, leaving behind an amusing medley of hashtags.

Whichever city or paradisiacal location heads the latest top-ten lists, it is no surprise to discover the freewheeling Carlos was often there first, mapping out the coolest "in" spots and hottest "in" folk, powered by his truffle-hound instincts for uncovering the shiniest examples of "nowness."

Inhabiting the epicenter of high fashion (he is currently Worldwide Brand Ambassador for the house of Valentino) has also afforded him numerous occasions for sampling hotels with the most superior facilities, restaurants that offer the most intriguing local fare, cultural scenes that promise the most heightened experiences, and beaches that hold the cutest crowds. Ever eager to explore diverse, fun events, his gregarious personality is as comfortable with a shopping mall gala in Shanghai as it is with a gallery opening in Mayfair.

It may well be that some will consider this hectic series of glossy and sybaritic experiences an unlikely manual for curious backpackers or cozy armchair travelers. It is not an obvious must-have for those less than impressed with celebrity lifestyles or those not inclined to think the view from a ski lift above Gstaad is the closest thing to heaven. Its appeal might also elude those aesthetes confronted by the glossy armada of multi-million dollar yachts lined up at the Venice film festival or anyone who has a deep-seated aversion to palatial furniture, red carpet shindigs, goofy selfies with Hollywood stars, and fondue parties in Swiss chalets. But for all who thrill to a non-stop agenda of sun-kissed lotus-eating, louche nightclubbing, couture fittings, and impressively deep perma-tanning, Carlos (a firm believer in living well being the best revenge) provides a celebratory peephole into all these otherworldly lifestyles through his one-of-a-kind lens. And for any who feel their stamina flagging the morning after, he can be relied on for the occasional health tip, too. For instance, the last time we met, on the sidewalk of Rio de Janeiro, he ushered me off to a local juice bar and inveigled me into drinking a glutinous, unappealing pick-me-up of berries. It turned out to be the most nutritious and invigorating thing I ever tasted.

Michael Roberts

GSTAAD

GSTAAD IS A SMALL, *idyllic* SWISS VILLAGE WHERE I HAVE CELEBRATED NEW YEAR'S EVE WITH VALENTINO AND A GROUP OF FRIENDS FOR *the past thirty years*. PART OF THE CHARM IN COMING TO GSTAAD IS THAT THINGS SEEM TO STAY THE SAME. ALL THE BUILDINGS MUST BE BUILT IN THE SWISS *chalet style*, AND THIS HAS THE EFFECT OF CREATING A VERY *traditional feeling*. I ENJOY WALKING AROUND THE QUAINT MOUNTAIN VILLAGE, REVISITING OLD HAUNTS LIKE HOTEL OLDEN, THE HOTEL ALPINA, AND THE *exclusive* EAGLE SKI CLUB.

#SLOW LIFE

Wasserngrat mountain reminds
me of the permanence of nature,
and the slow life. When I was
younger the pace of life in Switzerland
was too slow for my vibrant energy,
but now I really love the sense
of serenity I get when I am here.

#LA
VIDEMANETTE

Above (left): Émincé de veau à la zurichoise with rösti, one of my favorite traditional Swiss meals. *Above (right):* Frost covers the trees here in a way unlike anywhere else, and creates a beautiful lace pattern that I can look at and photograph for hours. *Left:* Such beautiful mountains in Gstaad, like La Videmanette.

#RACLETTE
I LOVE RACLETTE

The original, traditional fondue, that is best had with *Pfümli*— alcohol blanc—otherwise you will have a tennis ball in your stomach the next day.

#NEW YEAR'S EVE PARTY
WITH ANNE HATHAWAY
In front of a Claude Lalanne "gorilla" wood-burning fireplace.

#THE GANG

Right: Valentino and me in his chalet.
Below: Every year a gang of friends
meets at Valentino's chalet in Gstaad.
The house has numerous pieces
by Claude Lalanne, including these
sheep, where we take a group photo
every year. We now have decades of
photos from this fun occasion.

> *66 Gstaad beats St. Moritz and the others because of its strict building regulations. Only traditional chalets are permitted. 99*

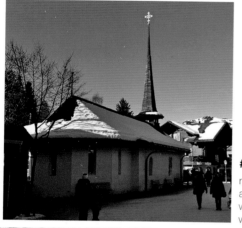

#SLEIGH HORSES

near the Hotel Rialto. Not far away, there is a nice oyster stand where you can enjoy the delicacy with a glass of white wine.

Above: Eagle Ski Club emblem; the Club is home to wonderfully large Swiss-style buffet lunches.

#HOTEL OLDEN

This is one of the best hotels in Gstaad. I have been going here for many years to listen to the owner, Heidi, sing cabaret songs—sadly Heidi is now retired, so don't show up expecting to hear her beautiful voice, but feel free to bring your own.

#CHAT

The bathrooms of Hotel Olden have these great tiles with plays on the word "chat" on them, like "chat-tellite" for satellite.

#CANTON DE VAUD'S

symbol is a stylized eagle. *Right:* In gstaad you can get these wonderful creme-filled pastries.

#SKI TIME

HOTELS

Gstaad Palace
Palacestrasse 28
3780 Gstaad
Tel: +41 33 748 50 00

Hotel Alpina
Alpinastrasse 23
3780 Gstaad
Tel: +41 33 888 98 88

Hotel Olden
Promenade 35
3780 Gstaad
Tel: +41 33 748 49 50

RESTAURANTS

Berghaus Rellerli
(great ski lunch)
Rellerliweg 35
3778 Schönried

Charly's Tea-Room and Confiserie
Dorfstrasse
3780 Gstaad
Tel: +41 33 744 15 44

La Fromagerie
Gstaad Palace
3780 Gstaad
Tel: +41 33 748 50 00

Gasthaus Rössli
Gsteigstrasse 161
3784 Feutersoey
Tel: +41 33 755 10 12

Restaurant Sonnenhof
3792 Saanen, Gstaad
Tel: +41 (0)33 744 10 23

Rialto
Promenade
3780 Gstaad
Tel: +41 33 744 34 74

SHOPPING

Blumen Stricker
(for flowers)
Promenade Unter Gstaad
3780 Gstaad
Tel. 033 748 62 77

Boutique Pupa
Bahnhofstrasse 1
3780 Gstaad
Tel: +41 33 744 36 76

von Siebenthal Cookshop
Promenade 21
3780 Gstaad
Tel: +41 33 744 12 81

SKIING & MOUNTAIN ACTIVITIES

Eggli
(great for beginners)
Talstation Eggli
Egglistrasse 43
3780 Gstaad
Tel. +41 33 748 82 12

Gstaad Ice Rink
Tel: +41 33 748 80 90

Gstaad Snow Park
(snowboarding)
Talstation Saanersloch
Alte Strasse 2
3777 Saanenmöser
Tel: +41 33 748 82 42

Hiking Routes
Col du Pillon-Lake Retaud
(circular)
Gstaad-Oberbort-Turbach
(intermediate)
Saanenmöser-Schönried
(panoramic route)

La Videmanette
Talstation La Videmanette
1659 Rougemont
Tel: +41 26 925 81 61

Wasserngrat
Wasserngrat 2000 AG
Talstation Bissen
3780 Gstaad
Tel: +41 33 748 96 72

L.A.

FOR ME, L.A. REPRESENTS *the red carpet* OF LIFE. I COME HERE TO DRESS THE ACTRESSES WHO GO TO *the Oscars* AND THE GOLDEN GLOBES (AND HOPEFULLY WIN). ON TOP OF ALL THE THINGS I LOVE IN L.A., FROM EATING GREAT FOOD TO SEEING *art* AND *shopping*. BUT THERE IS ONE THING I CAN DO IN L.A. THAT I DON'T DO IN OTHER CITIES: DRIVE. I ALWAYS DRIVE DOWN *the palm tree-lined* STREETS OF THE CITY OF ANGELS LISTENING TO MUSIC ON THE RADIO.

THE #HEARTBEAT
OF MY L.A.

Whenever I am in L.A. I like to stay at the Sunset Towers, where friends and the beautiful view keep bringing me back. As with many places in L.A., breakfast here is busy with meetings and Hollywood buzz—and it's also really good.

#GOOD
TO BE BACK

A little chocolate "welcome back" snack.

NOBU MATSUHISA
Yellowtail with jalapeño is my absolute favorite dish here.

#VANITY CALENDAR

Vanity Fair hosts the best Oscars party. It took place at Morton's for years, but then moved to Sunset Towers, which was good for me because I can just walk down from my room.

#EVERYONE WANTS TO BE INVITED

After the Oscars, everyone changes out of their gowns and black ties and heads to Madonna's famous after-party. And everybody is looking to dance. In 2013, my sons Sean and Anthony were the DJs. Everyone wants to go, but the list is very exclusive, and even for those on it, it is kind of a CIA experience getting in.

#DRESSES

I love dressing people in Valentino, especially my friends, like Rosie Huntington-Whitely.

#NO PHOTOS

Leaving Madonna's party I asked Leroy Barnes Jr., aka Hypnosis, if I could take his picture—despite the photo ban—and he said "yesssss"!

#DRIVE

I love to drive down Burton Avenue
with the radio on, discovering new music.

Clockwise from top left: street art; beauties at Mario Testino show; new orange kicks from Sportie LA; James Perse designs the best t-shirts; Sportie LA is my favorite place to buy sneakers–casual, stylish L.A.; Lapo is a *force de nature,* always in good spirits, always adding energy to the party.

#RODEO DRIVE
VALENTINO STORE

View out the window of the Valentino store on Rodeo Drive. There are some wonderful shops nearby, including Tom Ford, Prada, and Céline.

#SUNRISE
AT SUNSET

Jet lag after flying from Paris to L.A. can be fierce, so why not use it creatively? I like to take early-morning hikes in the canyons; I also like to take sunrise shots like this from my room at Sunset Towers.

#BREAKFAST

at The Fountain in The Beverly Hills Hotel. L.A. is a breakfast city, and The Fountain is a great place for meetings. I always get the eggs benedict with salmon.

#CLASSIC L.A.

I first stayed at The Beverly Hills hotel 25 years ago with my ex-wife, Charlene. We stayed in a bungalow and it was fantastic.

#ACE

The new Ace Hotel in downtown L.A. occupies the old United Artist's Building and is home to a lot of very fun, late-night parties.

#GALLERIES GALORE

There are so many great galleries in L.A.; I like visiting Honor Fraser, Matthew Marks, Prism, and the BOX Gallery.

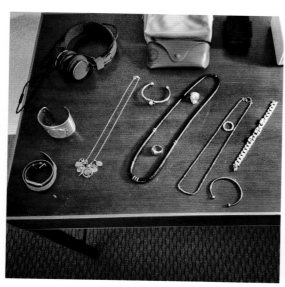

#OCD

Even whille traveling I like to keep my jewelry organized— we're all a little OCD sometimes.

#GAGOSIAN
WITH MARINA ABRAMOVIC

at Mr. Chow, where Larry Gagosian always hosts his after-opening parties—so much fun.

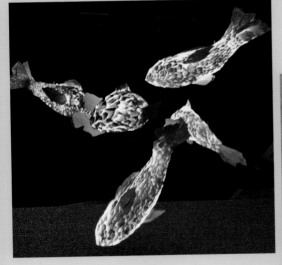

Right: My friend Ginerva admiring a Richard Prince painting.
Above: Frank Gehry: Fish Lamps.

#JUST ONE EYE

A kickass new boutique combining art, design, and fashion—including my jewelry line, Most Wanted Design.
Right and below: Diane von Furstenburg's pre-Oscars picnic is a cool, casual fixture of the Oscar season, where I always run into friends.

#SAN FRANCISCO

**WONDERFUL ARCHITECTURE
IN SAN FRANCISCO**

My eye is drawn to those unusal juxtapositions of angles, like this building. down near the Embarcadero.

#CAFÉ ZUNI

The brick oven-roasted chicken here is amazing—but you have to order it one hour in advance!

#GOLF

At the Lincoln Park Golf Club you get this view—how spectacular with the Golden Gate Bridge and the bay in the background.

Beautiful pottery at the Asian Art Museum. I love color!

#COTOGNA

At Cotogna the desserts are inspired by Valentino designs, like this peach jelly with flowers creation. Pastry chefs Alen Ramos and Carolyn Nugent have done a beautiful job.

#SF NIGHTS

Out on the town with Bubbles and Squeeze after the SFMOMA Gala.

#BIG SUR

Big Sur, about 3 hours south of San Francisco, is a truly magical place. The sea views and the rough coastline are beautiful and make a perfect setting for a wedding. I was lucky enough to go to Anne Hathaway and Adam Schulman's wedding in Big Sur, and took this photo on the way out of the woods where the wedding was. Gorgeous!

L.A. HOTELS

The Ace Hotel
929 S Broadway
Los Angeles, CA 90015
Tel: +1 (213) 623-3233

Chateau Marmont
8221 Sunset Blvd
West Hollywood, CA 90046
Tel: +1 (323) 656-1010

The Sunset Tower
and The Tower Bar
8358 Sunset Blvd
Los Angeles, CA 90069
Tel: +1 (323) 654-7100

RESTAURANTS

E. Baldi
375 N Canon Dr
Beverly Hills, CA 90210
Tel: +1 (310) 248-2633

The Ivy
113 N Robertson Blvd
Los Angeles, CA 90048
Tel: +1 (310) 274-8303

Nobu Matsuhisa
129 N La Cienega Blvd
Beverly Hills, CA 90211
Tel: +1 (310) 659-9639

The Fountain
at The Beverly Hills Hotel
9641 Sunset Blvd
Beverly Hills, CA 90210
Tel: +1 (310) 276-2251

Mr. Chow
344 N Camden Dr
Beverly Hills, CA 90210
Tel: +1 (310) 278-9911

Spago
176 N Canon
Beverly Hills, CA 90210
Tel: +1 (310) 385-0880

MUSEUMS, GALLERIES, & SIGHTS

Disney Concert Hall
111 S Grand Ave
Los Angeles, CA 90012
Tel: +1 (323) 850-2000

Getty Center
1200 Getty Center Dr
Los Angeles, CA 90049
Tel: +1 (310) 440-7300

Prism
8746 Sunset Blvd
West Hollywood, CA 90069
Tel: +1 (310) 289-1301

Gagosian Beverly Hills
456 North Camden Dr
Beverly Hills, CA 90210
Tel: +1 (310) 271-9400

LACMA
5905 Wilshire Blvd
Los Angeles, CA 90036
Tel: +1 (323) 857-6000

TCL Chinese Theatre
6925 Hollywood Blvd
Hollywood, CA 90028
Tel: +1 (323) 461-3331

SHOPPING

Decades
('60s and '70s vintage couture)
8214 Melrose Ave
Los Angeles, CA 90046
Tel: +1 (323) 655-1960

Just One Eye
(bitter-cool concept store)
7000 Romaine St
Los Angeles, CA 90038
Tel: +1 (888) 563-6858

Robertson Boulevard
(shopping, restaurants, and
people watching in Beverly
Hills and West Hollywood)

Fred Segal
8100 Melrose Ave
Los Angeles, CA 90046
Tel: +1 (323) 655-9500

Maxfield Los Angeles
8825 Melrose Ave
Los Angeles, CA 90069
Tel: +1 (310) 274-8800

Sportie LA
(must-have kicks)
7753 Melrose Ave
Los Angeles, CA 90046
Tel: +1 (323) 651-1553

SAN FRANCISCO HOTELS

The Battery
717 Battery St
San Francisco, CA 94111
Tel: +1 (415) 230-8000

The Fairmont
950 Mason St
San Francisco, CA 94108
Tel: +1 (415) 772-5000

**The Inn
at The Presidio**
42 Moraga Ave
San Francisco, CA 94129
(415) 800-7356

St. Regis
125 3rd St
San Francisco, CA 94103
Tel: +1 (415) 284-4000

Big Sur Lodge
Pfeiffer Big Sur
State Park
47225 Highway One
Big Sur, CA 93920
Tel: +1 (831) 667-3100

Ventana Inn & Spa
48123 California 1
Big Sur, CA 93920
Tel: +1 (831) 667-2331

RESTAURANTS

Bi Rite
(for ice cream)
3692 18th St
San Francisco, CA 94110
Tel: +1 (415) 626-5600

Coqueta
Pier 5, The Embarcadero
San Francisco, CA 94105
Tel: +1 (415) 704-8866

Cotogna
490 Pacific Ave
San Francisco, CA 94133
Tel: +1 (415) 775-8508

Jane Café
(for baked goods and juice)
2123 Fillmore St
San Francisco, CA 94115
Tel: +1 (415) 931-5263

Tosca Café
262 Columbus Ave
San Francisco, CA 94133
Tel: +1 (415) 986-9561

ZUNI Café
1658 Market St
San Francisco, CA 94102
Tel: +1 (415) 552-2522

MUSEUMS, GALLERIES, & MORE

Asian Art Museum
200 Larkin St
San Francisco, CA 94102
Tel: +1 (415) 581-3500

de Young
Golden Gate Park
50 Hagiwara Tea Garden Dr
San Francisco, CA 94118
Tel: +1 (415) 750-3600

**The Ferry Building
Farmer's Market**
1 Ferry Building
Marketplace
San Francisco, CA 94111
Tel: +1 (415) 291-3276

Hedge Gallery
(mid-century modern
furniture)
501 Pacific Ave
San Francisco, CA 94133
Tel: +1 (415) 433-2233

Legion of Honor
Lincoln Park
100 34th Ave
San Francisco, CA
Tel: +1 (415) 750-3600

SFMOMA
151 Third Street
San Francisco, CA 94103
Tel: +1 (415) 357-4000

PARIS

AFTER THE AWARDS SEASON IN L.A., I HEAD TO PARIS FOR THE *couture* AND *high fashion shows*. I HAVE BEEN COMING TO PARIS FOR OVER TWENTY YEARS. I ALWAYS ENJOY MY ROUTINE *walks* FROM WHERE I STAY, AT THE *Hôtel Costes*, THROUGH THE *Jardin des Tuileries*. RECURRING, CONSTANT ELEMENTS HELP ME TO STAY GROUNDED.

> **" *If you are lucky enough to have lived in Paris as a young man, then wherever you go for the rest of your life, it stays with you, for Paris is a moveable feast.* "**
>
> —Ernest Hemingway

#LADURÉE

The best *macarons* in Paris;
I always get a box of caramel,
my favorite flavor.
Above: Odorantes is the best
place to buy roses in Paris.

#AT BRASSERIE LIPP

You have to order the
choucroute—homemade
sauerkraut with sausage,
ham, potatoes, and
mustard—but don't forget to
order with a Heineken.

#PALAIS ROYAL

During Fashion week I walk by the Palais Royal. And I always stop in the Jardin des Tuileries for a breath of fresh air.
Above: A night view of a sculpture in the park, and another restful moment.

#SUNSET
PLACE DE LA CONCORDE

#HOME AWAY FROM HOME

I have been coming to Hôtel Costes for nearly 20 years, and it's where everyone in fashion comes too. It is my second office in Paris, and when my company wanted to put me up in another hotel, Mr. Costes said, "We will do whatever it takes to keep Mr. Souza; he is our good luck charm."

> **"** *I have often joked with Mr. Costes that one day I will open a hotel in Brazil and greet guests in a pareo, drink in hand.* **"**

#CHEZ OMAR
WITH OLIVA

The best couscous in town; my personal favorite,
vegetable and chicken.

#MIRACULOUS
140 RUE DU BAC

So many beautiful and inspiring churches and cathedrals in Paris. I always go to the Chapelle Notre-Dame-de-la-Médaille-Miraculeuse to buy medals to give to friends and their newborn children for good luck.

#ORCHIDS
AT VALENTINO STUDIO

The building was old, gold boisserie, rococo Paris, but Christian Liaigre made it very modern and very Valentino by painting some of the gold white!

> *Since childhood, it was my dream to go where all the poets and artists had been. Rimbaud, Artaud, Brancusi, Camus, Picasso, Bresson, Goddard, Jeanne Moreau, Juliette Greco, everybody— Paris for me was a Mecca.*

—Patti Smith

Mask balls in Paris are always so much fun, and everyone looks so glamorous. Here is a mix of Valentino and *Vogue* masquerade parties. Parisian nightlife never ceases to amaze me—people stay so elegant all through the night.

Fashion editor Suzy Menkes, with whom I've worked for many years.

#PLACE VENDÔME

#CLASSIC
LE VOLTAIRE

One of my favorite restaurants for traditional French food. Their cuisine is established, very French, and very traditional. We go for the *salade des haricôts verts* and the *poulet à l'estragon*. It's very close to the Tuileries, so it's the perfect spot for lunch during fashion week. As with so many places in Paris, you often see the same people at cafés, both workers and clientele, and this keeps me coming back.

#STYLE

I love to mix styles, especially with
my own brand, Most Wanted Design.

#CAMOUFLAGE

at Valentino—a big hit!

#KINUGAWA

HANDS DOWN THE BEST JAPANESE IN PARIS.

If you go, order the ikura oroshi, a perfect mix of salty salmon roe and
slightly sweet grated daikon radish—it's on Rue du Mont Thabor.

**#CAVIAR KASPIA—
FASHION'S CANTINA**

I usually have the crab salad in summer and borscht in the winter, but always with the Vladivostok potato with sevruga.

#LA MADELEINE

#THE NEW VALENTINO

Maria Grazia and Pierpaolo are the *ne plus ultra* successful creative desigers of Valentino. In only a few years they have conquered a whole new generation of followers and clients due to their modern vision and interpretation of the brand's DNA; they also make my life so much easier—I do not have to call, they are calling me for RED CARPET MOMENTS!

**#BACKSTAGE COUTURE
AND THE VALENTINO
SHOWROOM**

#CABINET DES CURIOSITÉS

Valentino Couture show.

HOTELS

L'Hôtel
13 rue des Beaux Arts
75006 Paris
Tel: +33 1 44 41 99 01

Hôtel Meurice
228 rue de Rivoli
75001 Paris
Tel: +33 1 44 58 10 10

Ritz
15 Place Vendôme
75001 Paris
Tel: +33 1 43 16 30 30

Hôtel Costes
239-241 rue Saint Honoré
75001 Paris
Tel: +33 1 42 44 50 00

Pavillon de la Reine
28 Place des Vosges
75003 Paris
Tel: +33 1 40 29 19 19

Royal Monceau
37 avenue Hoche
75008 Paris
Tel: +33 1 42 99 88 00

RESTAURANTS

L'Ami Louis
32 rue du Vertbois
75003 Paris
Tel: +33 1 48 87 77 48

Café de Flore
172 boulevard Saint-Germain
75006 Paris
Tel: +33 1 45 48 55 26

Ladurée
16 rue Royale
75008 Paris
Tel: +33 1 42 60 21 79

L'Avenue
41 avenue Montaigne
75008 Paris
Tel: +33 1 40 70 14 91

Chez Omar
42 rue de Bretagne
75003 Paris
Tel: +33 1 42 72 36 26

Le Stresa
7 rue Chambiges
75008 Paris
Tel: +33 1 47 23 51 62

Brasserie Lipp
151 blvd Saint-Germain
75006 Paris
Tel: +33 1 45 48 53 91

Kinugawa
9 rue du Mont Thabor
75006 Paris
Tel: +33 1 45 48 55 26

Le Voltaire
27 Quai Voltaire
75007 Paris
Tel: +33 1 42 61 17 49

MUSEUMS & GALLERIES

Centre Georges
Pompidou
Place Georges-Pompidou
75004 Paris
Tel: +33 1 44 78 12 33

Jeu de Paume
1 Place de la Concorde
75008 Paris
Tel: +33 1 47 03 12 50

Musée Jacquemart-
André
158 Boulevard Haussmann
75008 Paris, France
+33 1 45 62 11 59

Grand Palais
3 Avenue du Général Eisen-
hower
75008 Paris
Tel: +33 1 44 13 17 17

Musée des Arts
Décoratifs
107 rue de Rivoli
Paris 75001
Tel: +33 1 44 55 57 50

Musée du Louvre
Paris 75001
Tel: +33 1 40 20 50 50

Musée D'Orsay
1 rue de la Légion d'Honneur
75007 Paris
Tel: +33 1 40 49 48 14

Musée Rodin
79 rue de Varenne
75007 Paris
Tel: +33 1 44 18 61 10

Gagosian Gallery
800 avenue de l'Europe
93350 Le Bourget
Tel: +33 1 48 16 16 47

Galerie Perrotin
76 rue de Turenne
75003 Paris
Tel: +33 1 42 16 79 79

Galerie Yvon Lambert
108 rue Vieille du Temple
75003 Paris
Tel: +33 1 42 71 09 33

Thaddaeus Ropac
7 rue Debelleyme
75003 Paris
Tel: +33 1 42 72 99 00

SHOPPING

Assouline
35 rue Bonaparte
75006 Paris
Tel: +33 1 43 29 23 20

Annick Goutal
(perfumes)
14 rue de Castiglione
75001 Paris
Tel: +33 1 42 60 52 82
(additional locations)

Chez Estéban
(for incense)
49 rue de Rennes
75006 Paris
Tel: +33 1 45 49 09 39

Colette
(fashion boutique)
213 rue Saint Honoré
75001 Paris
Tel: +33 1 55 35 33 90

Galignani Bookstore
224 rue de Rivoli
75001 Paris
Tel: +33 1 42 60 76 07

Jacenko
(great menswear)
38 rue de Poitou
75003 Paris
Tel: +33 1 42 71 80 38

Jean–Paul Hévin
(for chocolate)
231 rue Saint Honoré
75001 Paris
Tel: +33 1 55 35 35 96
(additional locations)

Marché aux Puces
(Parisian "flea market"
for great vintage and antique
finds)
Grandes-Carrières
75018 Paris

Mariage Frères
(the best teas & marmelades)
30 rue du Bourg Tibourg
75004 Paris
Tel: +33 1 42 72 28 11

Moulié Fleurs
(for wonderful orchids)
8 Place du Palais Bourbon
75007 Paris
Tel: +33 1 45 51 78 43

Odoratnes
(perfect roses)
9 rue Madame
75006 Paris
Tel: +33 1 42 84 03 00

Serge Lutens
(perfumes)
142 Galerie de Valois
75001 Paris
Tel: + 33 1 49 27 09 09

WALKS

Avenue Montaigne, rue de Grenelle, les Trous des Halles

LONDON

I LOVE LONDON FOR ALL ITS *wonderful art* AND *architecture*. MY SONS, SEAN AND ANTHONY, WENT TO SCHOOL IN LONDON, AND I USED TO TAKE THEM TO *galleries* AND *museums* WHEN THEY WERE YOUNGER, SOMETHING THEY WEREN'T ALWAYS HAPPY TO DO. NOW, WHEN I COME TO LONDON, THEY TELL ME WHAT I HAVE TO SEE AT ALL THE MUSEUMS AND GALLERIES.

I usually stay in Cadogan
Square, in Knightsbridge,
with gorgeous Georgian
architecture.

#FOOD LOVE

There are so many good restaurants in London; try The Ivy, J. Sheekey, Lucio, or Amaya.

#FLOWERS

Rob Van Helden if you are looking for very chic flower arrangements.

THE THREE CARLOSES

Me with Carlos Mota at Carlos Place—where else?

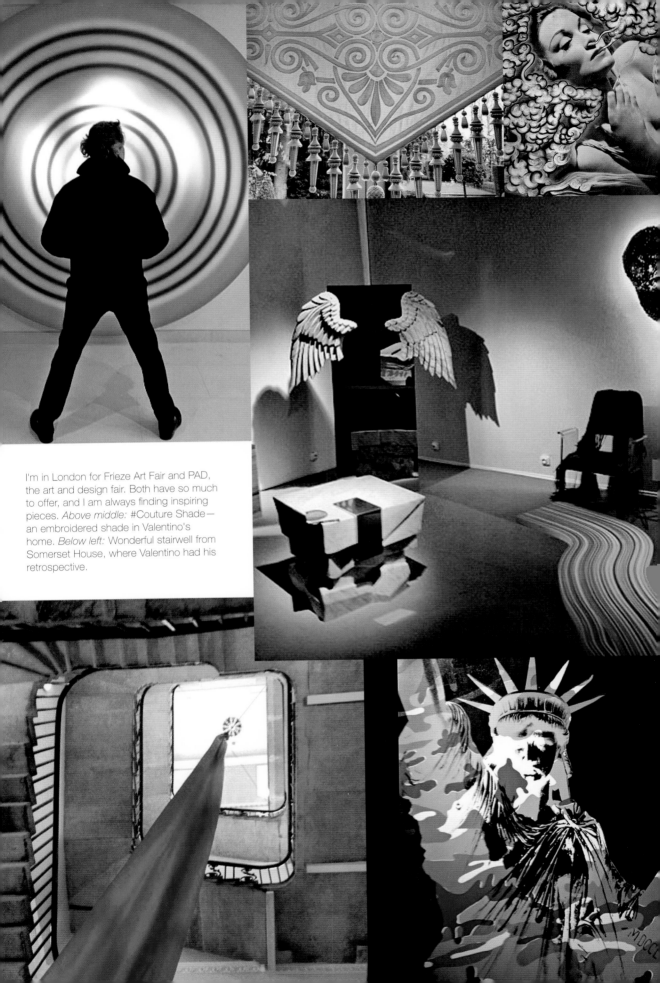

I'm in London for Frieze Art Fair and PAD, the art and design fair. Both have so much to offer, and I am always finding inspiring pieces. *Above middle:* #Couture Shade— an embroidered shade in Valentino's home. *Below left:* Wonderful stairwell from Somerset House, where Valentino had his retrospective.

Impressive entrance at Tate Britain, not far from where I stay in Knightsbridge.

#BUTTERFLIES

What's better than one Damian Hirst painting? Three! At Jay Jopling's house.

A LONDON #THANKSGIVING

I'm addicted to turkey. Absolutely amazing food at Valentino's thanksgiving dinner, and the table decor was simply stunning. *Above:* Dinner after the opening of Valentino's retrospective at Somerset House.

#THE BEST "PUB" IN LONDON
The bar at the Savoy Hotel.

#WONDERFUL INTERIOR
Interior of the Savoy Bar.

#LONDON ARCHITECTURE
Some of my favorite places to walk in London are around the mews near Cadogan Square, Holland Park, where you can see very British-looking homes, and the Westbourne Grove neighborhood.

#FRIENDS
The artist Francesco Clemente and Dorothea Mercouri, my Greek Sophia Loren.

#DESIGN
Color from Giancarlo Giammetti's office.

THE ENTERPRISE.

#AMAZING PAINTINGS

Left: Paintings with enamel and rhinestones by Raqib Shaw at Pace Gallery. *Above:* The artist's bonsai tree-lined studio. *Below (left):* An early start at Frieze! *Below (right):* Giancarlo Giammetti at home.

#GIANCARLO PEACE

#MUSEUMS

Such a thrill walking over the Millennium Bridge
on the way to the Tate Modern. The general exhibitions
at many museums in London are free, and I really enjoy
walking through them in spare moments; check out the
National Gallery on Trafalgar Square.

#PARTY

My son Anthony hand-painted a mask
and old suit to create this modern
interpretation of Keith Haring.

#POP-THEMED PARTY

Above: Colorful costumes from a pop-themed party for Giancarlo Giammetti's birthday. Giancarlo Giammetti and Valentino with someone who played the Queen for a night. *Below:* A light show at Hayward Gallery.

#CAB

I really love the gray, rainy London days.

#CLASSIC VALENTINO

Vintage Valentino designs at the retrospective from Somerset House.

Breakfast at Colbert in Sloane Square—a French twist on the classic English breakfast.

#YUMMY

Pastries and desserts at Ottolenghi.

HOTELS

ACE Shoreditch
100 Shoreditch High Street
London E1 6JQ
Tel: +44 20 7613 9800

Bulgari
171 Knightsbridge
London SW7 1DW
Tel: +44 20 7151 1010

The Cadogan
75 Sloane Street
Knightsbridge
London SW1X 9SG
Tel: +44 20 7235 7141

Claridge's
49 Brook Street
London W1K 4HR
Tel: +44 20 7629 8860

Chiltern Street
Firehouse Hotel
1 Chiltern Street
Marylebone
London W1U 7JA
Tel: +44 20 7073 7676

RESTAURANTS

Amaya
Halkin Arcade, Motcomb St,
London SW1X 8JT
Tel: +44 20 7823 1166

American Bar
at The Savoy
Strand
London WC2R 0EU
Tel: +44 20 7420 2111

C London (Cipriani)
23-25 Davies Street
London W1K 3DE
Tel: +44 20 7399 0500

Colbert
50-52 Sloane Square
London SW1W 8AX
Tel: +44 20 7730 2804

Moi-Polloi at ACE
100 Shoreditch High Street
London E1 6JQ
Tel: +44 20 8880 6100

The Ivy
1-5 West Street
London WC2H 9NQ
Tel: + 44 20 7836 4751

J. Sheekey
28-34 St. Martin's Court
London WC2N 4AL
Tel: +44 20 7240 2565

Koya
49 Frith Street
London W1D 4SG
Tel: +44 20 7434 4463

Lucio
257-259 Fulham Rd
London SW3 6HY
Tel: +44 20 7823 3007

Ottolenghi
287 Upper St
London N1 2TZ
Tel: +44 20 7288 1454

Quattro Passi
34 Dover St, London W1S
4NG, United Kingdom
Tel: +44 20 3096 1444

San Lorenzo
22 Beauchamp Place
Knightsbridge
London SW3 1NH
Tel: + 44 20 7584 1074

CLUBS

Annabel's
44 Berkeley Square
London W1J 5QB
Tel: + 44 20 7629 1096

Groucho
45 Dean Street
London W1D 4PZ
Tel: + 44 20 7439 4685

Loulou's
5 Hertford Street
London W1J 7RB
Tel: +44 20 7408 2100

Gagosian Gallery
6–24 Britannia Street
London WC1X 9JD
Tel: +44 20 7841 9960

17–19 Davies Street
London W1K 3DE
Tel: +44 20 7493 3020

Hamilton's Gallery
13 Carlos Place
London W1K 2EU
Tel: +44 20 7499 9493

Hayward Gallery
Southbank Centre
Belvedere Road
London SE1 8XX
Tel: +44 20 7960 4200

National Portrait Gallery
St. Martin's Place
London WC2H 0HE
Tel: +44 20 7306 0055

Pace London
6 Burlington Gardens
London W1S 3ET
Tel: +44 20 3206 7600

6-10 Lexington Street
London W1F)LB
Tel: +44 20 7437 1050

Royal Academy
Burlington House
Piccadilly
London W1J 0BD
Tel: +44 20 7300 8000

Saatchi
(The Duke of York's HQ)
King's Road
London SW3 4RY
Tel: +44 20 7811 3070

Sadie Coles
62 Kingly Street
London W1B 5PW
Tel: +44 20 7493 8611

Serpentine
Kensington Gardens
London W2 3XA
Tel: +44 20 7402 6075

Tate Modern
Bankside
London SE1 9TG
Tel: +44 20 7887 8888

Tate Museum
Millbank
London SW1P 4RG
Tel: +44 20 7887 8888

Victoria & Albert Museum
Cromwell Road
London SW7 2RL
Tel: +44 20 7942 2000

White Cube
144–152 Bermondsey Street
London SE1 3TQ
Tel: +44 20 7930 5373

SHOPPING

Harrods
87–135 Brompton Road
London SW1X 7XL
Tel: +44 20 7730 1234

Horioshi the III
19 Connaught Street
London W2 2AY
Tel: +44 20 7262 2121

LNCC
(by appointment only)
18–24 Shacklewell Lane
London E8 2EZ
Tel: + 44 20 3174 0741

Liberty
Regent Street
London W1B 5AH
Tel: + 44 20 7734 1234

Matches
87 Marylebone High Street
London W1U 4QU
Tel: +44 20 7487 5400

Rob Van Helden
(floral design)
8 Tun Yard
Peardon Street
London SW8 3HT
Tel:+44 20 7720 6774

WALKS

Brook Street, Cadogan Square, Elizabeth Street, Old Brompton Road, Savile Row, Walton Street

ROME

WHEN I WAS VERY YOUNG I ARRIVED IN ROME AND ASKED FOR *polenta*. THEY SAID, "EXCUSE ME, IT'S THE SUMMER." COMING FROM BRAZIL WHERE THERE IS NO CHANGING OF THE SEASONS, I DID NOT UNDERSTAND THAT THERE ARE *winter dishes* AND *summer dishes*. IN ITALY, THE FOOD IS ABOUT BEING VERY FRESH AND *always seasonal*. TODAY, ROME FOR ME IS STILL ABOUT *food*, BUT ALSO WORK, *culture, history,* AND ALWAYS A LITTLE TIME TO RELAX!

#PIAZZA DI SPAGNA

When I first moved to Rome, I lived not far
from here, on Via delle Carrozze.
Previous pages: I LOVE AIRPORTS!

#PANELLA

PANELLA IS MY GO-TO SHOP

I love this place for my bread, groceries, and even pizza. The Altamura bread, made from hard wheat flour and baked with a thick, crunchy crust, is wonderful.

#BEST

You can buy the best balsalmic vinegars and Setaro, the best pasta from Naples, at Panella—indispensible for traditional Italian cooking.

#CASTEL SANT'ANGELO

66 *The Ponentino—a wind that kisses the city at the end of the day—reignites my love for Rome every time I am here.* 99

#LOVE THIS CAR COVER

You can find style in the most unexpected places.

#PIAZZA,
RAINY DAYS

Top (left): Sculpture in the Galleria Borghese.
Above (left): My apartment; for my 40th birthday I bought myself
this Chinese rosewood opium bed—one of the many treasures that
I have collected from different places around the world. *Above (right):*
The view of Piazza Vittorio from my apartment.

#CASTAGNE
ROASTED CHESTNUTS

are my favorite smell when I arrive in Rome.
It reminds me of the first time I was here—it was
October and the shepherds had come down
from the mountains to sell their chestnuts.
The streets were filled with the smell. When
I first moved to Rome, I lived on Vie delle
Carrozze—a short walk to Piazza di Spagna.

#VESPA
SO ITALIAN

The Vespa is traditional
transportation. Ever since
Gregory Peck and Audrey
Hepburn in *Roman Holiday,*
the Vespa has been the
symbol of summer. But I
upgrade myself to a yellow
Ducati Monster for my summer
tours; there is nothing more
beautiful than going around
Rome at night through the
eternal city with its incredible
monuments, all very well-lit.

#AL MORO

Spaghetti al moro, the best
carbonara in the world.
Left: Babington's in the Piazza di Spagna
serves a lemon tartlet to die for.
Below (left): Piazza Farnese, in front of
the French Embassy.

#CHURCHES

If you go into any church, you will see
the riches of Rome. The families with papal
connections, like the Borghese and the
Pamphili, were the first art collectors.

#MITORAJ
**VALENTINO OFFICES,
PIAZZA MIGNANELLI**

#MAS

MAS IS AN INCREDIBLE
DISCOUNT STORE

where you can find really wonderful things. We jokingly call it the best boutique. For one euro I bought an impeccable jacket. When costume designers for films need to dress a lot of people they come here. What I like about fashion now is the mixture of up and down market—designer and discount.

#MAXXI MUSEO

Rome's contemporary art museum, designed
by the fantastic Zaha Hadid. The interior architecture
is just as amazing as the exterior.

#APPERITIVO TIME

Mortadella, focaccia, mozzarella—all
from Panella, of course!—with a
refreshing drink of Campari.
Right: Spaghetti frutti di mare.
Top, clockwise from left: San Carlo;
Cardinals during the Conclave before
the election of Pope Francis I;
Palazzo Borghese.

#FIORI DI ZUCCA

Zucchini flowers are traditionally filled with mozzarella and anchovies and deep fried for another spring favorite.

SPRING VEGETABLES, SO #FRESH

Behind my apartment in the Piazza Vittorio there is the best market. I go down at 7:30 in the morning with a handful of spare change and I'll buy my meal with these coins. It's all about the freshness of the season. You can first get artichokes, the king of Italian vegetables in Februrary. They are delicious fried or steamed with a glass of white wine.

#ESCAPE

OSTIA BEACH

is only 30 minutes by motorcycle from Rome. The first weekend of spring, everyone leaves the office pale, wearing their winter clothes, and spends all weekend frying on the dark sand beaches. On Monday they come back in tight white jeans and tan like it's August. Ostia beach has dark gray sand that attracts much more UV than one needs. Instant suntan!

HOTELS

Art Hotel
Via Margutta 56
00187 Rome
Tel: +39 06 328 711

Boscolo Palace
Via Veneto, 70
00187 Rome
Tel: +39 06 478 719

Hotel de Russie
Via del Babuino, 9
00187 Rome
Tel: +39 06 328 881

Boscolo Exedra
Piazza della Repubblica, 47
Rome 00185
Tel: +39 06 489 381

Hassler
Piazza Trinità dei Monti, 6
00187 Rome
Tel: +39 06 699 340

Westin Excelsior
Via Vittorio Veneto, 125
00187 Rome
Tel: +39 06 470 81

RESTAURANTS & BARS

Bar del Fico
Piazza del Fico, 26
Rome 00186
Tel: +39 06 6880 8413

Glass Hosteria
Vicolo del Cinque 58
00153 Rome
Tel: +39 06 5833 5903

Pastificio San Lorenzo
Via degli Ausoni, 1
00185 Rome
Tel: +39 06 4542 2960

Dal Bolognese
Piazza del Popolo, 1–2
00187 Rome
Tel: +39 06 361 1473

La Montecarlo
Vicolo Savelli, 13
00186 Rome
Tel: +39 06 686 1877

Pierluigi
Piazza De Ricci, 144
00186 Rome
Tel: +39 06 686 8717

Caffè Greco
Via dei Condotti, 86
00187 Rome
Tel: +39 06 679 1700

Al Moro
Vicolo delle Bollette, 13
00187 Rome
Tel: +39 06 678 3495

Roscioli
(restaurant, wine bar, deli-
roscioli has it all!)
Via dei Giubbonari, 21/22
00186 Rome
Tel: +39 06 687 5287

Etabli
Vicolo delle Vacche, 9
00186 Rome
Tel: +39 06 9761 6694

Nino
Via Borgognona, 11
00187 Rome
Tel: +39 06 678 6752

Il Sanlorenzo
Via dei Chiavari, 4/5
00186 Rome
Tel: +39 06 686 5097

Franchi
Via Cola di Rienzo, 204
00192 Rome
Tel: +39 06 687 4651

Ottavio
Via Santa Croce
in Gerusalemme, 9
00185 Rome
Tel: +39 06 702 8595

San Theodoro
Via dei Fienili, 50
00186 Rome
Tel: +39 06 678 0933

La Farnesina
Via della Lungara, 230
00165 Rome
Tel: +39 06 6802 7268

Galleria Borghese
Piazzale del Museo Borghese, 5
00197 Rome
Tel: +39 06 841 3979

Maxxi
Via Guido Reni, 4 A
00196 Rome
Tel: +39 06 320 1954

Museum Altemps
Piazza di Sant'Apollinare 46
00186 Rome
Tel: +39 06 3996 7700

Palazzo Borghese
Via dell'Arancio
00186 Rome

Palazzo Colonna
Piazza dei Santi Apostoli, 66
Rome 00187
Tel: +39 06 678 4350

Palazzo Farnese
Piazza Farnese, 67
00100 Rome
Tel: +39 06 0606 0884

Pantheon
Piazza della Rotonda
00186 Rome
Tel: +39 06 6830 0230

Vatican Museums
Viale Vaticano
00165 Rome
Tel: +39 06 6988 3332

Antica Fabbrica del Cioccolato
Via Tiburtina, 135
00185 Rome
Tel: +39 06 446 9204

Delfina Delettrez
(accessories)
Piazza di Tor Sanguigna, 13
00186 Rome
Tel: +39 06 6813 6362

Emporio delle Spezie
(for my favorite peperoncini)
Via Luca della Robbia, 20
00153 Rome
Tel. +39 327 8612655

Libreria Altroquando
Via del Governo Vecchio, 80
00186 Rome
Tel: +39 06 687 9825

Miki Way
(fashions by young Italian designers)
Via del Boschetto 40 b/c
00184 Rome
Tel: +39 064880914

Nuyorica
(fashion)
Piazza Pollarola, 36
00186 Rome
Tel: +39 06 9970 0829

Panella
(the best bread in town)
Via Merulana, 54
00185 Rome
Tel: +39 06 487 2651

Volpetti
(an Italian gourmet pantry)
Via Marmorata, 47
00153 Rome
Tel: +39 06 574 2352

Campo de Fiori, Pantheon (Piazza della Rotonda), Via Giulia, Via Margutta, Via San Teodoro

VENICE

AND THE *Film Festival* ARE THE PERFECT
EXCUSES TO VISIT THIS WONDERFUL
FLOATING CITY. FOR THE LAST
DECADE OR SO I HAVE BEEN GOING
TO THESE TWO INTERNATIONAL
EVENTS, AND JUST ARRIVING IN
VENICE IS LIKE BEING ON A HOLIDAY—
MAYBE THERE IS SOMETHING ABOUT
arriving by water. VENICE IS A SENSORIUM
OF ART AND FOOD, AND EACH VISIT

unlocks something new.

#THIS IS VENICE!!

#FRIULANE
These espadrilles are made from
recycled tires—practical and colorful.

#APERITIVO TIME
DA IVO VENEZIA

serves the most incredible little peaches drizzled with truffle oil.

#FOOD

From Da Ivo, you can see the gondolas, and you can arrive by them too.
Right: Noona Smith coming aboard...

66 *Venice is like eating an entire box of chocolate liqueurs in one go.* **99**

—Truman Capote

#PERFECT CONTRAST

Breath an eleven-meter tall inflatable sculpture
by Marc Quinn, was installed on the island
of San Giorgio Maggiore, gazing out across
the Giudecca canal.

#SCAMPI
ANTICHE CARAMPANE

is my favorite restaurant in Venice.

#MY VENICE
WATER, MARBLE, AND
ARCHITECTURE

The way the filtered light reflects on
the stone perfectly captures the spirit
of the city. *Below:* the fish market
bustling with shoppers.

Clockwise from top left: Art selfie; Brazilian artist Arthur Bispo do Rosário, who lived in an insane asylum for fifty years, stitched his assemblages with the thread from his old uniforms; installation by Walter de Maria at the Venice Biennale.

❝ I love the colors of Venice, especially the reflections off the water. ❞

#BAL MASQUÉ

DOLCE AND GABBANA

celebrated their couture collection with a costume party. They sent beautiful masks with the invitations and everyone dressed in black tie or wore a costume to match their mask.

#PALAZZO
PISANI MORETTA

After drinks on the first floor,
we moved downstairs for
dancing so we would not
ruin the beautiful floor. The
old palazzi do not have air
conditioning, so it was very
hot—especially for the ladies,
with their velvet dresses
and feathers!

HOTELS

Aman Canal
Palazzo Papadopoli
Calle Tiepolo 1364
Sestiere San Polo
30125 Venice
Tel: +39 041 270 7333

The Bauers Venezia
Multiple locations
Tel: +39 041 520 7022

Belmond Hotel Cipriani
Giudecca 10
30133 Venice
Tel: +39 041 240 801

Ca Maria Adele
Dorsoduro 111
30123 Venice
Tel: +39 041 520 3078

Oltre Il Giardino
San Polo, 2542
30125 Venice
Tel: +39 041 275 0015

Palazzo Barbarigo
Calle Corner
Sestiere San Polo 2765
30125 Venice
Tel: +39 041 740 172

RESTAURANTS & BARS

Antiche Carampane
Sestiere San Polo 1911
30125 Venice
Tel: +39 041 524 0165

Bistrot de Venise
Calle dei Fabbri 4685
30124 San Marco, Venice
Tel: +39 041 523 6651

Da Fiore
Calle del Scaleter 2202/a
30125 Venice
Tel: +39 041 721 308

Harry's Bar
Calle Vallaresso 1323
30124 San Marco, Venice
Tel: +39 041 528 5777

Harry's Dolci
Calle Vallaresso, 1323
30124 San Marco, Venice
Tel: +39 041 522 4844

Da Ivo
Calle dei Fuseri 1809
30124 Venice
Tel: +39 041 528 5004

Alla Madonna
Calle della Madona 594
30125 Venice
Tel: +39 041 522 3824

Met Restaurant
Riva Schiavoni 4149
30122 Venice
Tel: +39 041 52 40 034

Naranzaria
San Polo 130
30125 Venice
Tel: +39 41 724 1035

Il Ridotto
campo SS. Filippo e Giacomo
Castello 4509
30122 Venice
Tel: +39 041 520 8280

Alle Tesiere
Calle del Mondo Novo 5801
30122 Venice
Tel: +39 041 522 7220

Al Timon
Cannaregio, Fondamenta
2754
30121 Venice
Tel: +39 041 524 6066

MUSEUMS

Caterina Tognon
S. Marco 2746
30124 Venezia
Tel: +39 041 520 7859

**Galleria Massimo
de Luca**
Via Torino 105/Q
30172 Mestre, Venezia
Tel: +39 366 6875619

Fondazione Prada
Ca' Corner Della Regina
Calle Corner
30135 Venice
Tel: +39 041 810 9161

Museo del Vetro
Fondamenta Giustinian 8
30121 Murano
Tel: +39 041 739 586

Palazzo Grassi
Campo San Samuele 3231
30124 Venice
Tel: +39 041 523 1680

Palazzo Fortuny
San Marco 3958
30124 Venice
Tel: +39 041 520 0995

Palazzo Mocenigo
Santa Croce 1992
30135 Venice
Tel: +39 041 721 798

Peggy Guggenheim
Collection
Dorsoduro 704
30123 Venezia
Tel: +39 41 240 5411

Punta della Dogana
Dorsoduro 2
30123 Venice
Tel: +39 41 271 9031

SHOPPING

L'Angolo del Passato
(glassware)
Dorsoduro 3276
Campiello dei Squelini
30123 Venice
Tel: +39 041 528 7896

Antonia Miletto
(jewelry)
Calle delle Botteghe
San Marco 3127/3128
30124 Venice
Tel: +39 41 520 5177

Codognato
(jewelry)
San Marco 1295
30124 Venice
Tel: +39 041 522 5042

Frette
(fine linen)
2070/A San Marco
30124 Venice
Tel: +39 041 522 4914

Giberto
(glassware)
Tel: +39 041 277 0086
www.giberto.it

Laguna B.
(glassware)
Tel: +39 041 520 4775
www.lagunab.com

Libreria Studium
San Marco 337
30124 Venice
Tel: +39 041 522 2382

Nardi
(jewelry)
Piazza San Marco 69
30124 Venice
Tel: +39 041 522 5733

Pied à Terre
(furlane shoes)
S. Polo 60
30125 Venice
Tel: +39 041 528 5513

VizioVirtù Cioccolateria
San Polo 2898/a
30125 Venice
Tel: +39 041 275 0149

CAPRI, POSITANO & AMALFI

THEY TALK ABOUT THE CÔTE D'AZUR, BUT FOR ME THE TYRRHENIAN COAST IS *unbeatable.* IT'S *lovely* FROM MAY TO THE END OF JULY. AFTER, MOBS OF VACATIONERS ARRIVE AND EVERYONE ELSE LEAVES FOR *their boats,* OR COUNTRY HOUSES, OR GOES TO THE MOUNTAINS.

WALKING DOWN #PUNTA TRAGARA

You have the best view of Marina Piccola.

#FANTASTIC FRUITS AND VEGETABLES

The produce here takes on a wonderful flavor due to the volcanic, Vesuvian earth. Tomatoes grown in this soil are absolutely the best.

WHEN YOU WALK THROUGH #CAPRI AND #POSITANO,

the smell of geraniums and citrus wafts through the air. At night, the scent of jasmine takes over, and can intoxicate your dreams.

CAPRI PIAZZETTA

is a great spot for people watching—you can get a spot at Al Piccolo Bar and watch who is leaving and arriving on the island. *Opposite:* Vintage convertables take you from the port up to the piazzetta. From there you walk. In Positano and Capri you do a lot of walking and really exercise your derrière—just in time to lounge on the beach!

#TASTE OF SUMMER

This woman in the via Tragara makes the best lemonade and citrus juices. Look at the size of those lemons…

MY #SECRET SPOT

I love to rent a lounge chair at La Fontelina and lie on the rocks like an alligator. I usually walk down, which is very good exercise for keeping your posterior in shape!

#POSITANO WALLS

This wall is beautiful because the colors are so saturated even though it is *délaboré* — ruined.
Right: Il Saraceno Hotel, Amalfi, is built into the cliffs, and epitomizes Mediterranean elegance.
Below: Praiano rooftop with pigeon tower.

View of the terraces from
the rooftop of a friend's home,
from the previous page.

Gelato tastes a lot like ice cream, but it's just better for some reason.

—Winston Churchill

#GELATO

I AM ADDICTED TO GELATO! I LOVE VANILLA, PISTACHIO, CHOCOLATE, FRUITY MANGO, AND COCONUT.

#COOL WATER
A nice beach at Saraceno.

#TRE SORELLE
A great spot in Positano famous for their
wonderful spaghetti zucchini.

#MARKET VEGETABLES

I'm addicted to pepperoncini.
I buy my red pepper in Italy and travel
with a peppermill I bought at G. Lorenzi
in Milan. The food in Positano is so
good because of the rich soil and good
sun. Nothing beats it.

Left: Santa Caterina, a wonderful hotel located on the coast
of Amalfi, where the sunsets are divine.
Below (right): Amalfi Cathedral.
Below (left): My friend Francesco Clemente—always so chic—who
together with his wife Alba, the "empress of Amalfi," stages beautiful
and delicious dinners on their terrace that dominates the city.

HOTELS

Cà P'a
(Casa Privata)
Via Rezzola 41
84010 Praiano
Tel: +39 398 987 4078

Grand Hotel Quisisana
Via Camerelle 2
80073 Capri
Tel: +39 081 837 0788

Hotel La Scalinatella
Via Tragara 8
80073 Capri
Tel: +39 081 837 0633

Monastero
di Santa Rosa
Via Roma 2
84010 Conca dei Marini
Tel: +39 089 832 1199

Le Sirenuse
Via Cristoforo Colombo 30
84017 Positano
Tel: +39 089 875066

Villa Tre Ville
Via Arienzo 30
84017 Positano
Tel: +39 089 812 2411

RESTAURANTS

Da Adolf
Via Laurito 40
84017 Positano
Tel: +39 089 875022

Da Armandino
Via Praia
84010 Praiano
Tel: +39 089 874 087

Bar Al Piccolo
Piazza Umberto I
80073 Capri
Tel: +39 081 837 0325

La Conca del Sogno
Via Marciano 9
80061 Massa Lubrense
Tel: +39 081 808 1036

Gelateria Buonocore
Via Roma 36
80073 Capri
Tel: +39 081 837 6151

Da Gemma
via Fra Gerardo Sasso 11
84011 Amalfi
Tel +39 089 871 345

Maria Grazia
a Nerano
Via Marina del Cantone 65
80061 Massa Lubrense
Tel: +39 081 808 1011

Il Pirata
Via Terramare
84010 Praiano
Tel: +39 089 874 377

Pizzeria Aurora
Via Fuorlovado 18-22
80073 Capri Napoli
+39 081 837 0181

Quattro Passi
Loc. Nerano, 80061
Massa Lubrense, Napoli
Phone:+39 081 808 1271

Le Tre Sorelle
Via del Brigantino 27/29
84017 Positano
Tel: +39 089 875 452

Villa Verde
Via Sella Orta 6
80073 Capri
Tel: +39 081 837 7024

SIGHTS & WALKS

Amalfi Cathedral
Via Duca Mansone I
84011 Amalfi
Tel: +39 089 871 059

Arco Naturale

La Fontelina
Beach Club
Via Faraglioni
80073 Capri
Tel: +39 081 837 0845

Li Galli Islands

Villa Jovis
Via Tiberio
80073 Capri
+39 081 837 0381

Villa Malaparte
visible from the Pizzolungo coastal
path, but difficult to reach

RIO

WHEN I WAS YOUNG, I BOUGHT AN APARTMENT IN RIO. I WOULD GO TO *São Paolo* TO SEE MY FAMILY, BUT RIO WAS FOR FUN. RIO IS *the most amazing* CITY WITH THE MOST *beautiful* scenery—THEY CALL IT *the eighth wonder of the world* BECAUSE GOD WAS SO GENEROUS TO PUT THE CITY BETWEEN THE *beach* AND THE *mountains*.

Ipanema Beach, dominated by the
Dois Irmãos mountains and Pedra da Gavea.

#FASANO SELFIE
The Fasano Hotel is a must
for any trip to Rio.

#IPANEMA
People who live in Ipanema
stay in Ipanema—it's that
gorgeous. It's the young
side of the city, where I went
when I was 16. For me,
Ipanema is Tom Jobim and
Vinícius de Moraes, both
excellent musicians.

#MAR
I'M AN ART FANATIC!

I visited during an amazing Lygia Clark
exhibition, but was told "no pictures."
I took some anyway! Here are some
other great Brazilian artists:
Vik Muniz
Beatriz Milhazes
Adriana Verejão
Tunga

Rio is home to many fabulous beaches, like Ipanema, Copacabana, and Barra da Tijuca Beach, to name a few. For all your beachwear needs, go to Osklen *(upper left)* on Rua Maria Quitériam, Lenny Niemeyer, or Blue Man. Rio de Janeiro was founded by the Portugeuse colonizers in the 16th century and is home to a big melange of styles in its architecture, which intrigues the mind and fascinates the eye—old colonial Portugeuse buildings, like the town hall *(below left),* early 1920s modernists, like Oscar Niemeyer, and contemporary constructions that become the home of street art.

Oscar Niemeyer
1907–2012

"" People don't really go to the museums in Rio...
they go to the beaches. ""
—Francisco Costa

#MEDITERRANEAN MEETS
SOUTH AMERICA

#FRESH

Satyricon is my favorite restaurant in Ipanema and offers a Brazilian take on Italian Mediterranean classics; I like to order the *Mare Nostro,* which has a lot of flavors from crudo fish, as well as *Robalo a la Plancha* with risotto of Sicilian lemon.

#OLD RIO

I like to visit the old, colonial part
of Rio, especially the markets.

#PARATY

Is a small colonial town 3.5 hours away from Rio, or a 45-minute helicopter ride.

A GREAT #WEEKEND TRIP

Paraty is a beautiful colonial port village from which early colonizers would send a lot of gold in the *Naus*—Portugeuse ships—back to Portugal. It is also a pirate city, where streets are curved so you could escape musket fire. All of the buildings have colonial-style architecture and are painted beautiful vibrant colors.

Don Pedro II overlooking wedding sweets; it's a tradition to have sweets at Brazilian weddings. *Below (right)*: my niece, Yasmine, and João Felipe on their wedding day.

#COLONIAL
BRAZIL

#LOCAL
COLOR

THIS LITTLE SHOP

is filled with traditional Brazilian-Indian crafts, like baskets and thread. Just wander around and you are bound to find something unique.

HOTELS

Copacabana Palace
Avenida Atlântica 1702
Copacabana
Rio de Janeiro 22021–001
Tel: +55 21 2548–7070

Hotel Fasano
Avenida Vieira Souto 80
Ipanema
Rio de Janeiro 22420–000
Tel: +55 21 3202–4000

Marina Palace
Avenida Delfim Moreira 630
Leblon
Rio de Janeiro 22441–000
Tel: +55 21 3613–5150

RESTAURANTS

Academia da Cachaça
Rua Conde de Bernadotte 26
Leblon
Rio de Janeiro 22430–200
Tel: +55 21 2239–1542

Confeitaria Colombo
R. Gonçalves Dias 32
Centro
Rio de Janeiro 20050–030
Tel: +55 21 2232–2300

Pizzaria Capriciosa
Rua Vinicius de Moraes 134
Ipanema
Rio de Janeiro 22411–010
Tel: +55 21 2523–1169

Antiquarius
Rua Aristides Espinola 19
Leblon
Rio de Janeiro 22440–050
Tel: +55 21 2294–1049

Esplanada Grill
Rua Barão da Torre 600
Ipanema
Rio de Janeiro 22411–002
Tel: +55 21 2512–2970

Satyricon
Rua Barão da Torre 92
Ipanema
Rio de Janeiro 22411–000
Tel: +55 21 2521–0627

Brigite's
Dias Ferreira 247–A
Leblon
Rio de Janeiro 22431–050
Tel: +55 21 2274–5590

Gero
Rua Anibal de Mendonça 157
Ipanema
Rio de Janeiro 22410–050
Tel: +55 21 2239–8158

Siri Mole
Rua Francisco Otaviano 50
Copacabana
Rio de Janeiro 22080–040
Tel: +55 21 2267–0894

Casa da Feijoada
Rua Prudente de Moraes 10
Ipanema
Rio de Janeiro 22420–040
Tel: +55 21 2523–4994

Giuseppe Grill
Avenida Bartolomeu Mitre 370
Rio de Janeiro 22431–000
Tel: +55 21 2249–3055

Sushi Leblon
Rua Dias Ferreira 256
Leblon
Rio de Janeiro 22431–050
Tel: +55 21 2512–7830

MUSEUMS & SIGHTS

Corcovado
Rua Cosme Velho 513
Cosme Velho
Rio de Janeiro 22241–090
Tel: +55 21 2558–1329

Jardim Botânico
Rua Jardim Botânico 1008
Jardim Botânico
Rio de Janeiro 22460–030
Tel: +55 21 294–6012

**Museu da Imagen
e do Som**
Rua Visconde de Maranguape 15
Lapa
Rio de Janeiro 20021–390
Tel: +55 21 2332–9470

Museu Imperial
do Brasil
Rua da Imperatriz 220
Petrópolis
Rio de Janeiro 25610-320
Tel: +55 24 2245-5550

Museu National do Brasil
Quinta da Boa Vista
São Cristóvão
Rio de Janeiro 20940-040
Tel: +55 21 2562-6900

Museum of Modern Art
Avenida Infante Dom Henrique 85
Parque do Flamengo
Rio de Janeiro 20021-140
Tel: +55 21 2240-4944

Palacio do Catete
Rua do Catete 153
Catete
Rio de Janeiro 22220-000
Tel: +55 21 2127-0324

Pão de Açúar
Avenida Pasteur 520
Urca
Rio de Janeiro 04719-001
Tel: +55 21 2546-8400

Parque Lage
Rua Jardim Botânico 414
Rio de Janeiro 22461-000
Tel: +55 21 2127-1800

Sítio Roberto Burle
Marx
Estrada Roberto Burle Marx 2019
Barra de Guaratiba
Rio de Janeiro 23020-240
Tel: +55 21 2410-1412

Vista Chinesa
Estrada da Vista Chinesa 789
Alto da Boa Vista
Rio de Janeiro 20531-410
Tel: +55 21 2492-2253

Visit Paraty
the charming colonial city, four
hours from Rio by car

SHOPPING

Blue Man
(swimwear)
Fórum de Ipanema
Rua Visconde de Pirajá 351
Ipanema
Rio de Janeiro 22410-003
Tel: +55 21 2247-4905

Chocolate Q
Rua Garcia D'Ávila 149 Loja B
Ipanema
Rio de Janeiro 22410-010
Tel: 55 21 2523 5090

Fashion Mall
Estrada da Gávea 899
São Conrado
Rio de Janeiro 22610-001
Tel: +55 21 2111-4427

Feira Hippie
(Sundays)
Praça General Osório
Ipanema
Rio de Janeiro 20410-020
Tel: +55 21 8746-1082

Granado
(soaps and scents for the home)
Rua Primeiro de Março, 16
Centro
Rio de Janeiro 20010-000
Tel: +55 21 3231-6746

Lenny Niemeyer
(beachwear)
Galeria Forum, Loja 114 e 115
Rua Visconde de Pirajá 351
Ipanema
Rio de Janeiro 22410-003
Tel: +55 21 2523-3796

Osklen
(beachwear)
Rua Maria Quitéria 85
Ipanema
Rio de Janeiro 22410-040
Tel: +55 21 2227-2911

Shopping Leblon
Avenida Afrânio de Melo
Franco 290
Leblon
Rio de Janeiro 22430-060
Tel: +55 21 2430-5122

SÃO PAULO

SÃO PAULO

IS *the economic lung* OF BRAZIL, BUT DESPITE ITS HARD WORKING *nature*, THE CITY IS VERY *cosmopolitan*, HAVING BEEN INDUSTRIALIZED BY ITALIANS. AND MOST IMPORTANT, *the art* AND *the food are great*. THE SCENTS AND FLAVORS OF SÃO PAULO BRING BACK ALL OF THE *memories* OF MY YOUTH.

Top: Niemeyer-designed Oca building in the Ibirapuera Park. *Below:* Pavilhão Ciccillo Matarazzo, also designed by Niemeyer, together with Hélio Uchôa, is where the São Paulo Art Biennial is held. I love these curves.

Clockwise from top left: Sean and Anthony DJ for Valentino; Gallery Pivô, in the Copan building designed by Oscar Niemeyer; the Bandeiras memorial statue in Ibirapeura Park; exhibition from the MAC; Ibirapeura Park greenery.

#STREET LIFE

There are some wonderful streets for shopping
in São Paulo: I love Rua Oscar Feire,
and in Liberdade you have the Japanese colony
where I buy porcelain and incense.
I also love Ibirapuera Park.
Below: Edificio Copan designed by Niemeyer.

Above: The White Cube was one
of the first international galleries
to open in Brazil, showcasing
international artists. Paulistas have
money and love investing in art.

THE #ARCHITECTURE OF SÃO PAULO IS SO MIXED AND VIBRANT!

Top: Ohtake Building.
Left: Street art at Ibirapuera Park.
Below: Colorful street scene
—love her smile!

Clockwise from top left: Fasano hotel pool; view from my offices at Cidade Jardim shops; Isabelli at *Vogue* party at Baretto; Fasano Hotel bar.

#SEU JORGE
PLAYING AT AMFAR S.P.

The international gala by AMFAR for AIDS research held at the home of Dinho Diniz is a must event; they always have great hosts, like Sharon Stone and Kate Moss.

#NIEMEYER

The simplicity and clean lines of his designs continue to inspire me and others.

#DALVA E DITO

Great restaurant that serves traditional Brazilian cuisine with a contemporary flair. I enjoy the *farofa*.

#COPAN
BAR DA DONA ONÇA

Perfect place for end-of-the-day drinks.
I like Caipirinhas of Lima-da-Pérsia.

#SÃO PAULO
ART FAIR

is held in the
Niemeyer building
at Ibirapuera Park
in early April.
Below (left): MASP
Museum.

HOTELS

Hotel Emiliano
Rua Oscar Freire 384
Jardim Paulista
São Paulo 01426-000
Tel: +55 11 3068-4399

Hotel Fasano
Rua Vitório Fasano 88
Jardim Paulista
São Paulo 01414-020
Tel: +55 11 3896-4000

Hotel Unique
Avenida Brigadeiro
Luís Antônio 4700
Jardim Paulista
São Paulo 01402-002
Tel: +55 11 3055-4700

RESTAURANTS

Dalva e Dito
Rua Padre João Manuel 1115
Cerqueira César
São Paulo 01411-001
Tel: +55 11 3068-4444

Jun Sakamoto
Rua Lisboa 55
Pinheiros
São Paulo 05413-000
Tel: +55 11 3088-6019

Rodeio
Rua Haddock Lobo 1498
Jardim Paulista
São Paulo 01414-002
Tel: +55 11 3474-1333

Dom
Rua Barão de Capanema
549
Cerqueira César
São Paulo 01411-011
Tel: +55 11 3088-0761

Mani
Rua Joaquim Antunes 210
São Paulo 05415-010
Tel: +55 11 3085-4148

Spot
Alameda Ministro
Rocha Azevedo 72
Cerqueira César
São Paulo 01410-000
Tel: +55 11 3283-0946

BARS

Astor
Rua Delfina 163
Vila Madalena
São Paulo 05443-010
Tel: +55 11 3815-1364

Baretto
(at Hotel Fasano)
Tel: +55 11 3079-9008

Bar Brahma
(at the famous corner of Av
Ipiranga and Av São João)
Avenida São João 677
Centro
São Paulo 01036-100
Tel: +55 11 3367-3600

Bar da Dona Onça
Av. Ipiranga 200 loja 27-29
República
São Paulo 01046-925
Tel: +55 11 3129-7619

Número
Rua da Consolação 3585
Jardim Paulista
São Paulo 01416-001
Tel: +55 11 3061-3995

GALLERIES

Fortes Vilaça
Rua Fradique Coutinho 1500
Pinheiros
São Paulo 05416-001
Tel: +55 11 3032-7066

Leme
Avenida Valdemar
Ferreira 130
Butantã
São Paulo 05501-010
Tel: +55 11 3093-8184

Luisa Strina
Rua Padre João Manuel 755
Jardim Paulista
São Paulo 01411-001
Tel: +55 11 3088-2471

Mendes Wood
Rua da Consolação 3358
Cerqueira César
São Paulo 01416-000
Tel: +55 11 3081-1735

Nara Roesler
Avenida Europa 655
Pinheiros
São Paulo 01449-001
Tel: +55 11 3063-2344

Triangulo
Rua Pais de Araújo 77
Itaim Bibi
São Paulo 04531-090
Tel: +55 11 3167-5621

Vermelho
Rua Minas Gerais 372
Consolação
São Paulo 01244-010
Tel: +55 11 3138-1520

White Cube
Rua Agostinho Rodrigues Filho
550 50
São Paulo 04026-040
Tel: +55 11 4329 4474

SIGHTS

Auditório Ibirapuera
Avenida Pedro Álvares Cabral
Parque do Ibirapuera
São Paulo 04094-050

Copan
Avenida Ipiranga 200
São Paulo 01046-010

Mercado Municipal
Rua da Cantareira 306
Centro
São Paulo 01024-000

Oca
Avenida Pedro Álvares
Cabral, Portão 3

Parque do Ibirapuera
São Paulo 04094-000
Tel: +55 11 3105-6118

Pinacoteca
Praça da Luz 2
Luz
São Paulo 01120-010
Tel: +55 11 3324-1000

Terraço Italia
Avenida Ipiranga 344
Centro
São Paulo 01046-010
Tel: +55 11 2189-2929

SHOPPING

Adriana Degreas
(swimwear)
Rua Melo Alves 734
São Paulo 01417-010
Tel: +55 11 3064-4300

Etel Interiores
(super chic wood furniture and
home accessories)
Alameda Gabriel Monteiro
da Silva 1834
São Paulo 01442-001
Tel: +55 11 3064-1266

Hugo França
(sculptural furniture)
Rua Gomes de Carvalho 585
São Paulo 04547-002
Tel: +55 11 3045-6575
hugofranca.com.br

Jo de Mer
(swimwear)
Rua Oscar Freire 329A
Cerqueira César
São Paulo 01426-010
Tel: +55 11 3081-4232

Marcenaria
São Paulo
(Paulo Alves Design)
Rua Harmonia 815
Sumarezinho
São Paulo 05435-000
Tel: +55 11 3032-4281

Shopping Cidade Jardim
Avenida Magalhães de
Castro 12,000
Jardim Panorama
Sao Paulo 05676-900

BAHIA,

FRIBURGO,

BRASÍLIA &

ALTO PARAÍSO

BAHIA IS LOCATED IN THE *eastern part of Brazil*, AND HAS LUSH GREENERY AND GREAT BEACHES ALONG THE *Atlantic Ocean*. I GO THERE WITH MY FAMILY TO GET AWAY FROM IT ALL. FOR ME, TRAVELING TO BAHIA IS ALL ABOUT *relaxation*. I GO TO MY FARM IN NOVA FRIBURGO DURING THE *pruning season*. I LOVE TO SHAPE THINGS—I WILL GO OUT INTO THE GARDEN WITH MY SHEARS AND WHEN I'M FINISHED, EVERYTHING IS *transformed*.

CHARLENE'S BALINESE COMPOUND AT #UNA

is the perfect place to relax and recover from city life. The property is located on the Cacao Coast, famous for its cacao plantations. I come here with my family and we enjoy the downtime miles away from everyone. You have to fly to Ilhéus and then drive south by car.

#SECLUSION

#DETOX

We drink lots of coconut water and green juices—apples, carrots, celery, kale, cucumber, and ginger; it is a perfect cleanser and is part of my daily routine.
Above (right): the beach at Una is quiet and tucked away from the world.
Below: A little yoga never hurt anyone.

#GODDESS
THE SEA GODDESS, IEMANJÁ,

blesses us with sand dollars. She is the sea goddess in many parts of southern Brazil, and is the patron of fishermen and corresponds to the Holy Mary in the Catholic Church.

#CRAFT TIME

Below (right): We spend time together, painting hats and decorating eggs for Easter. *Below (left):* We spend hours at the beach collecting sand dollars. *Right:* Mangosteens, from Indonesia, are grown in this part of Brazil.

#UNA

JORGE AMADO,
BORN IN ILHÉUS, BAHIA,

is one of Brazil's best-known
authors, famous for his modernist
novel *Gabriel, Clove, and
Cinnamon.* Amado is from Bahia,
a state in eastern Brazil where there
are many small, beautiful villages. It
is also home to Salvador
de Bahia, said to be
"Brazil's capital of happiness."
Top right: Coconut equality!

#FRIBURGO

is where I have my beautiful, peaceful farm that is nestled in the Parque Estadual dos Três Picos. I come to this quiet retreat to detox with my nutritionist, Edna, to recharge after hectic traveling, and get away from it all. It is a secret garden that I planted 20 years ago—an organic *jardin potager*.

#MOUNTAIN
SOLITUDE

the mountains here are truly inspiring!

#BRASÍLIA
CATHEDRAL OF BRASÍLIA

The first time I entered this Niemeyer chef d'œuvre, I was very emotional. The light filtering from the stained glass designed by Marianne Peretti and the suspended angels by Alfredo Ceschiatti in collaboration with Dante Croce gave me an INCREDIBLE feeling of peace and holiness. (Oscar Niemeyer was a proclaimed atheist.)

Left: View of the National Congress of Brazil.
Above: Sede da Procuradoria Geral da República Brasileira.

#NIEMEYER

#PERFECTION

Left: Palácio do Planalto.
Above (left): Staircase in the Itamaraty Palace.
Above (right): Marlon Brando and Juscelino Kubitschek, the visionary president of Brazil who proposed the relocation of the government and oversaw much of the construction of Brasília.

#GRAND

Brasília's Monumental Axis.

> *Meditation can help us embrace our worries, our fear, our anger; and that is very healing. We let our own natural capacity of healing do the work.*
>
> —Thich Nhat Hanh

#ALTO PARAÍSO

A very small town located in the Chapada dos Veadeiros National Park, which is incredible!

BAHIA HOTELS

Hotel Canto das Águas
(near the Chapada Diamantina)
Avenida Senhor dos Passos 1
Juiz de Fora 36037-490,
Tel: +55 75 3334-1154

Pestana Convento
do Carmo
Rua do Carmo 1
Santo Antônio Além do Carmo
Salvador
Bahia 40301-330
Tel: +55 71 3327-8400

Txai Resort Hotel
Avenida Lomanto Júnior 528
Ilhéus
Bahia 45654-000
Tel: +55 73 3634-6956

RESTAURANTS & FOOD SHOPS

Bataclan
Avenida 2 de Julho 77
Ilhéus
Bahia 45653-758
Tel: +55 73 3634-0088

Cacau do Céu
(chocolate)
Avenida Soares Lopes 508
Ilhéus
Bahia 45653-005
Tel: +55 73 3231-7661

Capa
(wine and cheese)
Avenida Soares Lopes 1280
Ilhéus
Bahia 45653-005
Tel: +55 73 3231-1030

CHOR
(chocolate)
Rua Coronel Paiva 93
Ilhéus
Bahia 45653-310
Tel: +55 73 3231-0087

Pericles
(fabulous exotic flavors of ice
cream)
Rua Erotildes Melo 320
Ilhéus
Bahia 45654-450

Trapiche Adelaide
Rua Tupinambás 2
Salvadore 41940-090
Tel: +55 71 3241-4761

SIGHTS & VISITS

Catedral do
São Sebastião
Ilhéus
Bahia

Chapada Diamantina
(beautiful national park,
inland from Salvador)

Ecoparque de Una
(south of Ilhéus, near Una)

Fundação Casa de
Jorge Amado
Largo do Pelourinho 51
Pelourinho, Salvador
Bahia 40026-280
Tel: +55 71 3321-0070

Fundação Pierre Verger
Rua Vila América 6
Engenho Velho de Brotas
Salvador
Bahia 40243-340
Tel: +55 71 3203-8400

Roberto Ablan
Galeria de Arte
Rua Senta Pua 53
Ondina, Salvador
Bahia 40170-180
Tel: +55 71 3243-3982

Brasília Palace Hotel
SHTN, Trecho 1, Lote 1
Brasília 70800-200
Tel: +55 61 3319-3543

Golden Tulip
SHTN, Trecho 1, Conjunto 1B,
Bloco C
Asa Norte
Brasília 70800-200
Tel: +55 61 3429 8000

Royal Tulip
Tel: +55 61 34247000

Grand Bittar Hotel
Setor Hoteleiro Sul, Quadra
5, Bloco A
Asa Sul, Brasília 70315-000
Tel: +55 61 3704-5000

Meliá Brasil 21
SHS Quadra 6 Bl. B, D e F
Asa Sul, Brasília 70316-000
Tel: +55 61 3218-4700

RESTAURANTS

Gero Brasília
Shopping Iguatemi
Shin Ca 04 Lote A Loja 22
Térreo
Lago Norte 71503-504
Tel: +55 61 3577 5520

Limoncello
Rua CLS 402, Bloco A, Loja 33
Asa Sul
Brasília 70236-510
Tel: +55 61 3226-3208

Taypá Sabores Del Peru
SHIS QI 17 Bloco G Loja
208 - Fashion Park
Brasília 71645-500
Tel: +55 61 3364-0403

Tratoria do Rosario
Shis Qi 17 Conjunto 10 11
Brasília 71645-000
+55 61 3248-1672

Universal Diner
CLS 210, Bloco B, Lj. 30
Asa Sul
Brasília 70273-520
Tel: +55 61 3443-2089

SIGHTS & VISITS

Catedral Metropolitana
Esplanada dos Ministérios,
Lote 12
Brasília 70050-000
Tel: +55 61 3224-4073

Palácio do Itamaraty
Esplanada dos Ministérios
Bloco H, Eixo Monumental
Brasília 70170-090
Tel: +55 61 2030-8051

Palácio do Planalto
Praça dos Três Poderes
Brasília 70150-900
Tel: +55 61 3411-1221

Parque Nacional da
Chapada dos Veadeiros
Tel: + 55 62 3455-1114

Pirenopolis

Poço Azul
Tel: +55 61 3244-7959

Salto do Corumbá
Rod Br 414, km 383
Zona Rural, Corumbá de
Goiás 72960-000
Tel: +55 61 4063-8546

SHANGHAI THE *excitement*

OF THE *Pudong skyline* PROPELS MY LOVE FOR SHANGHAI—IT GIVES ME THE SAME FEELING I FELT FOR *New York in the '80s.* THE FIRST TIME I VISITED SHANGHAI, FIFTEEN YEARS AGO, IT WAS ALL THREE-STORY BUILDINGS AND THE PUDONG REGION DID NOT EVEN EXIST. NOW, SHANGHAI IS *the new frontier*, AN EXCITING PLACE TO BUILD *a career*, WITH ALL THE CULTURE AND *entertainment* OF A GLOBAL *capital.*

#YONGFOO ELITE

Sharing a meal with my sons at Yongfoo Elite restaurant in Shanghai. The dish of Mandarin fish was tart and delicious, but what makes the restaurant really special is the décor. The building used to be the British consulate and has beautiful antique furniture.

Above: IAPM shopping center, home to the Valentino store *(center)*. The show was at the Shanghai International Cruise Terminal — simply magnificent. *Below:* the Shanghai market, where I saw this traditional robe in beautiful oriental yellow. *Bottom (left):* There was a traditional lion dance representing luck for the opening of the Valentino store. And look at the buzz in this Chinese pharmacy.

#RELAXING AT THE DIVINE PULI HOTEL

after a day of Shanghai shopping.
Below: At 7:30 a.m. I take my daily swim
in the Puli pool—everyone else is still in
bed with je tlag. It is the most beautiful
hotel pool. I am so drawn to its oriental
elegance. I love the scale and symmetry.
It's the longest hotel pool I've seen and
the water is good—no chlorine, so your
hair stays beautiful!

#NIGHTLIFE

#DIVINE BIRTHDAY CELEBRATION

at my friend Yue-Sai's home.
Above: The Park Hyatt Pudong is simply majestic.
Fifteen years ago, Shanghai was all three-story
buildings—now it has the most beautiful skyline
in the world. The Pudong region was a swamp,
but they transformed it into a 21st-century city.
Top: My sons DJ for the Valentino party.

#OLD MEETS NEW
IN HANGZHOU

A one-and-a-half-hour train ride from Shanghai
is the marvelous city of Hangzhou, where a beautiful
21st-century white marble train station greets you
in this bucolic city. Famous for having the biggest
Buddhist temple in eastern China, Lingyin, and for
the famous Dragon Well tea.

> *When I saw these young monks going to pray in Hangzhou, I thought they were so elegant and beautiful. I went into the city and tried to buy the robes, but the shopkeeper said they only sell them to monks. I told him I pray a lot, but he said no.*

SPA
**#PERFECTION
AT AMANFAYUN
IN HANGZHOU**

In contrast to the amazing pace
and architecture of the modern city
of Shanghai, which is very 21st century,
I went with my family to this amazing
spa that catapulted us back 150 years
in time to a bucolic Chinese dream.
Very sophisticated in this almost monastic
décor, AMANFAYUN is a must-try
experience, and is very inspiring in
its simplicity. Zen-oriented indeed!

#BEST
FOOD
TEN VEGETARIAN

plates were like individual
sculptures, each decorated with
an incredible artistic approach at
Vegetarian House in Hangzhou.

#HANGZHOU

You can get here with a one hour bullet train from Shanghai. Lakes near Hangzhou have magnificent willow trees surrounding them.

#TEMPLE OF LINGYIN AND DRAGON WELL TEA FIELDS

Hangzhou is famous for the tea grown in the region. I went to many tearooms and learned that when you pour the tea you have to let the water splash— the ceremony has to be splashy to show abundance.
Above: The Aman walk, leading to Lingyin Temple and a rock garden of Buddhas.

HOTELS

Andaz
88 Songshan Road
Huangpu, Shanghai
Tel: +86 21 2310 1234

Pudong Hyatt
88 Century Avenue
Pudong, Shanghai
Tel: +86 21 5049 1234

Waldorf Astoria
2 Zhongshan East 2nd Road
Huangpu, Shanghai
Tel: +86 21 6322 9988

The Peninsula
32 Zhongshan East 1st Road
Huangpu, Shanghai
Tel: +86 21 2327 2888

PuLi
1 Changde Road
Jing'an, Shanghai
Tel: +86 21 3203 9999

RESTAURANTS

Crystal Jade
123 Xingye Road
Huangpu, Shanghai
Tel: +86 21 6385 8752

Mercato
(Italian)
3 Zhongshan East 1st Road, 6F
Huangpu, Shanghai
Tel: +86 21 6321 9922

Shintori
(Japanese)
803 Julu Road
Jing'an, Shanghai
Tel: +86 21 5404 5252

Franck
(French)
376 Wukang Road
Xuhui, Shanghai
Tel: +86 21 6437 6465

Mr & Mrs Bund
18 Zhongshan East 1st Road
Huangpu, Shanghai
Tel: +86 21 6323 9898

Yongfoo Elite
200 Yongfu Road
Xuhui, Shanghai
Tel: +86 21 5466 2727

NIGHTLIFE

The Apartment
47 Yongfu Road
Xuhui, Shanghai
Tel: +86 21 6437 9478

Hollywood
46 Yueyang Road
Xuhui, Shanghai
Tel: +86 21 6466 7662

No. 88
701 Yongjia Road
Xuhui, Shanghai
Tel: +86 21 6431 2353

Bar Rouge
at Mr & Mrs Bund
Tel: +86 21 6339 1199

MINT
318 Fuzhou Road
Huangpu, Shanghai
Tel: +86 21 6391 3191

MUSEUMS

Propaganda Poster Art Centre
868 Huashan Road
Xuhui, Shanghai
Tel: +86 21 6211 1845

Shanghai Museum
201 Renmin Avenue
Huangpu, Shanghai
Tel: +86 21 6372 3500

Shanghai Urban Planning Exhibition Center
100 Renmin Avenue
Huangpu, Shanghai
Tel: +86 21 6318 4477

Dongtai Road
Antique Market
Liuhekou Road
Huangpu, Shanghai
Tel: +86 21 5382 5254

Taikang Lu
or Tianzifang
(great for Chinese antiques
and curios)
210 Taikang Road
Huangpu, Shanghai
Tel: +86 21 3425 0265

Xintiandi
(open-air shopping with good
brands and Chinese goods.
Walking Huaihai Road
is a must.)
123 Xingye Road
Huangpu, Shanghai

MASSAGES

Dragonfly Retreat
Fuxing Park
84 Nanchang Road
Luwan, Shanghai
Tel: +86 21 5386 0060

Green Massage
202 Shang Cheng Lu
Jing'an, Shanghai
Tel: +86 21 6289 7776

Zen Massages
210 Wuyuan Road
Xuhui, Shanghai
Tel: +86 21 3368 1227

WALK

The Bund (Zhongshan East 1st Road—go early and see people exercising the Chinese way—practicing tai chi)

HANGZHOU

Amanfayun
22 Fayun Alley
Hangzhou
Zhejiang 310013
Tel: +86 571 8732 9999

Lingyin Temple
Fayun Lane Lingyin Road 1
Hangzhou City
Zhejiang 310013
Tel: +86 571 8796 8665

National Tea Museum
88 Longjing Road
Hangzhou
Zhejiang 310013
Tel: +86 571 8796 4221

NYC

NEW YORK CITY IS ONE OF THE MAIN CITIES WHERE I LIVE AND WORK. IN MY OPINION, IT IS THE EPICENTER OF THE *fashion, ballet,* AND *art world.* MY APARTMENT NEAR THE UNITED NATIONS BUILDING, PARTLY DESIGNED BY *Oscar Niemeyer,* KEEPS ME TIED TO MY NATION OF BIRTH. MARCH TO MAY AND OCTOBER TO DECEMBER ARE THE MONTHS I AM HERE, *attending events* LIKE THE *Met Gala,* BALLET PREMIERES, BROADWAY, AND THE FABULOUS *Halloween* PARTY THROWN BY MY FRIEND ALLISON SAROFIM.

United Nations headquarters,
designed by Oscar Niemeyer
and Le Corbusier.

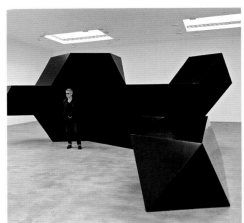

MY NEW YORK IS FILLED WITH #ART

You see beautiful and vibrant sculptures
even while walking down the street.
Left: Jeff Koons's *Hulk* at Gagosian.
Below: I always stop to take a picture.

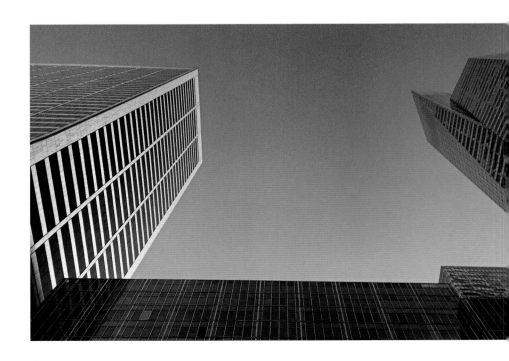

#GAGOSIAN

Jeff Koons's great *Lilo* sculptures
are so much fun to look at.

Above: Cecily Brown poses with
an abstract painting. Gagosian
is my favorite place to see
contemporary art in New York
—such wonderful art and spaces.
I go to the one uptown and the
one in Chelsea, which is filled with
galleries between 10th Avenue and
the Hudson River, and from West
27th Street all the way down to to
18th Street. I love Saturday morning
Chelsea gallery tours and getting
inspired by so much great art
and artists from all over the world.

#BOOMBOOM

I love this picture with the Boom Boom lights
reflecting on the glass, looking downtown.
The place is unique, and it's where I can see
all my friends in town in just a glance when
the city is sizzling during its peak months.
So many fun memories.

#BALLET, YES

The beautiful interior of Koch Theater before a performance by the New York City Ballet. *Right:* Soaking up some sun in front of the fountain at Lincoln Center. *Below:* Creel and Gow is a wonderful *cabinet de curiosités,* a great shopping destination for interior décor. *Below (right):* The Beaux Arts chandeliers at Grand Central Station add a wonderful glow to the main hall.

#GRAND CENTRAL

Stop by the Oyster Bar for lunch —it's a real American experience.

#STREET ART

Top (right): inside Comme des Garçons—no photos allowed, but I always try to snap one. *Right*: Pace Gallery, under the wonderful steel work of the High Line.

#BRUNCH
I CALL BAR PITTI

in the West Village my beach because I cannot go there without seeing all of my friends.

Clockwise from left: I love Sushi Yasuda, near my apartment—I always order ikura oroshi. John Chamberlain installation at the Lever House. Classic New York night street scene. James Turrell is one of my very favorite artists—his Guggenheim installation was breathtaking. Allison Sarofim's Halloween party is a highlight of fall in New York; last year the theme was the Tahitian paintings of Paul Gauguin. On the western wall of my apartment I have two photographs of Niemeyer's work taken by Todd Eberle.
Opposite: The Chrysler Building.

"Give me such shows —give me the streets of Manhattan!"

—Walt Whitman

#SERENITY

The Seagram Building on Park Avenue, designed by Philip Johnson, is one of my favorite structures in New York City. Look at these perfect angles.

#VERY ROMAN
IL POSTO ACCANTO

is a wonderful, tiny Italian restaurant near the Bowery. It has a nice Roman atmosphere and when I come for brunch on the weekend, it reminds me of home. Beatrice makes fabulous drinks.

#BIRTHDAY FUN

Sophia loves to host parties at Milon in the East Village. It's good Indian food, and the atmosphere is so fun! The ceiling is covered with Christmas lights and they play a recording of "Happy Birthday" with traditional Indian tablas. As soon as the song is over, someone unplugs the speakers and the room goes completely silent.
Left: show at Gagosian.

#ROMANTIC

On the lakes near Southampton the herons
come at dusk. They are so elegant.

#WEEKEND
GETAWAY

Southampton: the beaches in the Hamptons are a great
place to get away for the weekend. Along the way you
can get fresh fruits and vegetables. I love corn on the
cob and the sunflowers—such a summer experience.

New York City in the Hamptons: I love to get a little snack here.

#HAMPTONS FUN

Beaches aren't the only wonderful things here; the gardens are some of the best I have seen.

HOTELS

Ace Hotel
20 W 29th Street
New York, NY 10001
Tel: +1 (212) 679-2222

The Bowery Hotel
335 Bowery
New York, NY 10003
Tel: +1 (212) 505-9100

NOMAD
1170 Broadway
New York, NY 10001
Tel: +1 (212) 796-1500

RESTAURANTS

Saint Ambroeus
259 W 4th Street
New York, NY 10014
Tel: +1 (212) 604-9254
(additional locations)

Bar Pitti
268 6th Avenue
New York, NY 10014
Tel: +1 (212) 982-3300

Casa Lever
390 Park Avenue
New York, NY 10022
Tel: +1 (212) 888-2700

Cipriani
multiple locations

ESCA
402 W 43rd Street
New York, NY 10036
Phone: +1 (212) 564-7272

La Grenouille
3 E 52nd Street
New York, NY 10022
Tel: +1 (212) 752-1495

Marea
240 Central Park South
New York, NY 10019
Tel: +1 (212) 582-5100

Milon
93 1st Ave #2
New York, NY 10003
Tel: +1 (212) 228-4896

Narcissa
21 Cooper Square
New York, NY 10003
Tel: +1 (212) 228-3344

Il Posto Accanto
190 E 2nd Street
New York, NY 10009
Tel: +1 (212) 228-3562

NIGHTLIFE

The Diamond
Horse Shoe
Paramount Hotel
235 W 46th Street
New York, NY 10036
Tel: +1 (212) 706-7448

Top of the Standard
(formerly Boom Boom Room)
848 Washington Street
New York, NY 10014
Tel: +1 (212) 645-4646

New York City Ballet
David H. Koch Theater
20 Lincoln Center
New York, NY 10023
Tel: +1 (212) 496-0600

MUSEUMS & GALLERIES

Cheim & Read
547 W 25th Street
New York, NY 10001
Tel: +1 (212) 242-7727

David Zwirner
525 W 19th Street
New York, NY 10011
Tel: +1 (212) 727-2070

Gagosian
980 Madison Avenue
Tel: +1 (212) 744-2313
555 W 24th Street
Tel: +1 (212) 741-1111
522 W 21st Street
Tel: +1 (212) 741-1717

Gladstone Gallery
515 W 24th Street1
Tel: +1 (212) 206-9300
530 W 21st Street
Tel: +1 (212) 206-7606

Guggenheim
1071 5th Avenue
New York, NY 10128
Tel: +1 (212) 423-3500

Luhring Augustine
531 W 24th Street
New York, NY 10011
Tel: +1 (212) 206-9100

Mary Boone
745 5th Avenue
New York, NY 10151
Tel: +1 (212) 752-2929

Matthew Marks
523 W 24th Street
New York, NY 10001
Tel: +1 (212) 243-0200

Metropolitan Museum of Art
1000 5th Ave
New York, NY 10028
Tel: +1 (212) 535-7710

MoMA
11 W 53rd Street
New York, NY 10019
Tel: +1 (212) 708-9400

New Museum
235 Bowery
New York, NY 10002
Tel: +1 (212) 219-1222

Sonnabend
536 W 22nd Street
New York, NY 10011
Tel: +1 (212) 627-1018

The Pace gallery
32 E 57th Street
New York, NY 10022
Tel: +1 (212) 421-3292

Paul Kasmin
293 10th Avenue
New York, NY 10001
Tel: +1 (212) 563-4474

Whitney Museum
945 Madison Avenue
New York, NY 10021
Tel: +1 (212) 570-3600

SHOPPING

Century 21
(designer fashion
at great prices)
22 Cortlandt Street
New York, NY 10007
Tel: +1 (212) 227-9092

Chelsea Market
(shops, from food to fashion)
247 W 29th Street
New York, NY 10001
Tel: +1 (212) 594-8289

Creel & Gow
(a cabinet des curiosités)
131 E 70th Street
New York, NY 10021
Tel: +1 (212) 327-4281

De Vera
(beautiful objects)
1 Crosby Street
New York, NY 10013
Tel: +1 (212) 625-0838

Eataly
(gourmet Italian specialties)
200 5th Avenue
New York, NY 10010
Tel: +1 (212) 229-2560

Fivestory
(fashion and décor)
18 E 69th Street
New York, NY 10021
Tel: +1 (212) 288-1338

Global Table
(homewares)
109 Sullivan Street
New York, NY 10012
Tel: +1 (212) 431-5839

Mood Indigo
(accessories and homewares)
40 W 25th Street
New York, NY 10010
Tel: +1 (212) 254-1176

Les Toiles du Soleil
(colorful French fabrics)
261 W 19th Street
New York, NY 10011
Tel: +1 (212) 229-4730

WALKS

Bleeker Street, Crosby Street, Madison Avenue (from 57th to 78th)

#FAMILY
Souza family portrait by Donald Robertson

ABOUT THE AUTHOR

Carlos Souza is the Worldwide Brand Ambassador of the fashion house of Valentino. Mr. Souza has over twenty-five years of experience in fashion, beginning as a model for Valentino and working his way up. Known as an art world and fashion fixture, Souza is also an editor at large for *Architectural Digest*, a contributing editor for *Interview*, and a jewelry designer for his own line, Most Wanted Design.

Michael Roberts is a British fashion journalist, illustrator, and filmmaker. He is a former fashion and style director of *Vanity Fair*, fashion editor of *The Sunday Times*, and design director of British *Vogue*, to mention only a few of his positions. As a photographer and illustrator, Roberts has contributed images to *Vanity Fair*, *Vogue*, *The Sunday Times*, and *GQ*, among others. He has also published several books, including a book of illustrations, *Fashion Victims*.

ACKNOWLEDGMENTS

This book is dedicated to Sean and Anthony, my inspiration and guiding light in this world; to my beloved Charlene, who gave me the two most wonderful gifts in my life; to Valentino and Giancarlo for their friendship and constant unconditional support; and finally to my mother, Conceiçao, who implanted in my heart the seeds of optimism and good humor, and taught me to always see the bright side of life.
I also want to thank Martine and Prosper and the whole team at Assouline.